SEMPLE STADIUM

STADIUM

FIELD OF LEGENDS

I ndil chuimhne ar mo
thuismitheoirí Liam agus Cáit.

Is binne ceol mo chamán féin
Ná ceiliúr na n-éan ag fáinne an lae.

LIAM Ó DONNCHÚ is a native of Hollyford, County Tipperary, and now resides at Ballymoreen, near Thurles. Having spent over four decades as a primary school teacher, Liam, now retired, is director of Lár na Páirce, the museum of Gaelic Games in Thurles, and was for many years PRO of Semple Stadium. He is a former player, secretary and chairman of Thurles Sarsfields GAA club and at present its vice-president.

He is the author of such publications as *Tom Semple and the Thurles Blues*, *Thurles Sarsfields GAA Story* Vols 1 & 2, *Pouldine School: Inné agus Inniu*, and co-author of *Tipperary's GAA Ballads* and *Horse and Jockey, A Pictorial Record*, and has written numerous articles on Gaelic games.

Liam is married to Catherine and they have four adult children: Eoghan, Muireann, Neasa and Kilian.

SEMPLE STADIUM

FIELD OF LEGENDS

Liam Ó Donnchú

THE O'BRIEN PRESS
DUBLIN

First published 2021 by The O'Brien Press Ltd.
12 Terenure Road East, Rathgar, Dublin 6, D06 HD27, Ireland.
Tel: +353 1 4923333 Fax: +353 1 4922777
Email: books@obrien.ie. Website: www.obrien.ie
The O'Brien Press is a member of Publishing Ireland.

ISBN 978-1-78849-228-7

Thanks to the following for granting permission to use quotes, poems and extracts in this publication (see individual pages for more details): *Tipperary Star* (incl. John O'Grady, 'Cúlbaire'); *Sport*; *Cork Examiner*, *Irish Examiner* (Michael Moynihan); *Irish Independent* (Con Houlihan and Éamonn Sweeney); *The Irish Times* (Paddy Downey, Seán Kilfeather, Joanne Cantwell, Malachy Clerkin); *Irish Press* (Norman Freeman); *Magill* (Kevin Cashman); *Hogan Stand*; RTÉ's *The Sunday Game* and *Sport in Action*; TG4's *Laochra Gael*; Liam Ó Donnchú, *Tom Semple and the Thurles Blues* (2015); Philip F Ryan, *The Tubberadora Boherlahan Hurling Story* (1973); *Moycarkey-Borris GAA Story* (1984); Canon Edward J Whyte, *Kilruane MacDonaghs and Lahorna De Wets* (1985); Seamus J King, Liam Ó Donnchú, Jimmy Smyth, *Tipperary's GAA Ballads* (2000); Jimmy Smyth, *Ballads of the Banner* (1998) and *In Praise of Heroes* (2007); Séamus Ó Ceallaigh, *Gaelic Athletic Memories* (1945); Seamus J King, *A History of Hurling* (1996), *The Little Book of Hurling* (2014), *Tipperary's GAA Story 1935-1984* and *Tipperary's GAA Story 1985-2004*; Raymond Smith, *Decades of Glory* (1966) and *Clash of the Ash* (1981); Jim Cronin, *Munster GAA Story* (1984) and *A Cork GAA Miscellany* (2005); Philip F Ryan, *The Tubberadora Boherlahan Hurling Story* (1973); James Murphy, *The Poetry and Song of Black and Amber Glory* (2002); Brendan Fullam, *Giants of the Ash* (1991) and *Captains of the Ash* (2002); 'Carbery', Paddy Mehigan, *Hurling: Ireland's National Game* (1942); Séamus Ó Ceallaigh and Sean Murphy, *One Hundred Years of Glory* (1988) and *The Mackey Story* (1982); Seán Óg Ó Ceallacháin, *Tall Tales and Banter* (1998); David Smith, *The Unconquerable Keane* (2011); Diarmuid O'Flynn, *The Boy Wonder of Hurling: The Story of Jimmy Doyle Told in His Own Words* (2015); John Harrington, *Doyle: The Greatest Hurling Story Ever Told* (2011); John Scally, *The GAA Immortals: 100 Gaelic Games Legends* (2018); *Beyond the Tunnel: The Nicky English Story* with Vincent Hogan (1996); Blackrock's Centenary Year publication *The Rockies* (1984); Michael O'Hehir, *My Life and Times* (1996); Liam Ó Tuama, *Where He Sported and Played: Jack Lynch, A Sporting Celebration* (2000); Jim Fogarty, *The Dan Breen Cup* (2012) and *The Cross of Cashel* (2015); *Treasures to Share: The Collected Poems of Gerard Ryan* (1997); Munster, Tipperary and All-Ireland hurling programmes and yearbooks; Pat Mahon; Pat Costello; Jimmy Duggan; Jim Rhattigan; Dick Stokes; Noel Morris; Seán O'Callaghan; Ger Loughnane; Doireann Ní Bhriain; Bobby Ryan; Vincent Hanly; Aogán Ó Fearghail; Nickey Brennan; Tomás Ó Sé and Ruadhan King.

And to the following for use of their photographs in this publication (see individual pages for more details): Sportsfile: Ray McManus, Damien Eagers and Piaras Ó Mídheach; Tom Ryan Casey; George Hatchell; Eamon McGee; Bridget Delaney; Star Systems, Thurles; Waterford County Museum, Dungarvan; Mary Guinan Darmody, Tipperary Studies; Tipperary County Library, Thurles; Clare County Library, Ennis; the *Irish Examiner* Archive; Seamus O'Reilly; *Clare County Express*. Many photos are taken from Liam Ó Donnchú's personal collection.

10 9 8 7 6 5 4 3 2 1
25 24 23 22 21

Printed by EDELVIVES, Spain.
The paper in this book is produced using pulp from managed forests

Published in:

DUBLIN
UNESCO
City of Literature

CONTENTS

FOREWORDS

LABHRÁS MAC CÁRTAIGH
Uachtarán CLG

Is cúis mór áthais an deis a bheith agam réamhrá a scríobh don leabhar tabhachtach seo a thugann cur síos luachmhar dúinn ar cheann de na páirceanna is cáiliúla in ár n-eagraíocht.

As with many exciting and worthwhile projects placed before us, sometimes we are entitled to wonder how a body of work such as this was not undertaken before. To that end, we are indebted to Liam Ó Donnchú for embarking on a project to publish a book that will capture the history and stories associated with this iconic venue and ensure its special place in the organisation is passed on to future generations.

The mere mention of Tom Semple's field conjures up vivid memories of halcyon days for people from so many counties – not least Tipperary. For obvious reasons the town occupies a special place in the annals of GAA history, given it is the source from which the Association officially sprung in 1884.

Our founding forefathers couldn't have known it then, but the movement they unleashed on the country manifested itself in a way barely imaginable. Nowhere is this more striking than in and around Liberty Square in Thurles on a match day, when members and supporters throng the town before marching up the hill.

As with any large inter-county venue, the facilities have evolved and changed over the years to leave us with one of the largest stadiums in the country. We can be grateful to numerous pioneering administrators who fueled that process of development, ensuring that the venue has become and remains one of our most storied.

Whether it's sepia-toned images of trainloads of supporters arriving at the ground to witness the exploits of 'Hell's Kitchen' in the 1960s, the centenary final of 1984 or John Fenton's remarkable goal strike in 1987, Semple Stadium occupies a revered place on the

Irish sporting landscape.

It wasn't all hurling either. Who could forget Maurice Fitzgerald's golden moment in 2001, which earned his team a draw from a last-gasp sideline ball, when Kerry and Dublin played out two titanic quarter-final clashes?

Similarly, the creative fundraising required to upgrade the stadium saw concert-goers flock to the town for the Trip to Tipp and Féile, creating non-sporting memories for another generation.

Most of us will fondly recall trooping towards the venue in a sea of colour and bonhomie, either as neutrals or partisans, clutching or seeking tickets for the Old or New stands or the Town or Killinan End terraces. As I write in 2021, it is a scene I keenly await the repeat of, in these testing times.

I laud Liam for the work he undertook in bringing this project to fruition, and I look forward to delving into the final book. I wish him and everyone involved with it every success.

Go n-éirí go geal libh agus tá súil agam go mbeimid go léir bailithe ar ais arís i Staid Semple i nDurlas Éile go luath.

Le gach dea ghuí,

Labhrás Mac Cártaigh,
Uachtarán CLG

CONCHÚIR Ó HÓGÁIN
Cathaoirleach, Semple Stadium

PHOTO BY TOM RYAN CASEY

Wherever our Gaelic Games are spoken about, whenever people try to capture the essence and uniqueness of the GAA, whenever they describe the rivalry, the passion, the buildup, the great games, the thrill of victory, the agony of defeat, whenever they recount the deeds of the legendary players, inevitably the conversation will turn to Semple Stadium, and Munster, National League and All-Ireland Championship days. To be in Liberty Square on the morning of a Munster final, to mingle among the supporters, with their colours, their banners and their banter, to walk with the crowd over the railway bridge to the strains of the roadside musicians, to see the stadium before you, to enter and take your place in the famous ground, is an experience to be found nowhere else – and that is before the games even begin. After the GAA was founded in Thurles in November 1884, the town quickly established itself as a centre for organised games, and when the opportunity presented itself in 1910 to acquire their own grounds, the Gaelic-minded people in the area rallied round and raised the money to purchase the Showgrounds, thus putting the foundations in place for Semple Stadium as we know it today.

In this outstanding history of the stadium, Liam Ó Donnchú takes us through 130 years of striving and ambition, of development and organisation, of welcome and pride, of great games and personalities, as each succeeding generation made its contribution to the story of the Field of Legends.

A recurring theme in the stadium's history has been the record of continuous reinvestment in the pitch and facility. Major structural works were carried out in the 1920s, 1930s, 1960s and in the early 1980s, in preparation for the All-Ireland hurling final played in Thurles in the centenary year, 1984. In the early 2000s, following a consultant's recommendation that Thurles be designated the Association's second national stadium, its management committee was asked to prepare plans for major refurbishment, resulting in the expenditure of €18 million at the ground between 2008 and 2011. Plans are currently in place for the installation of a Centre of Excellence and the upgrading of the Kinane Stand area.

The other theme that is apparent to the reader is Semple Stadium's popularity among players, organising bodies and patrons. Hurlers have long regarded the pitch as the best playing surface in Ireland. From the earliest games at the venue, Tom Semple set the standards for organisation and stewarding which continue to this day, with all games, whether organised by Munster, Leinster or Croke Park, accommodated seamlessly in a friendly and welcoming manner.

The GAA in Tipperary is proud of Semple Stadium, its facilities, its uniqueness, and its part in the history of Gaelic Games. While change and new challenges are inevitable, one thing is certain: Tom Semple's field will always be front and centre in the evolving story of the GAA. Tipperary people will see to that.

It is entirely appropriate that Liam Ó Donnchú should be the author of this history of Semple Stadium. Having served for over forty years as its PRO, he is known throughout Ireland as 'the voice' of the stadium on big match days. Liam has given life-long service to his club, Thurles Sarsfields, as a player and administrator, and he is also a noted publicist and historian. His outstanding history, *Tom Semple and the Thurles Blues*, will be a companion volume to this history of Semple Stadium. Molann an obair an fear.

Go mbainfidh lucht a léite mór-thaithneamh agus sult as an stair an-thabachtach seo.

Conchúir Ó hÓgáin,
Cathaoirleach, Semple Stadium

LIAM Ó LOINEACHÁIN
Cathaoirleach, Comhairle na Mumhan

Is iontach an rud é go bhfuil stair Staid Semple á chur i gcló. Tá clú agus cáil ar an bpáirc, ní hé amháin in Éirinn ach i ngach áit ar fud na cruinne ina imrítar cluichí Gaelacha. Is mór an onóir domsa cúpla alt a chur le chéile mar gheall ar an bpáirc stairiúil seo.

Semple Stadium is famous for its lush green sward and immaculate playing surface. It's where all hurlers want to play, and there have also been many memorable football games played at the Field of Legends. We look and remember so many epic Munster hurling finals and the never-to-be-forgotten point scored by Maurice Fitzgerald in the All-Ireland football quarter-final against Dublin in 2001. It was fitting that the centenary All-Ireland hurling final in 1984 between Cork and Offaly was played in the birthplace of Cumann Lúthchleas Gael.

There is always a magical atmosphere in Thurles on Munster hurling final days. Many supporters come early and stroll around Liberty Square, soaking up the atmosphere. Cars and buses proudly displaying their county colours drive into town with horns signalling their arrival. There is always plenty of good humour and banter in the stadium between the partisan supporters. Children love wearing their county colours and waving their flags.

So much has been written about Munster finals by many famous sports journalists, but the late Raymond Smith has to be mentioned. Raymond, who had close links with Thurles, had a dream of dying at the Killinan End on the day of a Munster hurling final between Cork and Tipperary, and being gently laid out on the hallowed ground of Semple Stadium.

Let us never forget the visionary GAA people who purchased what was then the showgrounds in Thurles for £900 in 1910. Remember Croke Park was put up for sale in 1907 and bought by Frank Dineen, another GAA visionary.

Beir bua is beannacht,

Liam Ó Loineacháin

Liam Ó Loineacháin,
Cathaoirleach, Comhairle na Mumhan

SEOSAMH Ó CINNÉIDE
Cathaoirleach, Bord Thiobraid Árann

I t is a great privilege to be asked to pen these words in acknowledgement of a publication that is a superb addition to the GAA library, focusing as it does on a stadium that is synonymous with the GAA and most notably with the supporters of the wonderful game of hurling.

Semple Stadium has a rich history, and I compliment Liam Ó Donnchú on compiling it all in this book for the followers of the game to enjoy. Liam, through his many years of dedicated service to the stadium, has a unique understanding of the history associated with this iconic venue. He has been 'the voice' of the stadium for many years on big match days.

Every child who plays the game in Tipperary and even further afield dreams of playing in the 'Field of Legends' at some stage of their career. The stadium holds a unique prestige for all players and followers of the GAA in Tipperary. The quality of the playing surface is so high that all our sporting rivals love coming to Thurles to play games.

In my lifetime I can remember viewing county finals from the grass bank where Ardán Ó Riain is now situated. Since then there have been many improvements to the facilities, but the prestige and the allure of the stadium remains the same. It has hosted many wonderful and exciting games, such as the Munster and All-Ireland finals in 1984, the Munster final replay of 1991, and the football qualifier between Dublin and Kerry in 2001, to name but a few.

It is fitting that the contributions of all the committee members, officials and stadium staff, both past and present, are recorded in this book.

On my own behalf, and on behalf of my fellow officers and the GAA community, I would like to thank Liam for his tremendous work and research in putting on record this comprehensive history of Semple Stadium for generations to come.

Fearaim fíor-chaoin fáilte roimh an leabhar seo agus tá súil agam go mbainfidh a lán, lán daoine an-taitneamh as.

Seosamh Ó Cinnéide,
Cathaoirleach, Bord Thiobraid Árann

INTRODUCTION

For followers of Gaelic games, particularly hurling, Semple Stadium in Thurles is their Mecca. Situated in the heart of Tipperary – itself the centre of the hurling world, surrounded as it is by hurling strongholds – this is the venue for the game's greatest contests. It is the favoured ground for generations of hurlers; here, the sliotar bounces true, the crowds are close to the clashing ash, and reputations are created or shattered.

In my youth, the stadium was always referred to in Thurles as 'the Field', and over the years it has held a continuing attraction for me. Having enjoyed years as a member of the Semple Stadium staff, I have been encouraged by many to compile the story of this iconic venue, which had never before been attempted.

The stadium has always been blessed with great leadership – far-sighted, courageous people who strove with might and main to keep the standards high, to continue to refurbish, modernise and innovate. You cannot stand still with Semple Stadium. Through the pages of this book, their efforts are recorded. Credit, too, to the groundsmen through the decades, all of whom took immense pride in their work and knew that they were in charge of the stadium's greatest asset: the pitch itself.

Semple Stadium holds a fascination for so many people. Even on weekdays, when no

PHOTO BY TOM RYAN CASEY

game is on, I have occasionally met people who happened to be in Thurles and wouldn't pass without going in. They stand and gaze in silence at the vacant arena, but for them it's not empty. They are recalling the days their parents or neighbours first brought them here, the halcyon days of the epic battles, the legendary players … For them, the stadium has preserved their youth and vigour, and they have not grown old.

There are so many who helped me compile this book that listing them is impossible, but a deserved thanks to all. However, there are a few who deserve special mention: Jim Fogarty, for generous use of some images from his book *The Dan Breen Cup*; Joanne Clarke, Croke Park; Tom Beirne and Gerry O'Neill, Kilkenny; Peter Devine, Cork; Seamus O'Reilly, Clare; Ed Donnelly, Munster Council; Ger Corbett, Joe Tobin, Seamus J King, Seamus O'Doherty, Humphrey Kelleher, Michael and Noel Dundon, Con Hogan and the staff at Semple Stadium; photographers Ned O'Shea, Brendan O'Connor, Bridget Delaney, Eamonn McGee, George Hatchell, Star Systems, Thurles, John O'Loughlin, Tom Ryan Casey and Ray McManus of Sportsfile. A special thanks to my editor, Nicola Reddy, for her encouragement and enthusiasm, and to Michael, Ivan and Emma at The O'Brien Press.

This is not a history of everything that has happened at Semple Stadium – such a task would be impossible in one book. Consequently and regrettably, I have been unable to feature camogie, Peil na mBan, school and college competitions, Cumann na mBunscoil, Community Games, Bord na nÓg etc.

Over the years I've seen the best of players at Semple Stadium; they seem to shine when they step onto that green swarth, knowing instinctively that this is the place for which they have been preparing their bodies and honing their skills. This is the place and the time to shine in the heartland of hurling, before knowing eyes. Name and fame are on the line and can be made or shattered in this, our colosseum, our Circus Maximus, our Field of Legends.

Dom is dleacht a leacht do líonadh,
Dom is eól a scéal do scaoileadh …

Liam Ó Donnchú,
Meán Fómhair, 2021

'Thurles is to hurling as Milan is to Grand Opera and Nashville is to Country and Western music … Its centre, Liberty Square, seems like the centre of Ireland on days of big games … Then in Bowe's pub down by the railway station you feel that you are at the centre of the universe.'

Con Houlihan

'The old Thurles Sportsfield comes infused with so much history and cliché and all that whispery-echo stuff that it can tend to obscure the genius of the venue itself. But there's no need to be coy about it – Thurles is the best place to go to see a hurling match.'

Malachy Clerkin

'No Irish summer is complete without getting up close and personal with the hurling championships. There is nothing like it anywhere in the world. The atmosphere ferments into something quite electric once you get inside Semple Stadium. It's the action on the pitch, the commentary and craic from the stewards and the people that make the day. You don't hear songs at GAA games – what you hear are almighty roars.'

Joanne Cantwell

'Anyone who couldn't hurl in Thurles shouldn't bother handling a stick.'

Jim 'Tough' Barry

Above left: Hayes's Hotel, Thurles, where the GAA was founded in 1884.
Above right: GAA founder Michael Cusack.
Below left: Maurice Davin, founder and the first GAA president.
Below right: Archbishop Thomas Croke, first GAA patron.

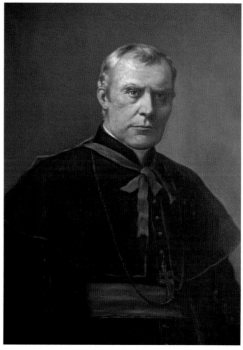

CHAPTER 1

IN THE BEGINNING

1884–1929

1884
Thurles, Birthplace of the GAA

Ever since the foundation of the Gaelic Athletic Association at Hayes's Hotel, Thurles, on 1 November, 1884, the town has been a focal point for supporters of Gaelic games. Not alone did that historic meeting take place in Thurles, but most GAA central council meetings and all GAA annual congresses for the following quarter century, until 1909, were held here too. This rich history, the centrality of Thurles within Ireland – with good road and rail links – and the fact that the patron of the GAA, Archbishop Thomas Croke, was a resident, ensured that Thurles will forever be in the hearts and minds of the GAA supporter.

Since GAA competitions began in 1887, Thurles was popular as a venue for major inter-county games in both hurling and Gaelic football. By 1910, when the grounds that would become Semple Stadium were purchased, three All-Ireland senior football finals had been hosted there. There was a growing desire among Tipperary and particularly Thurles GAA activists for a permanent home. By then, the GAA was well established in Thurles, and capable personnel were available in sufficient numbers to organise and run such events, all of which added to the demand for the town to have its own major sporting venue.

John Walsh.

James Maher.

Hugh Ryan, first chairman.

Edward T O'Meara, first treasurer.

Daniel A Butler.

The Tipperary hurling team, Thurles selection, photographed outside Clonmel Railway Station on Friday, 26 August, 1910, on tour to Brussels. Back row (l–r): William Butler, Thady Dwyer, James Kennedy, John Fitzgerald, Joe Cormack, Martin O'Brien, Eddy Flynn, William Carroll, Jack Mooney, Jimmy Bourke, Tom Kerwick. Middle row (l–r): Joe McLoughney, Richard O'Hanrahan, **Tom Semple** *(captain), Fr Michael O'Dwyer, Tim Gleeson, Jack Mockler. Front row (l–r): Pat Fitzgerald, Paddy Brolan, John Ryan Lanigan, Jim Bourke, Paddy Bourke, Anthony Carew.*

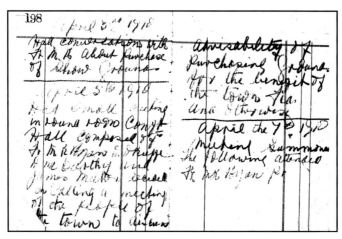

Jim Maher's diary, 1910.

1910
From Molloy's Field to Thurles Gaelic Sportsfield

In October 1909, the sale of Thurles Agricultural Society Grounds, about eleven acres, was a large topic for discussion around Thurles. The property had belonged to a local Thurles businessman, Joseph Molloy, and it passed into the possession of his wife, Mary, on his death. On 3 November, 1901, it was sold by public auction in two lots, at a price of £205 for one and £105 for the other, £310 in total, to the Thurles Agricultural Show committee.

> Whereas by indenture of lease dated the twenty-fourth day of September, one thousand nine hundred and three, William Daly and Denis St John Daly demised to the Thurles Agricultural Society Ltd., all that part of the lands of Thurles Townparks, known as Castle Meadows and that other part known as Muttonfield adjoining said lands of Castle Meadows both situate in the parish of Thurles … and containing in all eleven acres and thirty-five perches or thereabouts Irish plantation measure as then in the occupation of the lessees together with the rights, members and appurtenance thereunto belonging …
>
> Liam Ó Donnchú, *Tom Semple and the Thurles Blues* (2015)

This venture was a success for the show committee for some years, but by 1909, financial difficulties determined that the property be offered for sale. The local urban council convened a special meeting of its members to discuss the sale, as they had received an offer of the grounds from its directors, for the sum of £1,500. The need for a new burial ground in the town was high on the agenda, and many members considered that this property, if purchased, would make an ideal location. However, by year's end, Thurles Urban Council was finding it impossible to progress the deal.

Early in April 1910, a spirited civic attempt was made to hold the showground for the Gaels as a Gaelic field and for the good of the town. In his diary, Jim Maher, Parnell Street, wrote,

> 5 April 1910. Had a meeting in small room of Confraternity Hall, composed of Fr M K Ryan, Denis O'Keeffe, Denis McCarthy and myself. Decided on calling a meeting of the people of the town to discuss advisability of purchasing grounds for the benefit of the people of the town.

An offer of £900 was being gamely backed up. By the end of the month the *Tipperary Star* reported that 'the Thurles showground is now safe for the Gaels, the show and whatever will help the town – £900 is the purchase price'. To meet the cost of the purchase, an issue of shares was subscribed to by the townspeople. Shares were on sale, costing £1, from Hon Secretaries Denis O'Keeffe and William Butler. The grounds were then referred to as Thurles Sporting Grounds.

The election of the first committee, consisting of twelve members, took place in the Confraternity Hall on 24 May, 1910. The voting was by ballot of shareholders. It had been decided to limit the committee to fourteen members. By a unanimous decision, Thurles GAA and Mid Division GAA were each entitled to one permanent representative. The voting resulted as follows for the twelve remaining places: John Walsh, James Maher, Denis O'Keeffe, Edward T O'Meara, Hugh Ryan, Denis McCarthy, Thomas Semple, John Lambe, William Butler, D A Butler, J J Ryan and L J Ryan. The first officers elected were: Hugh Ryan, chairman; William O'Loughlin, secretary; and Edward T O'Meara, treasurer.

GAA Activity in Thurles
1886

Thurles GAA club undertook the onerous task of organising the first Gaelic tournament on Easter Sunday, 25 April, 1886. The idea of bringing clubs together to compete in friendly rivalry, in hurling and football, was new at the time and originated here. The chief organisers were Hugh Ryan, James Butler, Andy Callanan, Denis Maher, James Stapleton and John Gleeson, and the tournament attracted national attention and an attendance in the region of 15,000.

Suitable grounds were selected at Hackett's farm, Turtulla, just outside Thurles, and local teams were selected to meet the visiting teams. A huge gathering of the young men of Tipperary seemed to have collected there, their numbers increased by the arrival of special trains from Dublin. Taking part were Davitts and Faughs (both Dublin clubs), Dun Laoghaire, Two-Mile-Borris, Bray, Thurles, Nenagh, Moycarkey, Templemore, Holycross and Central Tipperary. Both hurling and football games were played, and the pitches for the tournament were in two linked fields marked out by Hugh Ryan, Thurles, and John Manning, Ballymoreen. Hugh spent much of the day on horseback, stewarding the sidelines and keeping the crowds under control.

When the ball was set rolling, every important official connected with the GAA at the time was on the field, from the patron, Archbishop Thomas Croke, to the president, Maurice Davin, the vice-presidents, J K Bracken and Frank Maloney, and the honorary secretaries, Michael Cusack, John McKay and J Wyse Power. Not a hitch occurred in the carrying out of the programme. As friends they met, as friends they parted. It was the day that planted the GAA in fruitful soil. As the games concluded, Archbishop Croke gave an impassioned speech, ending with these words:

> You have today safely planted the GAA and your magnificent tournament will ever constitute the premier page of Irish Gaelic history.

Sport, 1 May, 1886

1887

The First All-Ireland Hurling Champions

In the year 1887, the first county championships were organised, and Thurles GAA club affiliated a team in the inaugural hurling championship, winning their way to the Tipperary final. North Tipperary lined out against them. The teams were scoreless at half-time, but then the North began to weaken and gave way to the fitter Thurles team.

Three Thurles and Tipperary captains: Dinny Maher, Jim Stapleton and Tom Semple.

The final score was 3 points and 2 forfeit points to nil.

As Tipperary's champions, Thurles now had the right to select a team to represent their county in the All-Ireland championship. In their first game, they defeated Clare (Smith O'Briens) at Nenagh, and then accounted for Kilkenny (Tullaroan) at Urlingford. The All-Ireland final against Galway (Meelick-Eyrecourt) wasn't played until 1 April, 1888, at Johnny Farrell's field, Parsonstown (later Birr), County Offaly. A Tipperary victory resulted by 1 goal, 1 point and 1 forfeit point to Meelick's nil.

Above: The hurlers and athletes of the American 'Invasion' team assembled at St Patrick's College, Thurles, prior to their departure to the USA, in September 1888. Maurice Davin, first president of the GAA, stands on the left, holding a hammer.

Tipperary (Thurles selection), All–Ireland Hurling Champions 1887. Back row (l–r): Denis Maher (R), Jim Sullivan, Ned Murphy, Jim Ryan, Matty Maher (M), Ned Lambe, Tom Bourke, Con Callanan, Dan Davoren, Matty Maher (L). Middle row (l–r): Pat Ryan, Denis Maher (L), Jim Stapleton (captain), Tom Maher, John Leamy, Ger Ryan, Tim Dwyer. Front row (l–r): Mick Carroll, Martin McNamara, Tom Butler.

A Photograph More Than Twenty Years in the Making

On the last Sunday in June, 1910, the only photograph of the 1887 All-Ireland winning Tipperary (Thurles selection) team was taken at Thurles Sporting Grounds by Webster Photography, The Mall, Thurles. The players had to wait over twenty years for the occasion. As could be expected, they were not all available – three members had died and one had emigrated.

1888

The American 'Invasion'

In 1888, with the GAA running in smooth waters, the idea was fostered – mainly by GAA president Maurice Davin – of sending to America the best of Ireland's hurlers and athletes. The aim of the tour was to establish the GAA in America and to set up an annual athletics and hurling contest between America and Ireland. It was also hoped that the trip would prove financially worthwhile for the GAA. In order to facilitate the

Jim Stapleton, Thurles (far left) and Thady Ryan, Clonoulty (left), both Ivasion team hurlers.

tour, the 1888 inter-county championships in hurling and football were abandoned. This project became known in time as the American 'Invasion'. Sponsorship for the tour was sought and exhibition games were held for the purpose of fundraising, with the final one taking place on the grounds of St Patrick's College, Thurles, on 14 September, on the eve of departure. The tour party left Thurles for Cork on the late train, having been escorted to the railway station by an enthusiastic crowd.

The hurlers, athletes and officials, numbering fifty-one, were in high spirits as they sailed out of Queenstown (Cobh) aboard the SS *Wisconsin*. A great reception awaited them on their arrival in the USA, and they were fêted enthusiastically everywhere they went. They played exhibition games in New York, Boston, Providence, Philadelphia, Newark, Brooklyn, Yonkers, Lawrence, Lowell, Trenton, Patterson and New Jersey. However, the 'Invasion' was dogged by misfortune: bad weather resulted in poor atten-dances at matches; Irish–American societies were occupied with the excitements of the US presidential election, due on 6 November; and rivalry between the two main athletic bodies in America resulted in a lack of opposition teams – often the 'invaders' were left to put on exhibition matches among themselves. Financially, the expedition was a disaster. Far from raising money, the GAA was only able to fund the return journey thanks to a generous support of £450 from its patron, Michael Davitt.

Almost half of the 'invaders' remained in America, and others came back to Ireland only briefly before returning to live and work there.

T F O'Sullivan, *The Story of the GAA* (1916)

1895
A Much-Disputed Final

In the 1894 All-Ireland football final, Cork's Nil Desperan-
dum F C, remembered as Nils, drew with Dublin's Young Irelands at Clonturk Park, Dublin, on 24 March, 1895. The score
was 1-1 to 0-6 (goals counted for five points at the time). The
replay was fixed for 21 April at Ballycurrane, Thurles, about
a mile from the town, beside the railway line. Special trains
were commissioned to get supporters to the game, and it was
attended by about 10,000, including GAA patron Archbishop
Croke. GAA founder member J K Bracken of Templemore
received the archbishop at the ground. GAA secretary Dick
Blake, Navan, was referee. The crowd proved uncontrollably
large and finally spilled all over the ground. At times, the ball

*J K Bracken, Templemore,
GAA founder.*

was liable to strike spectators and still not be out of bounds, which caused frustration
between the players and fans. It was twenty-one players aside at the time, and with two
minutes left, the game was finely poised. Nils were leading by 1-2 to 5 points when an
incident occurred in a corner of the ground. The press reported:

> A Dublin player struck a member of the Cork team. A bystander, a Charleville man,
> shouted 'foul'. A Young Irelander (Dublin) ran at the spectator and struck him, but got
> promptly a knock down blow in return. The crowd then ran in and the match was inter-
> rupted. A few minutes later the Dublin team left the field and objected to Cork getting
> the match on the ground that the field was badly kept, and that one of their players had
> been struck.
>
> *Cork Examiner*, 22 April, 1895

Both sides claimed to have won. Crowd invasions were very common during this period.
Matches were also routinely abandoned due to players walking off the pitch in protest
at a refereeing decision.

GAA Central Council discussed the situation at a meeting at Hayes's Hotel on 28

April. They decided that the football match should be replayed, but that Cork would start two points ahead. Cork did not accept the decision and the game was never replayed, despite it being fixed for three weeks later. Dublin and Young Irelands were declared champions for the third time in four years.

1895
The Golden Square Mile

Tubberadora, referred to as the 'Golden Square Mile', is a townland close to Boherlahan village in County Tipperary. Its hurlers formed one of the greatest combinations in the annals of hurling. Many of their championship games were played in Thurles. The Tubberadora selection won three All-Irelands in four years – 1895, 1896 and 1898 – and were unbeaten in any championship contest in that period. Since their formation in 1895, they played in fourteen championship matches, scoring a total of 71 goals and 108 points, as against 17 goals and 46 points for their opponents. Tubberadora ceased to exist

Tipperary (Tubberadora selection), All-Ireland Hurling Champions 1898. Back row (l–r): Watty Dunne, Bill Devane, Ned Brennan, Mikey Maher (captain), E D Ryan, John Ryan, Tim Condon. Middle row (l–r): Thomas Leahy, Phil Byrne, John Connolly, Jack Maher, Denis Walsh, Jim O'Keeffe, Dick O'Keeffe, Michael Conlon. Front row (l–r): Tommy Ryan, Jack Maher (Fields), Ned Maher, Johnny Walsh. Note that caps were part of their playing gear.

following their 1898 All-Ireland success, but some of their players continued to further honours with neighbouring clubs.

> Now I'll sing in praise of home, no matter where I roam,
> And the many games and pleasures of the years,
> To see the Gaels all round upon the hurling ground,
> There are none to beat the Tubberadora team.
>
> Tom Leahy, quoted in Philip F Ryan,
> *The Tubberadora Boherlahan Hurling Story* (1973)

1899

World Athletic Records Broken in Thurles

The name of the Gaelic Athletic Association is indicative of its aim to make athletics more accessible to the masses and to revive and nurture traditional, indigenous sports and pastimes. From 1895 to 1914, the GAA staged their own Irish championships, and on 17 September, 1899, Thurles was the venue for the annual GAA Track and Field National Championships. These were a great success, chiefly owing to the outstanding performances of Thomas F Kiely, Ballyneale, Carrick-on-Suir, and Peter O'Connor, Wicklow, who established new records for the hammer and the long jump respectively.

Kiely started well by throwing the 16 lbs hammer 156 feet, which was 4 feet 1 inch better than his own British record. He also won the 56 lbs event, slinging the missile 37 feet 4 inches. However, Peter O'Connor was the hero of the day. His mighty leap of 24 feet 3 inches exceeded the world long jump record by 3.5 inches, and he also won the 220 yards, the high jump and the hop, step and jump (triple jump). Sadly for O'Connor, his long jump was not recognised as a world record, even though the record was set at a national championship. The reason given was that the jumping grounds were not properly laid out by the organisers and did not conform to the specifications necessary for establishing a record.

Long jumper Peter O'Connor from Wicklow.

1899

Kilfinane Capture the Croke Cup

The much delayed hurling final for the Dr Croke Cup of 1897 was held in Thurles on 9 July, 1899, in the presence of GAA patron Archbishop Thomas Croke. Limerick (Kilfinane selection), captained by Denis Grimes, won the competition by 3-8 to 1-4, against Kilkenny (Tullaroan selection). Seven thousand spectators saw GAA secretary Frank B Dineen present the teams to the archbishop, who imparted his blessing to the kneeling players before the start of the game. This was one of his rare appearances in public – he was in poor health at the time – and his final attendance at a hurling game. The Kilkenny team was composed of players from Tullaroan, Mooncoin and Three Castles. The referee was Patrick McGrath of Emly, Tipperary.

GAA General Secretary Frank B Dineen.

Kilfinane, Limerick, Dr Croke Cup Champions 1897. Back row (l–r): Pat Mulcahy, John Hynes, Michael Downes, Seán Óg Hanly, Mick Finn, Jim Flood, Patrick O'Brien, Jim Cattrell. Front row (l–r): Paddy Flynn, John Reidy, Tom Casey, Paddy Buskin, Maurice Flynn, Tom 'Goatee' Brazill, Denis Grimes (captain), John Finn, Frank Dunworth.

1900

Hayes Leads Two-Mile-Borris to Glory

'Tis well I remember, for the shield they did play

Against famous Kilkenny, always first in the fray,

For the Gaels of Moondharrig, strong and stout in their ways,

But still they went under to bold captain Hayes.

Moycarkey-Borris GAA Story (1984)

Two-Mile-Borris got a walk-over from Moycarkey in the Tipperary county final of 1900. The Borris selection won their way to the All-Ireland final, defeating London Irish by 2-5 to 0-6 at Jones's Road, later Croke Park.

Tipperary (Two-Mile-Borris selection), All-Ireland Hurling Champions 1900. Front row (l–r): Tom Allen, Matt Ryan, Ned Maher, Ned Hayes (captain), Mikey Maher, Paddy Maher (Best), Jack Gleeson, M F Crowe (referee), Denis O'Keeffe. Second row (l–r): Tom Duggan, Paddy 'Berry' Stapleton (Thurles), 'Big' Bill Gleeson, Paddy Hayes, Tom Semple (Thurles), Jack Maher, Tom Cantwell, David Cantwell. Third row (l–r): James Bowe, Johnny Walsh, Mick Purcell, Billy Maher, Mike Wall, 'Little' Bill Gleeson, Tommy Ryan, James O'Keeffe. Back row (l–r): ---, ---, Tom Fanning, Billy Maher, Jim Skehan, Ned Bowe, Charlie Maher, ---.

De Wets are Champions

The club Lahorna from Cloughjordan in north Tipperary added the name 'De Wets' in memory of the Boer general Christiaan de Wet, who opposed the British forces in the Boer war (1899–1902). They won the Tipperary Senior Hurling Championship in 1902 (team pictured above), defeating Carrick by 7-10 to 1-2 at Thurles Sportsfield.

Unconquered yet, are you De Wet
O may you never vary,
The magic name that gained such fame
For gallant Tipperary.

Canon Edward J Whyte, *Kilruane MacDonaghs and Lahorna De Wets* (1985)

Tipperary, Dr Croke Cup champions 1904.

1904
Cork and Tipperary Win Munster Double

A new competition, which had been inaugurated in 1902 and dedicated to the memory of the late Archbishop Thomas Croke, began in 1904. The Croke Cups, as they came to be known, were contested now by provincial champions in both hurling and football.

Jamesy Kelleher,
Dungourney captain.

Dungourney, Cork, All-Ireland Hurling Champions 1902. Back row (l–r): J Quirke (president), M Shea, W Daly, W Fitzgibbons, D McGrath, J Daly, J Shea, W O'Brien (county board), E Aherne (secretary). Middle row (l–r): J Desmond, P Leahy, S Riordan, Jamesy Kelleher (captain), T Coughlan, W O'Neill, T Mahony. Front row (l–r): J Ronayne, W Parfrey, J O'Leary, D O'Keeffe.

Faughs (Fág-a'-Bealach), Dublin, 1904. Back row (l–r): John Dillon, Stephen Spillane, Charles Dillon, William Connolly, Paddy Hogan, Pat Kinehan, Thomas Dillon. Middle row (l–r): Jack Hogan, Ned Egan, John Dwyer, Jack Connolly, Tom Hayes, Pat Flynn, James Riordan, Hugh Treacy. Front row (l–r): Jack Cleary, John Quinlan, Tim Gleeson, Danny McCormack (captain), Andy Harty, Tom Hogan, George Ryan.

The home finals were played at Thurles Agricultural Society Grounds (now Semple Stadium), on 6 November, 1904.

GAA patron Archbishop Thomas Fennelly was present, accompanied by a large number of clergymen. He threw in the ball to commence both games, which were won by Munster counties. In football, the Tipperary town club had the selection of the Tipperary team. Their captain, Bob Quane, was the best player on view as he led his team to victory over Bray Emmets by 2-4 to 0-4.

Tipperary: Bob Quane (captain), J Butler, Jack Ryan, John Wyse, Redmond Butler, Davy Quane, Jerry Noonan, P Heffernan (Tipperary Club), Pat Moloney (goalkeeper), Ned Kelly, John Kavanagh (Kilsheelan), Pat Wall, Jack Shea (Grangemockler), J Norris (Carrick), P Myers, Bill Barrett (Clonmel), Jack Hayes (Fethard).

The hurling was contested by Faughs of Dublin and Dungourney of Cork. This game was not finished as darkness set in about twenty minutes before the expiration of the hour. It was replayed, again in Thurles, on 27 November but was not finished due to a dispute. The referee had ordered a Dublin player off the field; he refused to leave and the match was awarded to Cork, with only eighteen minutes of the second half played. The final score was Cork (Dungourney) 1-1, Dublin (Faughs) 0-2. The final proper was played the following February at Jones's Road, Dublin, with the Munster counties again victorious against London Irish.

1904

Confraternity Hall Tournament

The new Confraternity Hall in Thurles was completed in the spring of 1904, but a large debt remained, so a major tournament was organised to recoup some of the costs. It proved to be a great success, with over 10,000 spectators thronging the town. The final featured two of the great names of Tipperary hurling, Tubberadora and Lahorna De Wets. Tom Semple of Thurles hurled with Tubberadora that day, the only Thurles player ever to wear the Tubberadora jersey. The day also had a special significance in that it was the last time a team bearing the name Tubberadora lined out in a hurling game. The final score was Tubberadora 10-13, Lahorna De Wets 0-3. The debt on the new hall was considerably reduced.

Tubberadora, 1904. Front row (l–r): Tom Ryan, Ned Maher, 'Big' Bill Gleeson, Tim Condon, Watty Dunne, Joe O'Keeffe, Dick O'Keeffe. Middle Row (l–r): Phil Byrne, Johnny Walsh, Paddy Hayes, Tom Semple. Back row (l–r): Tom Leahy (president), Mike Wall, Jim O'Keeffe, Jack Maher, Mikey Maher, 'Little' Bill Gleeson, Jack Gleeson, Mike Conlon (secretary).

1906
'Go Home, If You Won't Pull'

Tom Semple's team favoured a ground hurling style and worked hard to perfect it. This required anticipation, speed, concentration and great hand/eye coordination. It also

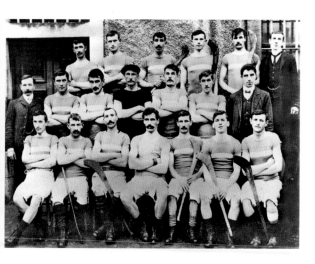

Tipperary (Thurles selection), All–Ireland Hurling Champions 1906. Back Row (l–r): Tom Allen, Jack Cahill, Jack Gleeson, Tom Kerwick, Paddy Maher 'Best', J M Kennedy (secretary). Middle Row (l–r): Denis O'Keeffe (chairman), Paddy Bourke, Jimmy Bourke, Paddy Riordan, Jer Hayes (vice-captain), Martin O'Brien, Phil Molony (treasurer). Front Row (l–r): Jack Mockler, Joe O'Keeffe, James 'Hawk' O'Brien, Tom Semple (captain), Tom Kenna, Michael Gleeson, Paddy Brolan.

required great courage to contest the 'clash of the ash' when closely marked by an opponent or opponents, or when your opponent had the advantage in contesting the ball. The aim was to deliver the ball with the minimum delay. Semple himself is remembered as having a strong ground stroke off either side and using it to good effect. Meeting the ball in the air, doubling on it overhead, was greatly encouraged. The rising and handling of the ball was kept to a minimum. As Paddy Brolan, one of Semple's star hurlers, recalled,

> And he [Semple] would drive a ball over the bar from sixty yards out off the ground, if he got half a chance. If he saw you stopping a ball he would shout, 'Go home, if you won't pull'.
>
> Ó Donnchú, *Tom Semple and the Thurles Blues*

1907
First Title for the Lilywhites: All-Ireland Senior Football Final

The All-Ireland football final of 1905, between Kerry and Kildare, was played at Thurles Agricultural Society Grounds on 16 June, 1907. Records of the attendance vary between 15,000 and 20,000. There were seventeen special trains into Thurles that day, and the mass of humanity broke down the gates in their eagerness to get into the ground. M F Crowe of Dublin was referee.

Kerry were bidding for a 'three in a row', but Kildare, captained by Joe Rafferty, took sweet revenge for their defeat two years before and won by double scores. The final score was Kildare (Roseberry) 1-7, Kerry (Tralee Mitchels) 0-5. Castleisland native Maurice McCarthy captained the Kingdom.

The All-Ireland senior football medal won by Kildare.

A long puck championship medal.   *Tom Semple, long puck champion.*   *Bob O'Keeffe.*

1907
Rising and Striking

The All-Ireland Athletic Championships, under GAA rules, were held at the Agricultural Showgrounds, Thurles, on 28 July, 1907. There were many champion athletes present, such as Thomas F Kiely of Carrick-on-Suir and Paddy Ryan of Pallasgreen. Local All-Ireland hurler Tom Semple won the event known as 'Rising and Striking the Hurling Ball'. The hurling ball weighed nine ounces and the distance was recorded at 96 yards, approximately 88 metres, a championship record. The runner-up was County Kilkenny native Bob O'Keeffe, who won the championship in 1903, played on the winning Laois team in the All-Ireland hurling final in 1915, and was president of the GAA from 1935 to 1938.

1909
The Kingdom Falls to the Dubs: All-Ireland Football (Home) Final

Over 10,000 football supporters headed for Thurles on 9 May, 1909, to attend the delayed 1908 All-Ireland home final at Thurles Agricultural Society Grounds. M F Crowe was the referee, and it was described as a splendid contest for forty minutes. In the final quarter, Kerry fell away as the Dubs assumed control. The final score was Dublin (Geraldines) 0-10, Kerry (Tralee Mitchels) 0-3.

Kerry's Dick Fitzgerald, famed in football lore, was on the losing side. Dublin, captained by Dave Kelleher, won that year's final proper, beating London Irish 1-10 to 0-4. Kelleher, also a noted hurler, was a native of Charleville, County Cork.

Dublin (Geraldines selection), All-Ireland Football Champions 1908. Back row (l–r): Paddy Sheehan, J J Keane, Paddy Fallon, Maurice Collins, James Brennan, Dan Kavanagh, Paddy Daly, L Tuite, J Lane. Middle row (l–r): J F Keenan, James Brennan, Bill Halinden, Jack Shouldice, Paddy Whelan, Mick Power, John Lynch, Hugh Hillard, W O'Flaherty. Front row (l–r): Tom Healy, Fred Cooney, Tom McAuley, Tommy Walsh. Missing from photograph: Dave Kelleher (captain) and Jack Grace.

Equestrian Events at Daly Park

Horse racing and other equestrian activities were popular in Thurles in the early days. A race meeting was held on Monday, 29 August, 1910, in which eighty horses contested five races, and another major meeting took place on the following St Stephen's Day. For horse-racing events, Thurles Sportsfield was often referred to during these years as Daly Park. The Daly family were former owners of the Llandaff estate, which included much of the town of Thurles.

1910

Double-Barrelled Shotguns

Shortly after the purchase of Thurles Sportsfield, committee member John Walsh expressed the opinion that it would be necessary to open with a first-class tournament, with proceeds in aid of the grounds. He voiced the view that, as the principal teams of Tipperary and other counties had medals 'go leor', there would be more enthusiasm for a different prize. According to him, there would be no prize more acceptable to a team than brand-new,

Right: J M Kennedy, secretary of Thurles GAA.

valuable double-barrelled shotguns. Thurles secretary James M Kennedy agreed. The committee decided that the guns would be purchased and stocked in the field at the first match, so the public would be satisfied that the tournament was bona fide.

Respectable People?

At a meeting of the Thurles Sportsfield Committee in 1910, chairman Hugh Ryan of West Gate (pictured) was amazed that some patrons were attempting to gain free entry to events by forcing a way through the galvanised enclosure. 'I am amazed that respectable people would be so lost to self-respect as to avoid a small payment,' he commented. They decided to appoint a caretaker and prosecute any trespassers.

1911
The 'Invasion' of the Irish-American Hurlers

Very little has been written about the 1911 Homegoing Tour of Ireland by the Irish-American hurlers of Chicago, Detroit and New York. Their plan was to arrive in Ireland in mid-July and play games at Wexford, Thurles, Waterford, Dublin, Cork and Limerick. Their colours were royal blue shirts/sweaters (with crests), white pants/shorts, and royal blue stockings. They would stay with friends or relatives after each game, reporting to their next venue on the Thursday before each match. As each player would bring only one hurley, the organisers requested that a few extras be made available just in case they were needed.

Among the games they played was one at Thurles Sporting Grounds, on 30 July, against a Tipperary selection of Thurles, Borris/Ileigh and Two-Mile-Borris players. The team's headquarters was at Lambe's Hotel, Thurles. Three bands, Thurles Brass and Reed, Clonmel and Urlingford Fife and Drum played the visitors through the town and onto the field, where a large crowd gave them a memorable reception. The team's vice-captain was the well-known All-Ireland hurler Paddy Riordan of Rosmult, Drombane. Paddy got an especially warm welcome from his old teammates around Thurles. As the 'Yanks' said, 'When Tipp does things, they are done thoroughly'. Tipperary won well, 7-2 to 1-3. The referee was Tom Irwin of Cork.

Irish-Americans: William Morgan (captain), Thomas Roche, Bill Heffernan, W Doyle, M McCarthy, Joe Mahon, J P Shortall, P Saunders, A Berkery, M Treacy, D Scully, Paddy Riordan, Joe Kavanagh, P Purcell, J Ryan, M Moriarty, M Fogarty. Overall, the tour proved to be a great success and the hurlers returned to the United States well satisfied with their momentous Irish 'Invasion'.

> What is your fear boys, whilst Semple is with you,
> That gallant old captain, who leads in the fray?
> Why should you doubt, when you think of the past boys?
> The one word 'Dungourney' ought all trouble allay.
>
> Seamus J King, Liam Ó Donnchú, Jimmy Smyth, *Tipperary's GAA Ballads* (2000)

1914

Raising the Banner: Munster Senior Hurling Final

The Munster senior hurling final, between Clare and Cork, was in Thurles for the first time on 20 September, 1914. There was a mighty hosting of Gaels, almost 20,000, from all over Ireland, and the match was fought out in the most dexterous and determined fashion. Clare were champions, and Tom Semple, who refereed the game, later conveyed

Clare, Munster and All-Ireland Champions 1914. Back row (l–r): Dr T Fitzgerald, J P McGuire, P E Kenneally, Willie Redmond MP, John Rodgers, Canon O'Kennedy, Patrick McDermott, Rev J M McCreedy, Batt Culligan, Patrick 'Bucky' Moloney, John Jones. Third row (l–r): Dr H McDonagh, Tom McGrath, John Fox, Rob Doherty, Michael Flanagan, James 'Bawn' Clancy, Joe Power, Stephen Clune. Second row (l–r): James O'Regan, Jim Guerin, Patrick 'Fowler' McInerney, William 'Dodger' Considine, Amby Power (captain), Martin 'Handsome' Moloney, Edward Grace, John Shalloo, Jim O'Hehir (trainer). Front row (l–r): Brendan Considine, James 'Sham' Spellissy.

the ferocity of the encounter when he stated that 'it was as hard fought a Munster final as ever I saw. The issue was in doubt up to the last minute. It was a strenuous game, but nevertheless a sporting one'. The final score was Clare 3-2, Cork 3-1.

Further evidence of the game's intensity was provided in the *Clare Journal* on 8 October, 1914, when it was reported that the Quin selection committee had in advance of the All-Ireland final appealed for hurleys as 'a reserve was absolutely essential given the large number broken during the match in Thurles'.

The prolific poet and journeyman blacksmith Martin Kennedy from Belvoir penned the poem '1914 Munster Final' with this final verse:

Now they're back in County Clare and there's music everywhere,
The boys are full of frolic and of fun,

The Banner County bred them and Maria Reddin fed them,

And Amby Power led like a father with his son,

He led the gallant hurlers all the way to Thurles,

And the Munster Final Championship, they won.

Jimmy Smyth, *Ballads of the Banner* (1998)

Clare's team trainer was Jim Hehir, Ballynacally, father of renowned sporting commentator Michael O'Hehir (Mícheál Ó hEithir).

Left: Jim Guerin, Ballycar, played in two Munster finals at Thurles Sportsfield, in 1914 and 1918. Jim died on 16 December, 1918, as a result of the 1918 'Spanish flu' pandemic. Courtesy of Clare County Library.
Right: Pat 'Fowler' McInerney, Clare goalkeeper in 1914. Below: Denis Morgan, Irish Volunteer activist and Thurles Urban Council Chairman in 1920. He was the grandfather of Father Ted *star Dermot.*

1914
The Tramp of Men:
Volunteer Training at Thurles Sporting Grounds

In May 1914, news of the successful passing of the Home Rule Bill through its final stages in the House of Commons was greeted with delight all over Tipperary. A remarkable demonstration was held in Thurles. Hundreds of Irish Volunteers paraded through the town behind the local band. 'A Nation Once Again' was sung with gusto, and bonfires were lit as the news was celebrated.

Volunteer activity increased as the year progressed, with regular parades in the town. Drilling was arranged to take place at Thurles Sporting Grounds on four nights weekly, and competent military instructors were secured. At the conclusion of the drilling, it was customary that the three companies would form in fours and, headed by the band, march in soldierly fashion along Bohernanave, down Friar Street, West Gate and the Square, forming up along Main Street and dismissing at the word of command.

A major Volunteer fundraising effort took place in the town through church-gate donations and collections at Thurles Sporting Grounds. The collection tables carried a poster stating 'We Want Rifles'. Joseph MacDonagh – brother of Thomas, future leader of the Easter Rising of 1916 – worked in Thurles and was a regular at the Volunteer meetings. D H Ryan of Thurles GAA club chaired many of the meetings. Tipperary County Volunteer Board meetings were chaired by Pierce McCan, Dualla, and James M Kennedy, Thurles, was acting honorary secretary.

In August, the outbreak of the Great War convulsed Europe, and Home Rule was suspended. John Redmond, leader of the Irish Parliamentary Party, called for the Irish Volunteers to support the British war effort. This caused a split: a minority opposed to the war retained their original name. The Redmondite majority was renamed the National Volunteers. In October, the Thurles Corps of the National Volunteers used Thurles Sporting Grounds as a rifle range. Three targets were set up, with a range of 200 yards.

Tipperary (Toomevara selection), All-Ireland Hurling Finalists 1913. Back row: (l–r) Jack Kennedy, Jack O'Meara, Ned Cawley, Jack Raleigh, Mick Ryan, Jim O'Meara, Paddy Kennedy. Front row (l–r): Bill Kelly, Jim Murphy, Hugh Shelly, Elias 'Bud' O'Keeffe. Middle row (l–r): Ned Guilmartin, Jack Harty, Frank McGrath, Patrick 'Wedger' Meagher (captain), Stephen Hackett.

1914
Toomevara 'Greyhounds' to the Fore: Tipperary Senior Hurling Final

In 1914, Toomevara, captained by Pat 'Wedger' Meagher, completed a three-in-a-row of Tipperary hurling championships, beating Boherlahan in the county final at Thurles

Sportsfield by 5-2 to 3-1. Before one of their games, Tom Semple advised the players to 'keep close to your men from the start, make the pace and the day is yours'. He then sprinkled them with holy water.

> Then hurrah for Toomevara! May your banner never fall,
> You beat Galway and Queen's County, you're the boys can play the ball.
> But I never will forget the day, Kilkenny's pride went down
> Before the skill of Wedger's men in sweet Dungarvan town.
>
> Michael Bourke, Newport

Male Support Predominated

This is a rare view of Thurles Sportsfield, taken about 1915. The match supporters, predominantly male, some hatted and mostly capped, are engrossed in proceedings. Since the days when the venue was used for horse racing, the classic picket fence was a feature separating the onlookers from the sporting arena.

The low-sized gentleman leaning on the railing in the centre of the photograph is Andy Mason from Drombane. Andy was the first secretary of the Mid Tipperary GAA Board, established in 1907, a position he held until his death in 1930.

1917

The Soldier's Song

On 5 August, 1917, Boherlahan and Toomevara played an epic hurling game in the Tipperary semi-final at Thurles Sportsfield, with Boherlahan victorious. With the county's top two teams in action, it was of little surprise that a huge crowd gathered. There was a profuse display of the republican tricolour in evidence, and for the first time 'The Soldier's Song' was sung at the venue. Written by Peadar Kearney, it was a popular marching song of the Irish Volunteers. This song would, within a few years, become Ireland's national anthem, 'Amhrán na bhFiann'.

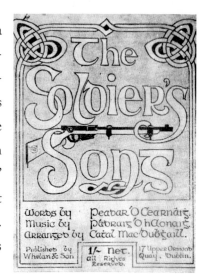

Sheet music for 'The Soldier's Song'.

1918

Gaelic Sunday

In July 1918, following months of civil unrest, strikes and protests, the British authorities informed the GAA that no hurling or football games would be allowed unless a permit was first obtained from Dublin Castle. The GAA unanimously agreed that no such permit should be applied for under any conditions and instead defiantly organised a series of matches throughout the country. On 4 August, at 3pm, the GAA staged approximately 1,500 hurling or football matches throughout the country in defiance of the ban on what became known as 'Gaelic Sunday'. In Mid Tipperary, chairman Tom Semple organised the playing of fourteen games, with Thurles Sportsfield as one of the venues.

1918

Limerick's Scoring Spree: Munster Senior Hurling Final

The Great War was drawing to a close as Limerick and Clare faced each other in the Munster final at Thurles Sporting Grounds, on 15 September, 1918. Tom Semple was referee, but this was mostly a one-sided affair as Clare made a very poor show and the

Above left: Willie Hough, Limerick captain in 1918.

Above right: Limerick (Newcastle West selection), Munster and All-Ireland Champions 1918. Back row (l–r): B Croke, J Kelly (chairman), D Hennessy, Mick Rochford, Paddy Kennedy, Willie Ryan, W Gleeson Snr, Dinny Lanigan, James Ryan (Limerick GAA secretary), Mick Murphy, C Ryan, M Bourke, M Ryan. Middle row (l–r): Jimmy Humphries, W Penny, Tom McGrath, Rev S Connolly, Willie Hough (captain), Rev J O'Keeffe, Jack Keane, Willie Gleeson, F Shanny. Front row (l–r): J Foley, Dick Ryan, Dan Troy, Bob McConkey, Paddy Barry, M Hogan.

The Tipperary (Boherlahan selection) team that won the 1916 All-Ireland. Back row (l–r): Tom Leahy, Dan O'Brien, Phil Fogarty (with hat), Ned Croke, Anthony Carew, Willie O'Dwyer (L), Tom Dwan, Arthur O'Donnell, Jack Doherty, Tom Shanahan, Dick Walsh, Jer Collison, Michael Myres, Willie O'Dwyer. Front row (l–r): Joe Nagle, Mick Leahy, Jimmy Murphy, Willie O'Dwyer, Hugh Shelly, Joe Fitzpatrick, Johnny Leahy (captain), Denis Walsh, Paddy Leahy, Jack Power.

Shannonsiders, led by Willie Hough of Monagea, swept to an easy victory. The final score was Limerick 11-3, Clare 1-2.

1918

Boherlahan Four-in-a-Row: Tipperary Senior Hurling Final

In 1918, Boherlahan completed a four-in–a-row of Tipperary hurling championships. Their 1916 Tipperary selection beat Kilkenny's Tullaroan in the All-Ireland final at Croke Park, by 5-4 to 3-2. Due to the political unrest in the country, this final wasn't played until 21 January, 1917.

1920

Black and Tans

William O'Loughlin, first secretary of Thurles Sportsfield.

In 1920, a British officer and a military sergeant called on William O'Loughlin, secretary of Thurles Sportsfield Committee, and warned him that unless the ticket slots in the sportsfield wall were closed within forty-eight hours, the British military would blow the entire wall away. Such threats from the British military were always ignored.

The Black and Tans were a notorious force recruited to support the Royal Irish Constabulary (police) during the War of Independence. They were mostly unemployed former World War One soldiers from Britain, and were deployed to troubled areas. They targeted the GAA as they associated it with the growth of nationalism and suspected that some members were involved in republican activities. The 'Tans' did much damage to the stand and fences in Thurles Sportsfield. The gates were flung open, the grounds were made a commonage, and woodwork of every kind was burned to ashes. A claim for compensation by the committee resulted in the payment of £300 from the British Treasury. (Thurles Sportsfield Minutes, 26 April, 1926.)

Horse racing continued at Thurles Sportsfield into the 1920s. For this meeting, M F Meagher was judge, Tom Semple was starter, and W H Ryan was measurer.

Above: Limerick, All-Ireland Champions 1921.
Left: Frank McGrath, referee.

1922

Limerick Upset the Odds: Munster Senior Hurling Final

The political upheaval in Ireland that came with the signing of the Anglo-Irish Treaty and the subsequent partition of the country militated against the efficient running of games, and many delays and postponements were experienced. Consequently the 1921 Munster senior hurling final wasn't played until 28 May, 1922. It was the only game in the Munster championship played that year as Munster GAA Council decided that the finalists of 1920 would contest the 1921 final. Cork were favourites, but Limerick really upset the odds by winning by 5-2 to 1-2. The referee was Frank McGrath, Nenagh, who was commandant of the 1st Tipperary Brigade of the IRA at the time. Limerick went on to beat Galway in the All-Ireland semi-final and Dublin in the final, becoming the belated 1921 All-Ireland champions on 4 March, 1923.

Limerick: Bob McConkey (captain), Michael Murphy, Willie Gleeson, Jimmy Humphries, Denny Lanigan, Dave Murnane, Willie Hough, Jack Keane, Willie Ryan, Garrett Howard, Paddy McInerney, Tom Mangan, Mick Mullane, Christy Ryan, Tom McGrath.

1923

Tipperary Takes the Title: Munster Senior Football Final

The 1922 championship was postponed due to the Civil War; torn up railway lines, broken bridges and blocked roads made travel hazardous. Having beaten Cork, in Cork, by the narrowest of margins in the Munster semi-final, 2-2 to 2-1, Tipperary met Limerick in the final at Thurles Sporting Grounds on 1 July, 1923. The home team, captained by Ned O'Shea, Fethard, were the deserving winners, 1-7 to 0-1. However, they lost the All-Ireland semi-final to Sligo by 1-8 to 0-7.

Tipperary: Ned O'Shea (captain), Arthur Carroll, Vincent Vaughan, Mick Tobin, Tom Lanigan, Mick Arrigan, Bill Barrett, Jim Doran, Ned Cummins, Bill Grant, Jim Ryan, Tommy Ryan, Tom Dunne, Mick Nolan, Dick Lanigan.

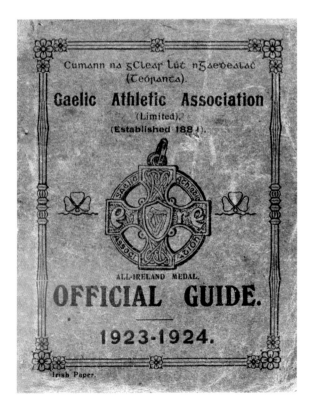

Left: The GAA Official Guide, 1923–1924.
Above: Referee Pádraig Ó Caoimh of Cork.

Above: Tipperary senior hurling team, 1923. Back row (l–r): Anthony Carew (secretary), John Conway, Bill Ryan (K), Jack O'Meara, Frank McGrath, Pat Browne, Tom Semple, Arthur O'Donnell, Stephen Hackett, Jack Kennedy, John Cleary, Patrick 'Wedger' Meagher. Middle row (l–r): John Darcy, Martin Kennedy, Tom Shanahan, Pakie Spillane, Johnny Leahy, Bill Dwan, Jim Gleeson. Front row (l–r): Jack Power, John Joe Hayes, Tom Dwan, Paddy Power, Martin Mockler. Below: Tipperary captain Johnny Leahy.

1923

A Game of Thrills: Munster Senior Hurling Final

The 1922 Munster hurling final, between Tipperary and Limerick, at Thurles Sportsfield on 1 July, 1923, was described as 'a game of thrills', with the hurling exceptionally good. Twenty thousand attended, and from the throw-in, an unusually fast pace was set, which lasted the hour. Limerick led by double scores at half-time, but they failed to score in the remaining half. Arthur O'Donnell saved the Premier with a late goal. A draw, 2-2 apiece, was seen as a fair result. Pádraig Ó Caoimh, Cork, later a GAA general secretary, was referee. Tipperary won the replay in Limerick, but lost the All-Ireland final to Kilkenny.

In praise of Tipperary's Martin Kennedy:

The fastest foot that ever sped around the dusty square,

The flying ball he never missed on ground or in the air.

His steel-like wrists and lightning twists, we'll ne'er forget;

He beat the best full-backs with ease as raspers shook the net.

King, Ó Donnchú, Smyth, *Tipperary's GAA Ballads*

Memories of Thurles

Jim Bolger, a noted sports journalist, recalled,

My first experience of a Munster final at Thurles was in the summer of 1923. The playing pitch as I recall it, even then, was well-nigh perfect; but accommodation for the crowd was not anything like what it is at present. Thurles has ever been noted for efficiency in stewarding; and if a word of praise in this respect is due to no one more than another, it goes to Tom Semple, one of the greatest hurlers of his time. His towering figure commanded respect and he took a pardonable pride in the welfare and improvement of the ground, his aim to ensure the utmost comfort for everybody. I will always remember with gratitude the personal interest he took in the press, seeing that we were adequately seated and that our view from the sideline was not obstructed. Best of all, however, was the cheery greeting. We were always sure of a hearty welcome in Thurles and when the game was over and the day's work done, there was the usual exchange of views on the merits of the teams, invariably merging into recollections of great struggles of the past. As a rock, where firmness is required, yet genial and open in manner, Tom Semple was a grand character.

Séamus Ó Ceallaigh, *Gaelic Athletic Memories* (1945)

1923
First-Time Pulling

Jim Power from Tynagh (pictured) won an All-Ireland with Galway in 1923. He was full-back and recalled,

It was the awfullest place on the field; all the tough going was there.

The only thing for it was first-time pulling. When I trained, I had a man thirty yards away from me and he banged in balls, left and right, overhead, this side, that side. I never tried to stop that ball or catch it: I was all the time pulling first time. In the end very few balls passed me.

Seamus J King, *A History of Hurling* (1996)

Sportsfield Caretaker Tom Butler

Tom Butler was born in the Derheen, Thurles, in 1860. He was a useful hurler in his youth, as were his brothers, Dick and Mikie. Tom was caretaker at Thurles Sportsfield for many years. In 1910, he represented his brother Dick in the team photograph of the first All-Ireland. Tom died in 1954, aged 94, and had seen every All-Ireland final from the early days until 1950. His nephew, Tommy Butler, won All-Irelands with Tipperary in 1930 and 1937.

1926

New Stand

Early in 1926 a fine roofed stand was completed at Thurles Sportsfield. It was 125 feet long and 25 feet wide, and there were twenty-one commodious tiers. The contractor was Tim Brophy, Thurles, and the iron-work was supplied and erected by E J Delahanty, Kilkenny. Beneath were added dressing rooms and all the most modern adjuncts for the benefit of the players.

1926

Thurles Established as a Major Venue: Munster Senior Hurling Final

The 1926 Tipperary/Cork Munster final at Cork's Athletic Grounds was abandoned due to crowd-control issues, as spectators encroached onto the playing area. The replay was fixed for Thurles on the following Sunday, 19 September.

Feverish preparations were made at Thurles Sportsfield. Over one hundred men with twenty-five horses and carts had been busily engaged banking the enclosure. More than 10,000 tons of earth and rubble were moved into position. This new

Many workmen were engaged at Thurles Sportsfield in 1926, constructing the main embankment.

Far left: Martin Kennedy, Tipperary.
Left: Tipperary hurlers Paddy Leahy and John Joe Hayes.

Cork team, Munster Hurling Champions 1926. Seán Óg Murphy (captain), John Coughlan (goalkeeper), Eudie Coughlan, Jim Hurley, Edward O'Connell, Mick Murphy, Paddy 'Balty' Aherne, Mick 'Gah' Aherne, D J Kearney, Bill Higgins, Maurice Murphy, David Aherne, Dinny Barry-Murphy, Jim O'Regan, Phil O'Sullivan. Substitutes: Matt Murphy, Paddy Delea, Mick O'Connell.

Above left: A match programme cover from the 1926 Munster hurling final.
Above right: Celebrations as Tipperary draw with Cork at Thurles Sportsfield on 19 September, 1926.

embankment permitted well over 20,000 to watch the game without interference. The roofed area had recently been named the Canon Ryan Memorial Stand, after the erst-while chairman of the Tipperary County Board, and a temporary wooden stand was also erected for the occasion. Between them, the stands could accommodate 6,000. A limited number of sideline seats were also provided. The Thurles Sportsfield officers at this time were John Walsh (chairman), Tom Semple (vice-chairman), Jim Maher (treasurer) and E J Gorman (secretary).

This game ranks among the classic finals. It was a treat to witness and brought renewed lustre to the ancient game. It was the first Munster GAA match to be broadcast on radio, as Paddy Mehigan – known as 'Carbery' – brought the news to many listeners. At half-time Cork led by 2-3 to 1-0, but a spirited Tipperary response culminated in a Martin Kennedy goal five minutes from the end, securing a draw – Tipperary 3-4, Cork 4-1 – amid scenes of wonderful enthusiasm and wild excitement. Sports journalist Jim Bolger wrote, 'I have yet to hear a cheer to equal that which greeted Tipperary's drawing level with Cork in the second half hour' (Jim Bolger, 'Glamour of Thurles', in Séamus Ó Ceal-laigh, *Gaelic Athletic Memories*, 1945).

It was back to Thurles Sportsfield for the replay, on 3 October, a venue that was grow-ing in status for the excellence of its hosting. More than 30,000 saw Archbishop John Harty throw in the ball, and all seemed well for the Tipperary side in the first ten min-utes, until Martin Mockler was ordered off the field. From then on, Tipperary were playing a rearguard action, struggling tenaciously but yet retreating. 'The Banks' and the Cork shouts of jubilation filled the air as the Leesiders relished in their victory of 3-6 to 2-4. Denny Lanigan, Limerick, refereed all three games.

A Unifying Influence

In these years following the Civil War, the unifying influence of the GAA was seen to fine effect at the 1926 Munster Final in Thurles. Those of the most opposing political views were in attendance such as prominent army officers General Richard Mulcahy (pictured) and Major General Felix Cronin, and Republican TDs Dan Breen and Paddy Ryan Lacken.

Health and Safety

Today's health and safety inspectors would raise an eyebrow at the following account of the crowded stand at the 1926 final:

> The Canon Ryan Memorial Stand was packed to its utmost capacity. So great was the congestion that at times the entire stand moved as one man and swayed from side to side, as the scene of the game shifted from one end of the pitch to the other. Now and again, too, the pressure on those on top would force the unfortunates below out on the level ground in front of the stand.
>
> *Tipperary Star*, 9 October, 1926

'As Good as Four Fair Days'

Munster final day 1926 was 'as good as four fair days' for the traders in Thurles, at least according to one publican on Liberty Square. The masses that thronged Thurles for these games were amazed at the ability of the townspeople to cater for all requirements. Throughout every street numerous facilities were arranged to feed the people. The whole town seemed transformed into a gigantic restaurant, from the fronts of shops and ordinary dwelling houses to the haysheds at the rear. Signs with inscriptions such as 'Plain or Meat Teas', 'Luncheons' and 'Dinners' caught the eye. The name and fame of Thurles for its ability to cater for large crowds was made and affirmed by such days.

Semple's Blackthorn Stick

In *Decades of Glory* (1966), journalist Raymond Smith described the former Tipperary captain on the day of the Munster final,

> Tom Semple, like Napoleon, had sent out the call for an army of helpers and stewards, and they rallied to the flag of the Old Blues captain. He strode the sideline that Sunday like a general making a final inspection of the barricades, his word was law, the match was watched in comfort and the name of Thurles was made.

The reputation of Thurles as a popular hosting centre was enhanced, and with the games gaining in strength and appeal, the committee in charge went on improving their ground. The year 1926 marked a big uplift in the fortunes of the GAA. Stewarding was tested as perhaps never before, but the crowds behaved splendidly and the games were thoroughly enjoyed.

Full-Blooded Rebel

In his profile of Cork full-back Seán Óg Murphy in *A Cork GAA Miscellany* (2005), Jim Cronin records:

> His pluck was almost reckless at times. One day in a Munster final at Thurles, when Cork were hard pressed, he went in 'late' on a pull and got the full blow, which knocked him to the ground and broke four teeth. Like a roused lion he sprang up, spat out teeth and mud and rushed to the goalmouth and cleared the ball to safety. When defeat threatened, he would swell to the challenge, dash into the fray, sweep the ball upfield and swing the game around. Fearless he was but was never known to strike a false blow or commit a deliberate foul.

Boherlahan, Tipperary Senior Hurling Champions 1927. Back row (l–r): Phil Fogarty, Pat Maher, Paddy O'Dwyer, Mick Ryan, Tom Coffey, Larry O'Brien, Jimmy Ryan, Jack Moylan, Jack Doherty. Centre row (l–r): Paddy Leahy, Jim McGrath, Tom Butler, Johnny Leahy, Arthur O'Donnell, Jim Hayes, Willie O'Dwyer. Front row (l–r): Tom Power, Tommy Leahy, Martin Flanagan, Johnny Maher.

1927

Boherlahan are Tipperary Champions: Tipperary Senior Hurling Final

Boherlahan defeated Toomevara in the county final at Thurles Sportsfield on 2 October, by 4-1 to 1-1.

Up the boys from Boherlahan,

Gallant hurlers every man,

Ireland's choice and Ireland's champions

Are the boys of Boherlahan.

Phil O'Neill, 'Sliabh Rua', quoted in Philip F Ryan,

The Tubberadora Boherlahan Hurling Story (1973)

Opposite top left: Cork centre-forward Mick Leahy, Tubberadora, was a significant figure in Cork's No 1 Brigade during the War of Independence.

Opposite top middle: Dinny Barry-Murphy.

Opposite top right: Enjoying the 1928 Munster final at Thurles Sportsfield. The group includes Most Rev Dr Harty (GAA patron), Seán Ryan (GAA president), Rev J J Meagher (chairman of Tipperary GAA), General Eoin O'Duffy, Major Fitzmaurice, Chief Supt Hannigan (Thurles) and William Myles (editor, Tipperary Star*).*

Opposite middle: Thurles Gaelic Sportsfield, Munster Hurling Final 1928. A packed stand and sideline enjoy the spectacle.

Opposite bottom: GAA patron Archbishop John Harty throws in the ball to start the final.

Above: Munster GAA council officers with Archbishop John Harty at the 1928 final.

1928

Rebels on Fire in Replay: Munster Senior Hurling Final

An attendance of 27,000 came to Thurles to see Cork and Clare battle for provincial honours on 15 July, 1928. None regretted the trip, as they were treated to an exhibition of the highest order, played in a most sporting manner. Cork were lucky to get a draw, 2-2 apiece, and they could thank Eudie Coughlan, who moved to centre-back and quenched the Clare sting.

The replay, two weeks later, back at Thurles Sportsfield, set an attendance record in excess of 37,000. It was a strenuous battle in every way, but Cork were really on fire, winning by 6-4 to 2-2.

> Dinny Barry Murphy, boy,
> Great hurler, boy!
> He'd take the ball out of your eye, boy,
> And he wouldn't hurt a fly, boy!

Seamus J King, The Little Book of Hurling (2014)

Cork team: Seán Óg Murphy (captain), Miah Burke (goalkeeper), Jim O'Regan, Jim Hurley, Eudie Coughlan, Dinny Barry Murphy, Tom Barry, Paddy Delea, Paddy 'Balty' Aherne, Mick 'Gah' Aherne, Mick Leahy, Morgan Madden, Mick O'Connell, Peter O'Grady, Edward O'Connell.

1929
'Let Them Flake Away'

The hurling was fierce but not foul – men crashing into each other, one, two, three, four men went down in sequence. Virile manhood was manifested in all its power and glory. The wise referee knew his men and let them flake away. It was grand to see Cork and Tipperary hurlers engage in friendly conversation on their way back to the dressing room, when the fray was over.

A description of the Cork/Tipperary Munster semi-final 1929,
from Jim Cronin, Munster GAA Story (1984)

Offaly, All-Ireland Junior Hurling Champions 1929. Back row (l–r): Tony Hannon, Mick Digan, Joe King, Dick Conway, Mick Brien, P J Grogan (captain), Tom Carroll, Jim Dooley, Bill Guinan, Jim O'Donnell. Front row (l–r): Mick Dooley, Mick Carroll, John Verney, Jim Brien, Mick Corrigan, Jim Holligan, 'Skull' Brien, Jack Kinnarney, Sonie Wrafter, Ted Downey. Players not included were Mick Coughlan, Tom Dooley, Joe Carroll and Ned Nolan.

1929

Junior All-Ireland for 'The Faithful County'

Offaly won their second junior hurling All-Ireland when they defeated Cork by 6-1 to 3-2 in the final at Thurles Sportsground. Played on the third Sunday in December in front of fewer than 1,000 spectators, Cork trailed by three points at the interval in spite of playing with wind advantage. Offaly confirmed their superiority in the second half and won by 6-1 to 2-3. The referee was J J Callanan (Tipperary).

Joe King from Shinrone, who lined out at wing-back for Offaly on the day, recalled later walking from his home in Rathcahill to get the train at Brosna Station and changing at Roscrea for Thurles to play the All-Ireland. There was little or no preparation for the game. Joe had a good game, scoring a goal early on and dominating the mid-field area in the second half. Afterwards there was no shower and no meal with his victorious teammates. There were no flags and no crowd to greet him on his return to Brosna, and he believes that few people realised, until years later, that the county had won an All-Ireland junior championship.

Kilkenny, All-Ireland Senior Hurling Champions 1911-1912. Richard 'Drug' Walsh is in the back row, third from the left.

1929

One More Game

Richard 'Drug' Walsh (1878–1958), speaking in July 1929, aged fifty-one, said: 'If I could play in one more game – just one ... I think I could die happy.'

'Drug', from the famous Mooncoin club in south Kilkenny, won seven All-Ireland medals and was the winning captain on three occasions.

With eagle-eyed vision and speed of a deer,
No matter how hectic, in combat – no fear.
His wristwork – an artist's, Kilkenny's own doyen,
Reigned the prince among hurlers, 'Drug' Walsh from Mooncoin.

Fr Michael O'Hanlon, from James Murphy,
The Poetry and Song of Black and Amber Glory (2002)

CHAPTER 2

THE MAKING OF LEGENDS

1930–1945

Tipperary, 1930: Back row (l–r): Phil Cahill, James Harney, Tommy Treacy, Tom Butler, Jack McKenna, Tom Leahy, Jack Stapleton. Fifth row (l–r): Jim Lanigan, M F Cronin, Jimmy Heaney, Phil Purcell, J J Callanan (senior captain), Mick Ryan, John Maher, Jimmy O'Loughlin, Dan Looby. Fourth row (l–r): Rev M J Lee, Tommy Butler, Seán Harrington, Tom Rainey, Paddy Harty (junior captain), Jimmy Ryan, Tom Hayes, Tom Power, Martin Kennedy, Mick Ryan, Jack Dwyer, John Connolly. Third row (l–r): William O'Gorman, Ned Wade, Tom Harty, Tim Connolly, Martin Brown, Mick McGann, William Ryan, Joe Fletcher, Mick Ryan, Paddy Furlong. Second row: Frank McGrath, Pat McGrath (Munster GAA secretary), Paddy Ryan, Tom Kennedy, Joe Dunne, Gerry Heavey, Paddy Ryan, Ned Maher, Timmy Harney, Johnny Semple, John Lanigan, Jim Close, Dinny O'Gorman, Mick Maher. Front row (l–r): Peter Flanagan, Jack Russell (minor captain), Rev J J Meagher (Tipperary GAA chairman), Archbishop John Harty, Rev Philip Fogarty, Johnny Leahy (Tipperary GAA secretary), Jack Coffey, Jack Quinlan, Tommy Semple, Mick Boland, Willie O'Neill, Jack Gleeson. Unable to be present: Tom Semple, Martin Kennedy, Tom O'Meara, Paul McKenna.

1930
'Tiobraid Árann Abú'

In 1930, Tipperary won the senior, junior and minor All-Ireland hurling titles, remembered as the Treble Crown. On Sunday, 15 February, 1931, all three teams assembled at Thurles Sportsfield for the historic photograph on the previous page.

> Tiobraid Árann Abú! Tiobraid Árann Abú!
> That's our watchword and war-cry for aye;
> For Tipp'rary's brave men from the hill and the glen,
> Are the champions of Ireland today.
>
> Tom Keating, quoted in King, Ó Donnchú, Smyth, *Tipperary's GAA Ballads*

1931
Lory and Eudie, Hurling Icons of the 1920s and 1930s

Eudie Coughlan (Blackrock), was born in 1900 and won his first senior All-Ireland medal in 1919 when he was a substitute in the final. He won a total of five senior All-Ireland medals and captained Cork to the 1931 title after two replays against Kilkenny. Lory Meagher (Tullaroan) also won three All-Irelands and has been repeatedly voted onto teams of hurling's greatest players, including as midfield partner to Jack Lynch on the GAA's Hurling Team of the Century in 1984 and the Hurling Team of the Millennium in 2000.

> And they'll oft retell the story
> Of the glory that was Lory's,
> When Meagher graced the Black and Amber
> Of Kilkenny by the Nore.
>
> Brendan Fullam, *Captains of the Ash* (2002)

Toomevara, Tipperary Hurling Champions 1931. Back row (l–r): Jack Donovan, Bill O'Meara, Malachy Collison (Moneygall), Stephen Hackett, Jack Kennedy (Moneygall), Jack Guilmartin, Paddy O'Meara. Middle row (l–r): Tom Gleeson (Moneygall), Tom Byrne (Moneygall), Martin Kennedy (captain), Paddy 'Major' Collison (Moneygall), Din Kelly, Paddy Guilfoyle (Moneygall). Front row (l–r): Tom O'Meara, Mick 'Swimmer' O'Brien, Garrett Howard, Jack Gleeson.

1931
The Dan Breen Cup Goes to Toomevara: Tipperary Senior Hurling Final

In 1931, Toomevara retained their Tipperary county title, beating Moycarkey/Borris 5-4 to 0-2. Captain Johnny Leahy was referee in a one-sided affair. Martin Kennedy, who captained the team, was top scorer with 3-1. This was the first year that the Dan Breen Cup was presented to the county champions. Tipperary native Breen (1894–1969) was a veteran of the War of Independence and the Civil War, and in later years, a Fianna Fáil TD. The cup had been purchased by Breen in the US and brought to Ireland by the Tipperary team returning from their American tour in 1931.

1932
Thurles Gaelic Sportsfield Society Ltd.

In February, the proprietors of Thurles Sportsfield considered a resolution proposing the acceptance of an offer from Thurles Gaelic Sportsfield Society Ltd., a Friendly

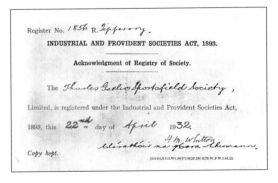

Society, for the purchase of the grounds. On 5 September, the Tipperary GAA Board unanimously agreed to a deed of conveyance of Thurles Sportsfield from Thurles Sportsfield Committee to Thurles Gaelic Sportsfield Society Ltd. Chairman: Thomas Semple. Secretary: E J Gorman. Treasurer: W J Dwan.

1932

Rebels Fall to Gallant Banner: Munster Senior Hurling Final

Clare won the Munster hurling final at Thurles Sportsfield on 31 July with a classic performance before a capacity attendance. It was an epic clash, played at a terrific pace, and had Clare ahead at the break by 3-2 to 1-0. The second half was pulsating as Clare's defence fought back a furious Cork onslaught. Tull Considine flashed in a goal past John O'Donovan, between the Cork sticks, to secure a Banner success as the 'Rebels' went down by 5-2 to 4-1.

Oh, to be in Thurles, at a Munster final game,

Regardless of the teams engaged, the thrills are much the same,

But surely the Olympian gods would ask no finer fare,

Than this sporting epic battle of old rivals Cork and Clare.

Joseph Senan Considine, Ennis, quoted in King, Ó Donnchú, Smyth,

Tipperary's GAA Ballads

Clare, Munster Senior Hurling Champions 1932. Back row (l–r): Robbie Lawlor (trainer), Mick Falvey, Jim Hogan, Jimmy Flanagan, Turlough 'Tull' Considine, Tom Burnell, John Joe 'Goggles' Doyle (captain), Pat 'Fowler' McInerney, Sean Hurley, Jack Gleeson, Martin 'Bocky' Connery, Tom O'Rourke, Jim 'Jimmo' Higgins. Front row (l–r): Jim Houlihan, Mick O'Rourke, Tommy Daly, Jim Mullane, Larry Blake, Tom 'Fowler' McInerney. Seated: Art McGann Jnr.

1932
On the Wind-Swept Hill of Tulla

Tommy Daly of Tulla (pictured) was considered to be one of the greatest goalkeepers of his era, 1917–1933. His hurling career began in 1914 when he won an All-Ireland junior medal with Clare. More glory was to follow on his move to Dublin to study medicine. He won senior titles with Dublin in 1917, 1920, 1924 and 1927 as well as six Leinster championship medals. With UCD Tommy won six Fitzgibbon Cup medals. He was a member of the Collegians side to win three Dublin county championships in a row, 1917–1919. His lone county championship success back home came with his native Tulla in 1933, the year after he was between the posts for Clare as they defeated Cork in the Munster final. He was commemorated by the Tulla club with the opening of the Dr Tommy Daly Park in 1941.

On the wind-swept Hill of Tulla,
Where the Claremen place their dead,
Four solemn yews stand sentinel
Above a hurler's head,
And from the broken north lands
From Burren bleak and bare,
The dirge of Thomas Daly
Goes surging on through Clare.

Bryan MacMahon, in *Smyth, Ballads of the Banner*

The Blues in '32

Thurles Sarsfields senior hurlers at Thurles Sportsfield, 1932. Back row (l–r): Tom Semple, John Maher, Jim Lanigan, Jack Stapleton, Jimmy O'Loughlin, James Maher (D), William 'Billix' Quinn, Jim Maher. Middle row (l–r): Denis 'Bunny' Murphy, Denis Max, John Lanigan, Fr J J Meagher, Fr Philip Fogarty, Tim Connolly, Tommy Butler, Jimmy (Skinny) Harney, William Leahy. Front row (l–r): Micil Callanan, Dick Ryan, Paddy Bowe, Con Keane, child unidentified, Timmie Harney, Paddy Maher (W), Willie Bowe.

Squeeze 'Em Up Moycarkey / And Hang 'Em Out to Dry

Moycarkey/Borris won the Tipperary senior hurling championship on four occasions in the 1930s. Here is the 1932 team, captained by Phil Purcell. In the final at Thurles Sportsfield on 11 September, they defeated near neighbours Killenaule by 7-6 to 5-1. Back row (l–r): John Maher (D), Jim Mullins, Jack Grant, Tom Dunne, Paddy Molo-

ney, Tom Bourke, John Fitzger-
ald, Neddy Bannon, Phil Cahill,
Tommy Kelly, Paddy Ryan (S),
Tom Allen, Mick Healy, Dan
Delaney. Middle row (l–r):
Jackie Ryan, Martin Dwyer, Jack
Fanning, Jack Gleeson (S), Phil

Thurles Traders' Association

IMPROVEMENT
— OF THE —
SPORTSFIELD

The Association, having decided at a Special Meeting held on the 22nd inst.,

To Raise a Fund for the Improvement of the Sportsfield

So as to secure the 1934 All-Ireland Hurling Final, earnestly appeal to all Traders, Hotel Proprietors, Restaurateurs, and Caterers to Subscribe Generously to the Fund.

The Proposed Improvements, it is estimated, will Cost from £1,500 to £2,000.

All are asked to regard the proposition as a business undertaking. Once the Sportsfield is made capable of accommodating visitors, it is possible that Thurles will become the venue of many other important matches, thus establishing a permanent source of revenue for the town.

Subscriptions will be gratefully received by :—
Mr. James Maher, Parnell Street.
Mr. W. H. Ryan, West Gate.
Mr. Ed. Finn, Liberty Square.
Mr. D. Maher, Liberty Square.

Above: Workmen extending the embankment at Thurles Sportsfield. Tom Semple is standing on the far left. Right: The Thurles Traders' Association help with fundraising, Tipperary Star, *26 August, 1933.*

Purcell (captain), Martin Maher, Tom Hayes, Bill Kennedy. Front row (l–r): John Mullins, Joe Maher, Bill O'Brien, Jimmy Heaney.

1934

Congress Says No

Thurles Sportsfield Committee – and particularly its chairman, Tom Semple – was almost certain that the 1934 All-Ireland final would be played in Thurles, as part of the Association's golden jubilee celebrations. But they also knew that to host such an event successfully, the grounds would need major investment. Munster Council agreed to match whatever sum was raised by the Sportsfield Committee, the Thurles traders and the friends of Gaelic sport in Mid Tipperary. All Munster counties favoured Thurles as the venue for the final, although Cork had reservations. Thurles traders called a special meeting to organise the raising of funds. Estimated costs were £1,500 to £2,000.

The committee began to upgrade the venue, with ambitious plans to accommodate a crowd of 60,000. Between £2,000 and £3,000 was spent erecting new stands on either side of the existing covered stand, which was also enlarged. On Easter Sunday, the GAA annual Congress was hosted at the Confraternity Hall, Thurles, but to the bitter disappointment of Tom Semple and the Sportsfield Committee, the decision was made not to stage the All-Ireland hurling final in the town.

Above left: Golden jubilee souvenir in the Irish Independent, *1934.*
Above right: GAA president Seán McCarthy addresses a thronged Liberty Square, Thurles, at the GAA golden jubilee celebrations, Easter Sunday, 1934.

1934
GAA Golden Jubilee Celebrations in Thurles

For Thurles and Tipperary, the highlight of the golden jubilee celebrations was the hosting of the Congress in the town on Easter Sunday. The town lived true to tradition in providing a rallying centre for Gaeldom. Proud of the honour conferred on them, the townspeople spared neither expense nor effort to have everything in keeping with the historic event. Houses were decorated and the streets ornamented with bunting, flags and streamers with appropriate mottoes.

Congress delegates, numbering two hundred and representing every county in Ireland, attended High Mass in the cathedral, at which Archbishop Harty presided. After the Mass, all marched in procession through Liberty Square, led by the Cassestown Fife and Drum Band and the Moycarkey Pipers' Band, circled the Croke memorial and formed up in front of Hayes's Hotel. It was here that Archbishop Harty unveiled a bronze memorial plaque to commemorate the foundation of the GAA on 1 November, 1884.

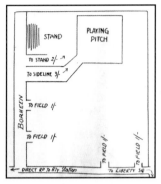

Left: New access arrangements and admission prices at Thurles Sportsfield in 1934.

Below: The searing heat of mid-summer matching the white heat of torrid Munster hurling, as Cork and Limerick vie for a Munster final place against Waterford in 1934. Hats, handkerchiefs and newspapers protect the sweating brows, as apples and minerals slake the thirst.

Bottom: The Cork goalmouth under pressure at the Killinan End, as Limerick launch another attack.

69

1934

Blood, Sweat and Tears: Munster Senior Hurling Semi-Final

The Munster semi-final was at Thurles Sportsfield on 8 July, 1934. A great save by Paddy Scanlon proved crucial. 'Micka' Brennan had got possession on the edge of the square and his bullet-like drive looked unstoppable, but Scanlan rapped the leather down sharply and cleared. Final score: Limerick 3-4, Cork 2-2.

Top: Thurles Sportsfield thronged to capacity for the 1935 Munster semi-final. Arriving at the grounds, one got an eloquent idea of what the crowd would be like later on. Entrances to all parts of the field were crammed with sweating humanity, and any price was offered for admission.
Above left: The scene at Liberty Square, Thurles, on Munster semi-final day 1935.
Above right: Mick Mackey of Ahane, Limerick.

1935

Miracle at Thurles Sportsfield: Munster Senior Hurling Semi-Final

Once again, Limerick met Cork in the Munster semi-final at Thurles Sportsfield on 28 July, 1935. Limerick won well, 3-12 to 2-3, but the game left two abiding memories. Mick Mackey's performance for Limerick is regarded as one of the most brilliant and spectacular individual displays of hurling ever. Many good judges of the game hold that Mackey reached the height of hurling perfection that day. The other abiding memory concerns an accidental injury suffered by Cork hurler Tommy Kelly in a collision with Limerick midfielder Mick Ryan. For a time, Kelly's condition appeared so grave that the Last Rites of the Catholic Church were administered, as players and spectators knelt in prayer. Rumour quickly spread around that he was dead. Phil O'Neill, in the *Tipperary Star* of 3 August, 1935, reported, 'As I knelt in prayer with thousands of others for the happy passing of this young soul, I feared greatly in my heart for the future of our Gaelic games'. The player was later removed to Thurles District Hospital, where he quickly recovered and was discharged the following day.

Travelling by Lorry to Thurles

GAA historian Seamus J King recalls an unusual means of transport to Thurles:

Getting to Thurles for Munster championship games could be a problem during World War Two and after. With the cars off the road and the trains not always suitable, support- ers had to depend on bicycles or shanks mare. Travelling by lorry was another possibility. My uncle, Son Slevin, who lived in Eglish, Borrisokane, had a lorry with a very valuable thirty-two-county licence plate, which allowed him do business all over the country. He also provided a valuable service on match days at Thurles and other venues. Of course it wasn't legal, as the vehicle wasn't licenced to carry people and he had no insurance for carrying passengers. That didn't stop him, especially when some of his neighbours and friends expressed a desire to see the match.

Most of the lorries ran on petrol and it was a scarce commodity at the time. Getting caught by the Gardaí was another problem, so he usually left early on the Sunday morning and travelled the by-roads to the vicinity of Thurles, where his load of supporters were dropped off and walked the rest of the way to the match in order to avoid the attention of the law. The load could be as many as thirty, and the ride was anything but comfortable as they trudged along bumpy roads. There was also a charge, but the prize at the end was seeing the match.

I don't believe he was ever caught or if all his passengers made their way back to the rendezvous after the game. His son, Harry, remembers seeing a picture of the truck with people in it and the big headlamps on the front mudguards. What a pity he can't find it!

Thurles Sarsfields, Tipperary Senior Hurling Champions 1935. Back row (l–r): Tom Butler, Jim Maher, Jimmy O'Loughlin, Paddy Brolan, William Leahy. Third row (l–r): Joe Campbell, John Joe Ryan, John Maher, Jer Cornally, Denis 'Bunny' Murphy, Dan Mackey, Mick Murphy, Paddy Bermingham, Pat d'Arcy Russell, William Bowe. Second row (l–r): Tommy Max, Denis Max, Br Ryan, Tom Semple (chairman and trainer), Jim Lanigan (captain), Fr J J Meagher, Br Lynam, Rody Curran, John Lanigan. Front row (l–r): Michael Callanan, Mick Maher, John Semple, Paddy Bowe, Dick Ryan, Tommy Lanigan, Tommy Butler, Paddy Maher (W), Tommy Semple, Paddy Connors, Seamus Bowe. Dermot Butler (mascot).

1935

Sarsfields Have It Easy: Tipperary Senior Hurling Final

Thurles Sarsfields and Carrick Swan met in the county final at Thurles Sportsfield on 10 November. Carrickman Pat Davin, brother of the GAA's founder and first president,

Maurice, threw in the ball. A close first half resulted in the half-time score with Thurles ahead by 1-3 to 0-1. But at the final whistle, the score was 6-5 to 0-2. The Thurles supremacy was due to the magnificence of their backline, preventing all Swan attacks. Thurles Sarsfields were champions again after a lapse of five years.

1936

Mackey's Master Class: Munster Senior Hurling Final

The Munster final was at Thurles Sportsfield on 2 August. Tipperary's opponents were Limerick, who were seeking their fourth successive title. Tipperary lived with them for about fifteen minutes, then the floodgates opened and the Shannonsiders went on to record an 8-5 to 4-6 victory. Mick Mackey, on his first day as Limerick's captain in championship hurling, was at the height of his powers, and this was one of his greatest triumphs, scoring no less than five goals and three points. Mackey's willingness to put the sliotar on the hurley and run at opposition defences caused havoc. He rampaged the field from end to end, giving and taking hard knocks with a smile, while his trademark bursting solo runs devastated the Tipperary defence.

> We followed you through Munster and we shouted for your fame
> In Dublin's far famed pitch we stood, that bears a glorious name.
> We jumped for joy each man and boy, each maid and matron when
> We saw the sheen of the white and green for Mick Mackey and his men.
>
> Tommy Power, Effin, Limerick, quoted in Jimmy Smyth, *In Praise of Heroes* (2007)

Striding to success: Mick Mackey leading Limerick in a pre-match parade at Thurles Sportsfield in the mid-1930s.

Limerick, Munster Senior Hurling Champions 1936. Back row (l–r): Paddy Scanlan, Tom McCarthy, Jim Roche, Dave Clohessy, Mick Mackey (captain), Paddy McMahon, Garrett Howard, Sergt Major Browne (trainer). Middle row (l–r): Jim Close, Micky Cross, Paddy Carroll, John Mackey, Mick Kennedy, Mick Ryan. Front row (l–r): Timmy Ryan, Paddy Clohessy.

Mackey had injured one of his knees on the American tour before the Munster championship. As this was widely known, he expected that the Tipperary back men would have a special interest in the welfare of his knee – to mislead them, he put the bandage on the 'good' knee before taking the field in Thurles.

King, *The Little Book of Hurling*

1936–1938
Expansion: The 'Croke Park' of Munster

In 1937, Munster Council agreed to match whatever finances the local committee could raise. The support from the townspeople of Thurles for the fundraising events gave great encouragement to the Sportsfield Committee to proceed. By April 1938, the following works had been completed:

- The pitch was moved forward from the stand side so as to enlarge the sideline accommodation

Above left: Eight new rows of sideline seating were added, and terracing of the embankment was completed in 1938.

Above right: Dancing till 3am in support of the Sportsfield works. Tipperary Star, *20 November, 1937.*

- The embankment on the opposite side was moved backwards and repositioned
- Eight rows of sideline seats were laid on concrete blocks all around the pitch, curving at the corners. The front rows were sunk below pitch level
- A concrete wall was built all around, behind the sideline seats
- Bridge-like entrances were provided to the sideline, with corridors for turnstiles
- 30,000 extra tons of material were used to raise and extend the embankment
- 2,000 railway sleepers helped to raise and terrace the embankment
- The main entrance was improved and extra stiles provided
- A score-board was installed.

The entire contract was carried out by James Skehan & Sons, Thurles, while Thomas J Hyland, B.E., acted as architect. The grounds were capable of accommodating 50,000 people in comfort and safety, and Thurles Sportsfield was now the largest embanked playing area in Ireland.

Above, from left to right: Ger Cornally, John Maher, Jim Lanigan (captain) and Dinny O'Gorman.

Opposite middle left: Fr Phil Purcell, Paddy 'W' Maher, Tom Kennedy, Martin Maher.
Opposite middle right: Denis 'Bunny' Murphy, Willie Wall, Philly Ryan, Bill O'Donnell.
Opposite bottom left: Gerry Doyle, Paddy 'Sweeper' Ryan, Tommy Butler, Dan Mackey.
Opposite bottom right: Rev J J Meagher, Tipperary GAA Chairman, pins the 'Blue Riband' on the
jersey of Tipperary captain Jim Lanigan. Also included is Tipperary secretary Captain Johnny Leahy.

1937

Tipperary All-Ireland Training

Traditionally Tipperary inter-county teams have used Thurles Sportsfield as a training venue. Most of their championship games, meanwhile, were played elsewhere, as teams usually insist on neutral venues, particularly in finals.

Here we see images of the Tipperary 1937 hurling team training in the weeks prior to the All-Ireland final, which was held at Fitzgerald Stadium, Killarney. Construction of the new Cusack Stand at Croke Park was eleven months behind schedule, and a strike by builders left the venue unusable. Tipperary won the 1937 final, beating Kilkenny by 3-11 to 0-3.

Archbishop John Harty, GAA patron, throws in the ball to start the 1938 Munster championship at Thurles Sportsfield on 22 May. Refereed by Phil Purcell (Tipperary), Cork defeated Limerick by 5-4 to 2-5.

1938
The Stratosphere Girl

One of the red-letter days of the Thurles calendar was the annual carnival and bazaar organised by Thurles Sportsfield Committee to fundraise for their developments. In 1938,

the highlight of each evening was a performance by 'The Stratosphere Girl'. This young German fräulein, Camille Mayer, dressed in a sailor costume, thrilled the crowds with her acrobatics on top of a steel mast, 137 feet (42 m) above the ground.

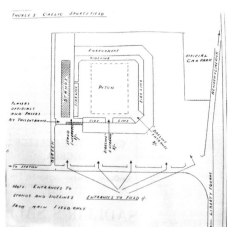

Opposite middle left: Access arrangements for the Munster hurling final in Thurles Sportsfield.
Tipperary Star, *29 July, 1939.*
Opposite middle right: Twenty-two special trains brought the crowd to Thurles for the Munster final.
Opposite bottom: Cork, Munster Senior Hurling Champions 1939. Back row (l–r): Jim Buttimer, Alan Lotty, John Quirke, Jack Barrett, Jim Young, Connie Buckley, Micka Brennan, Jim Barry. Middle row (l–r): Paddy O'Donovan, Willie 'Long Puck' Murphy, Jack Lynch (captain), Bobby Ryng, Bobby Dinneen, Ted O'Sullivan. Front row (l–r): Batt Thornhill, Willie Campbell.

1939
Cork Survive Classic: Munster Senior Hurling Final

The Munster final, the plum fixture of the year, was in Thurles on 30 July. No less than 40,986 people saw Cork, captained by Jack Lynch, beat Limerick by 4-3 to 3-4. This was 10,000 more than the previous attendance record. Twenty-two special trains brought much of the crowd to a game remembered as one of the greatest of all time. One report described it thus:

> It was a glorious, thrilling all-exciting game, an event that set hearts throbbing madly and blood pulsating wildly. Class hurling at any time is the fastest ball game on earth. Sunday last at Thurles it was 'grease lightning' and of such play adequate description is inadequate. On the forty odd thousand that thronged Thurles, it left an indelible impression that can never be erased. Those not present can never get an adequate description.
>
> Cronin, *Munster GAA Story*

Level scoring and fluctuating fortunes never left a dull moment, and right up to the last second it was anybody's game. Sides were level at 2-2 apiece at half-time and Limerick, holding a point lead, were being hailed as victors as the game entered its last lap, but to dash the cup from their lips was a dramatic Cork rally and a great goal by Ted O'Sullivan from a Micka Brennan pass.

Milk in Gallons, Tea in Streams

Catering for such an influx of people into the town for the Munster final was a serious challenge. A local correspondent described in the *Tipperary Star* on 5 August, 1939,

'Bread simply vanished in heaps, milk in gallons, tea in streams and meat in cwts. By the time that all demands had been met and those who were catering had time to have a bite themselves, it was none too easy to scrape a meal together. It was the general opinion that this event eclipsed all other occasions in the volume of business done.'

It was conservatively estimated that the day meant a taking of £20,000 in the town. The attendance at the All-Ireland final, known popularly as the 'Thunder and Lightning' final, in Croke Park on 1 September was over one thousand less than the Munster final attendance in Thurles.

Jack Lynch, Cork captain, 1939.

1939

A Future Taoiseach

Jack Lynch, Glen Rovers, won six All-Ireland medals in a row with the small ball between 1941 and 1944, in football in 1945 and another in hurling in 1946. He recalls, 'I played practically all my games for Cork at midfield, although I started at left half-back and played a few times at right half-forward. Towards the end of my career, when I was slowing down, I was moved to full-forward.'

'In Praise of Lynch'

I see him still on Thurles field as his gallant team he led,
So tall and straight, with manly gait, togged out in white and red –
With Tipp's men marching by his side, all eager for the fray,
Behind Seán Treacy's piper's band on a Munster final day.

> Jack Ryan, Greystones, Limerick (formerly Newport, Tipperary),
>
> quoted in Smyth, *In Praise of Heroes*

Jack Maher lived at Bohernanave, Thurles, and was caretaker of Thurles Sportsfield during the 1940s. In the background of this photo are the open and covered stands of that time. These were the war years, the 'Emergency', when some of the greatest games were played at Thurles Sportsfield. John O'Grady, former Tipperary goalkeeper and sports writer (known as 'Cúlbaire') recalled, 'It was the series of Cork v Limerick games in the late 1930s and on into the next decade that gave Thurles the uplift into glamour. Its primacy has not since been questioned – matches intrude into a city setting; they occupy Thurles.'

Above: Munster Hurling Final 1940 match programme.
Top right: Limerick, Munster and All-Ireland Champions 1940. Front row (l–r): Paddy Clohessy, Mick Mackey (captain), Mick Kennedy, Ned Chawke, Dick Stokes, Peter Cregan. Back row (l–r): Mick Hickey, Jim McCarthy, Tommy Cooke, Paddy Scanlon, Tony Herbert, Jim Roche, Paddy McMahon, John Mackey, Paddy Mackey, Timmy Ryan, Dave Hurley, Jackie Power, Martin 'Robbie' Lawlor.
Bottom right: The pre-match parade at Thurles Sportsfield.

1940

'No Place for Weak Hearts': Munster Senior Hurling Final

The Munster final between Cork and Limerick was in Thurles Sportsfield on 28 July. After an hour's hurling, the score stood at Limerick 4-3, Cork 3-6. 'Carbery', the popular correspondent, described it thus,

> Thurles was no place for weak hearts in Sunday's broiling heat and excitement . . . Many of us thought that the 1939 Munster final had reached hurling meridian. Yet this year's memories switched 1939 into limbo of forgotten things and battles long ago. Scribblers are bankrupt of phrases. Our vocabulary is exhausted – we must invent a new language to describe modern hurling. So overwhelming was the closing delirium of surging scores – like a crescendo of brass music – that all spectators were hushed and awestruck. Good men and true, all in action to the stirring finish. And there is more to come for they finished all square.

'Carbery', Paddy Mehigan, *Hurling: Ireland's National Game* (1942)

The replay was at the same venue the following Sunday, and the game was equally good. The first thirty minutes produced hurling hardly ever before witnessed. The pace was a cracker, with first-time striking and bouts of perfect overhead play that had the crowd at fever pitch. At half-time Cork led by one point to nil. Then in the third quarter, Limerick hit a golden patch with goals from Power, McMahon and Stokes that brought them ten points in ten minutes, putting them seven ahead. Cork rallied with a goal from Jack Lynch, and a Quirke point from the puck-out had them back in contention. But for brilliant Limerick back play and the unbeatable Paddy Scanlan between the sticks, they might have succeeded. The final score was Limerick 3-3, Cork 2-4.

Right: The replay match programme, courtesy of the GAA Museum & Archive.

Then Timmy Ryan at centre-field,
You heard his name before,
His prowess at the ancient game
Is known from shore to shore.

Fullam, *Captains of the Ash*

Limerick's midfielder Timmy Ryan (pictured) was master of the art of overhead striking. He was known to have doubled on puck-outs and sent them over the bar. He believed in first-time hurling, whether on the ground or in the air. Timmy dominated midfield in most games and was also known as 'Golden Miller' after the great steeple chaser of the time.

A Nail in Cork's Coffin

Micka Brennan, Cork's corner-forward from Sarsfields, was renowned for testing the opposing goalkeeper's resolve early and often. In this game Paddy Scanlon, in goal for Limerick, borrowed Brennan's hurley in a break in play to hammer in a dangerous-looking loose nail in the brace of his camán. Brennan took the hint and stayed out of the square. (Michael Moynihan, *Irish Examiner*, 12 July, 2013.)

The Rub

Dick Stokes from Pallasgreen, a member of the winning 1940 All-Ireland hurling team and one of Limerick's best, recalls:

Massage was a major item in those days. Our physical trainer, Martin Lawton, was an athlete in his younger days and then a well-known dog trainer. He had a special mixture of olive oil, camphorated oil, a shot of whiskey and poteen (no doubt the dog rub) which when properly applied would stimulate any human being to greater things.

The style of hurling in those days was also very different. The common features were overhead striking, with or against the ball, first-time ground play with the ball 'doing the work', very much man-to-man play. Running with the ball was not a feature, with very odd individual exceptions. Bunching was rare and four or five players trying to catch a falling ball in the hand would never occur. Thurles, the Mecca of hurling, had a special atmosphere for hurling fans, not found in other centres.

Pilgrims to Mecca

Stokes's teammate, Mick Mackey from Ahane, remembers:

> There will never be games, believe me, to equal these two games in Thurles in 1940. It was, you might say, the last years of the cars, for the restrictions on travel really began to bite in the succeeding seasons and yet they seemed to get there like pilgrims to Mecca. Nobody gave us a chance the first day, but we drew and beat them in the replay by two points.
>
> Raymond Smith, *Clash of the Ash* (1981)

Mícheál Ó hEithir

In this photo we see commentator supreme Michael O'Hehir (Mícheál Ó hEithir) at Thurles Sportsfield in the early 1940s. Front row (l–r): Mícheál's father, Jim; Fr Maurice Morrissey; Mícheál himself; his assistant, Tommy O'Reilly; and Hugh Ó hEithir, Mícheál's uncle. Clerical support aplenty in the back row. Mícheál was the voice of the GAA for decades, and his broadcasts helped to popularise Gaelic games. Fr Seamus Gardiner, former Munster Council PRO, recalls:

> In those far off days, a special section on the sideline seating in Thurles was reserved for priests. It was mainly to accommodate priests who said late Masses and also some who may have dined with the Archbishop of Cashel and Emly in Thurles before the game. There was a similar reserved area at Limerick's Gaelic Grounds also.

Boherlahan/Dualla, Tipperary Senior Hurling Champions 1941. Back row (l–r): Jerry Darmody, Tommy Leahy, Ned O'Dwyer, Jer Looby, Danny Maher, Jerry Coffey, Tom Power, Jack Doherty, Pad Dunne. Middle row (l–r): Willie O'Dwyer (secretary), Jimmy Wade, John Coffey, Tommy Wade, Philly O'Dwyer (captain), Jack Quinlan, Jimmy Maher, Sonny Maher, Dick Croke. Front row (l–r): Flor Coffey, Jackie Maher.

1941
Boherlahan/Dualla Win the Battle: Tipperary Senior Hurling Final

Thurles Sportsfield was the venue for the county final on 30 November. Boherlahan didn't get it easy from a fit, fast and eager Éire Óg Annacarty side, but goals from Tommy Leahy and Jer Looby ensured them success by 2-2 to 0-6. It was Boherlahan's first victory since 1928.

Four great Gaels at Thurles Sportsfield in the late 1920s. From left to right: John Walsh (Thurles Sportsfield chairman), Phil O'Neill ('Sliabh Rua'), Tom Semple and Paddy Mehigan ('Carbery').

1943

Death of Tom Semple

The untimely death of Tom Semple in 1943 was a major loss to Thurles Sportsfield Committee. Tom had been central to all the developments since the grounds were bought in 1910. He was on the first ever committee and was chairman at the time of his death. Semple was born to lead, a commanding figure; his magnificent physique and easy manner earned the respect of thousands of patrons, as he built up the reputation which Thurles Sportsfield gained for excellent stewarding on the days of major games.

Priests in a Pickle

Noel Morris of Borrisokane recalled:

During the Second World War, petrol supplies were seriously rationed and most cars were off the roads. There were a number of exceptions. Priests were given an allowance of petrol to help them fulfil their ministries but not to be used to travel to matches. But the temptation was there when a match was in Thurles. On one such occasion Fr Johnny Minihan, a native of Puckane, got a lift with his friend Fr Dan Woods. To avoid detection, they parked up in a farmyard some distance from the town. They walked to the field and enjoyed the match. When they returned to the car, it was gone! Someone had spotted them and reported the matter to the Gardaí, who removed the car during the course of the match. The two Reverends had no alternative but to report the matter to the Garda Station and were surprised to find the car there before them! They had some explaining to do and were delayed for some time to their great embarrassment, before being eventually let off home late with a warning!

Above left: Éire Óg Annacarty/Donohill, Tipperary Senior Hurling Champions 1943. Back row (l–r): Tom Burke, Bill O'Donnell, Denis Condon, Jack Cooney, Jerry Ryan (W), Jimmy O'Donnell. Middle row (l–r): Philly Ryan (C), Tom Joy, Michael Ryan (C), Johnny Ryan (W). Front row (l–r): George Ryan, Jerry Ryan, Jim Hanley, Tom Ryan (C, captain), Jack Dee.
Above right: Dan Breen presents the Dan Breen Cup to Éire Óg Annacarty captain Tom Ryan (C).

1943
Moycarkey Stunned: Tipperary Senior Hurling final

On 3 October, Éire Óg Annacarty upset all the predictions by beating Moycarkey/ Borris in the county hurling final at Thurles Sportsfield. With eight minutes to go, Moycarkey were ahead by four points and looking safe, but a goal rush was impending. Bill O'Donnell hit the net first, to be followed by two goals from Tom Joyce in two minutes. The Dan Breen Cup was heading west for the first time to Annacarty and Donohill. Indeed, Dan Breen himself was there to present his cup to captain Tom Ryan.

Jack Lynch: On Hurling

I think that hurling typifies the Irish character and tradition more than anything else, with the exception of our language. It has the combination of skill, courage, speed of thought and action, and calls for a spirit to give and take more than most games … Can anything be more racy of the soil – the game itself, the camán, the men who play it!

Brendan Fullam, *Giants of the Ash* (1991)

FROM TWO FRONTS
WE TAKE OUR CUE, BUT THAT WAS IN JUNE, 1939. WAIT FOR THE THIRD FRONT NEXT WEEK, THE EVE OF THE

Thurles Sportsfield Carnival
JUNE 4th ———— JUNE 18th

Prior to the Carnival in June, 1939, we published feature articles dealing with the Sportsfield in both the "Irish Independent" and "Irish Press," from which we take the following excerpts:—

"IRISH INDEPENDENT":
"Things thus dragged on for a number of years. The Thurles Field, unquestionably the most popular in the provinces, witnessed great triumphs — the Mecca of players and spectators alike. It was realised, however, that haphazard methods for improving and extending the embankment and sideline accommodation would have to be discarded.

"The problem was definitely grappled with towards the end of 1936, when a public meeting of the townspeople was convened by Rev. P. Fogarty, C.C., Chairman, Mid Division Board. A start on right lines having been made, enterprising local citizens subscribed individual amounts to meet the cost of the proposed scheme of improvements, this financial backing being ultimately responsible for securing invested commitments of £2,000 and £500 from the Munster and Central Councils, respectively."

"In all, the scheme of reconstruction has cost a little over £5,000 to date. The contract for the work, according to plans originally prepared by Mr. T. J. Hyland, B.E., being carried out in a most satisfactory manner by Messrs. James Skehan and Sons, Thurles."

"IRISH PRESS":
"Seeing that year after year the crowds gathered in increasing numbers to witness the hectic encounters between leading Munster hurling counties, Thurles gradually gripped the public imagination, eventually acquiring a kind of spell which sports writers were gracious enough to call an 'atmosphere.' In those days—and with pardonable justification—complaints occasionally arose when unusually large crowds found the over-taxed accommodation around the playing pitch not sufficient to meet their needs. This in time became a kind of hardy annual, the volume of voiced grievances growing noticeably louder as the crowds grew larger. The glorious playing pitch was the one bright spot all the time—a sort of soothing balm to the blister of discontent. To understand the position properly, it is only fair to mention that the Sportsfield Committee, with only very limited resources, valiantly did all in their power to improve the embankment, sideline and stand accommodation prior to every big game. But at best, it must be candidly admitted, it was only a temporary expedient, meeting, as a rule, with only partial success. And so we come to a task that was long deferred, but at last accomplished."

There will always be a Sportsfield—
THE ONE AND INCOMPARABLE!

'Wartime' advertisement for Thurles Sportsfield Carnival 1944.

Opposite top: Cork, Munster and All-Ireland Hurling Champions 1944. Front (l–r): Jim Young, Jack Lynch, Seán Condon (captain), Jim Morrison, Con Cottrell, Christy Ring, Din Joe Buckley. Back (l–r): John Quirke, Con Murphy, Alan Lotty, Willie 'Long Puck' Murphy, Joe Kelly, Tom Mulcahy, Paddy O'Donovan, Batt Thornhill, Jim 'Tough' Barry.

1944
From UCC to Thurles on Wheels

Tommy Leahy, who lived at Marlhill, New Inn, was doing chores around his farmyard on the eve of the 1944 Munster final at Thurles, when he saw two cyclists coming in the driveway.

His unexpected visitors were Alfie O'Rahilly, President of UCC, and Jim Hurley, the College Bursar. They were on their way to the match, and Tommy was delighted to feed them and give them a bed for the night. They had a great chat about the game before they retired for the night. When morning came the visitors crossed the fields to early Mass in Rockwell College, and when Tommy finished the milking he saw them at the pump washing off their shoes before they came in for breakfast. Following a hearty meal they hit on for Thurles and Cork's victory over Limerick in what came to be known as the 'Bicycle Final'.

Séamus Leahy, Clonmel

1944

The Great Bicycle Finals: Munster Senior Hurling Final

The Munster final between Cork and Limerick was played at Thurles Sportsfield on 16 July. Seldom had a contest gripped the imagination of the hurling public to the same extent as this one. Cork were going for three in a row in Munster and their fourth consecutive All-Ireland. Because of the war and 'Emergency' travel restrictions, the bicycle was the mode of conveyance for eighty per cent of the attendance of 20,000, so this came to be known as 'The Great Bicycle Final'. On the Saturday afternoon the ordinary rail and bus services were bursting at the seams when they arrived in Thurles, and later in the evening hordes of cyclists joined them; soon all the hotels and boarding houses were taken up. Fortunately the weather was kind so the latecomers were able to sleep in the open air or in some convenient hay barn or outhouse.

From dawn on Sunday morning all roads leading to the town were black with lines of cyclists and horse-drawn vehicles of every description stretching back for forty miles. Nor were the foot-slogging brigade outnumbered; indeed many walked all the way from Limerick. By midday the scene in Thurles was unforgettable. Under the broiling sun, Liberty Square presented an old-world atmosphere, chock-a-block with bicycles. There were cycle parks in every street. The day was glorious and the match was a cracker.

Mick Mackey, who had been playing senior hurling for Limerick since 1929, was on fire, whipping over points from acute angles and pitching in with two goals. After scoring his second one, he ambled past his marker, twenty-two-year-old debutant Con Murphy, a future president of the GAA, and smilingly commented, 'They'll surely be taking you off now.' Johnny Quirke, Blackrock, scored his third goal in the final minutes to pull Cork a point clear, but at the death, Dick Stokes equalised for Limerick, 6-7 to 4-13.

Cork lineout: Tom Mulcahy (goal), Willie 'Long Puck' Murphy, Batt Thornhill, Con Murphy, Din Joe Buckley, Alan Lotty, Jim Young, Con Cottrell, Jack Lynch, Christy Ring, Paddy Healy, Seán Condon (captain), John Quirke, Jim Morrison, Joe Kelly. Substitute: Paddy O'Donovan.

Towed to Thurles

'I met a man and his young sons at Thurles who had cycled from Cork,' wrote an *Irish Press* columnist. 'As all the hotels and guest houses were full, these brave travellers slept the Saturday night in a hay barn. On the way to Thurles, the chain of the fifteen-year-old boy's cycle broke. His two companions made sugán ropes in a field, tied his bike to their own and towed him the rest of the way to Thurles.'

Ring's Wonder Goal

The replay back in Thurles on 30 July caused huge excitement as well. With the country ravaged by war-time petrol restrictions, thousands set off for Thurles Sportsfield by every improvised means of transport, and once again the footsloggers took to the roads. Sixty-five-year-old Peter Ryan from Lisnagry, Limerick, walked the thirty-five miles to Thurles – such was the spirit of the times. Eighteen thousand spectators turned up, an estimated 15,000 of them on bicycles.

Hard to believe, but the replay was every bit as good as the drawn game. These were two of the finest hurling games ever played. With seven minutes left in the match, it looked as if Cork were done for. Trailing by four points, Mick Mackey burst through for his second goal, but, in the days before the advantage rule, play was called back for a foul on him. Limerick missed the resulting free. Cork nicked a goal and a point to equalise.

With a minute left, Mackey's effort for a winning point went wide. As the final seconds ticked away, Christy Ring collected a ball in his own half-back line and soloed to within forty yards of the Limerick posts, where he unleashed a rasper. Amid the clash of ash the ball ended in the net to give Cork the verdict, 4-6 to 3-6. 'Someone asked him,' maintained his teammate Din Joe Buckley, 'why he had not taken a point to win the game. "Anyone could do that," he said.' For those who were in Thurles that day, the goal remained a cherished memory of a wonderful artistic effort by a master hurler.

How oft I watched him from the hill move here and there in grace,
In Cork, Killarney, Thurles town or by the Shannon's race;
'Now Cork is bet, the hay is saved!' the thousands wildly sing –
You speak too soon, my sweet garsún, for here comes Christy Ring!

Bryan MacMahon, quoted in Smyth, *In Praise of Heroes*

For years, it was a badge of honour to proclaim, 'I was in Thurles in 1944'. Never since, according to many, has anything been witnessed to approach the grand true spirit of friendship and togetherness that prevailed, a bright beacon of light in the midst of wartime gloom.

Paddy O'Donovan: 'You Breathe It in the Very Air of the Place'

Four-in-a-row All-Ireland winner with Cork, Paddy O'Donovan from Glen Rovers, stated,

There is more atmosphere in Thurles on the day of a Munster final than you will get anywhere else – even at Croke Park on All-Ireland day. Once you put your foot inside Liberty Square on the morning of the match until you leave in the evening, you will feel completely tied up in this hurling atmosphere. You breathe it in the very air of the place. You feel more at one with the crowd at Thurles than at Croke Park, where the stands seem to make them more remote from you. A Munster final at Thurles, too, is a greater ordeal: you feel you cannot afford to fail before a crowd of 50,000 – almost every one of them with a direct interest in the contest.

Smith, *Decades of Glory*

Séamus Leahy: 'How far to Thurles, lads?'

GAA historian Séamus Leahy remembers the crowds travelling by bicycle on match days:

I was still ten years old when I arrived in Thurles from Tubberadora on a pony and cart and I was awed by the sight of Liberty Square stacked with row after row of bicycles. Motor cars, which had disappeared from the roads as a result of wartime restrictions, had not yet returned to the roads and many of the bikes had been ridden from Cork. Walking back to Tubberadora from Mass in Boherlahan in the morning, we had been amused by the shouts of, 'How far to Thurles, lads?' and we thought ourselves quite funny in assuming what we thought to be Cork accents as we shouted back, 'about six miles.'

Tipperary, All-Ireland Senior Hurling Champions 1945. Back row (l–r): Jack Mockler, Ger Cornally, John Maher (captain), Henry Gouldsboro, Tom Wall, Rev Fr Meagher, Flor Coffey, Jim Devitt, John Coffey, Tony Brennan, Johnny Ryan, Paddy Leahy, Jim Maher, Dan Breen. Front row (l–r): John Joe Callanan, Phil Purcell, Tommy Butler, Mick Murphy, Paddy Ryan (S), Jimmy Maher, Tommy Doyle, Mutt Ryan, Tommy Purcell, Eddie Gleeson, Johnny Leahy, Tommy Semple.

Tipperary hurlers returning in triumph to Thurles in 1945.

1945

Maher's March to Glory: Munster Senior Hurling Final

Tipperary played Limerick in the Munster final in Thurles Sportsfield on 15 July. The talk was of the two Mackeys, Mick and John, and how Tipp's backline would cope. It is remembered as a great Munster final with 25,000 spectators on their toes with its swaying fortunes. The hurling was hard, with men standing shoulder to shoulder and pulling first time in the air or on the ground with an abandon that was almost reckless.

Limerick dominated the first half but did not convert their superiority into scores. This was mainly due to the excellence of the Tipperary full-back line of Johnny Ryan, Ger Cornally and Flor Coffey, where Cornally was the star. Jimmy Maher, behind them, was outstanding between the sticks. Limerick led at half-time by 0-5 to 1-1. Goals and points were exchanged early in the second half as the tide of battle ebbed and flowed. Over the hour, Mackey was well held and though he careered around in his usual style, John Maher, Tipperary's captain, was successful on many occasions in spiking his guns. A goal by substitute Jack Dwyer gave Tipperary a four-point advantage. This was followed by a hectic Limerick onslaught, which yielded a Mackey point and left the victory to Tipperary by 4-3 to 2-6.

In the *Tipperary Yearbook* 1986, Séamus Leahy describes this great day in Thurles:

For me there was never quite another day in Thurles, or anywhere else for that matter like that in 1945, when John Maher and his men stopped Cork in their run for five-in-a-row. It was Cuchulainn in the gap facing the strangers, only there were fifteen Cuchulainns the whole way up the field from Jimmy Maher between the posts to John Coffey above in the corner. Gloriously sunny and the war just over, there was an atmosphere down through the town that day, that lighted many a dull night afterwards. It was great to be alive and Tipperary on the way to Croke Park and the minors were going with them and Cork was beat and the hay was saved and what else could anyone want out of life!

Close to the Action

Speaking with this author on 17 May, 2020, former Tipperary captain Tony Wall (pictured) described his early introduction to Thurles Sportsfield:

When I was growing up on Fianna Road in Thurles, one of my great childhood friends was Mícheál Gorman, who lived a few doors down from me. His father was Ned Gorman who was the sportsfield secretary and because of this, as young fellas, we were able to get into the field to have a few pucks, on the quiet. I remember maybe five or six of us playing three-goals-in on the sacred sod.

I remember also, in the mid-1940s, I was about ten years of age and Ned gave me a special important job to do on big match days. I had to collect a flag from the sideline, immediately the match was over. Supporters had the habit of taking these flags as souvenirs. So, I was given a seat on the sideline, as close to the action as you could be. And what action, I saw all those famous games and players of the time, up close.

I remember Mackey was bottled up one day by three Cork backmen, just in front of me. There seemed no way out for him, but he just palmed the ball off one of them over the sideline and off he went with the biggest grin you ever saw on his face.

Thurles Sarsfields, Tipperary Senior Hurling Champions 1945. Back row (l–r): Bill Leahy (club chairman), Gerry Doyle, Tom Mason, Nicholas Mockler, Jack Ryan (G), John Maher (captain), Ger Cornally, John McGuire, Mícheál Maher. Front row (l–r): Mick Murphy, Mickey Byrne, Tommy Doyle, Tommy Ryan, Paddy Gorman, Mikey Doyle, Eddie Gleeson.

1945
Gleeson's Goal, Sarsfields Success: Tipperary Senior Hurling Final

Roscrea were bidding for their first county title at Nenagh on 11 November but had to settle for a draw, 4-4 to 3-7. The replay was at Thurles Sportsfield a fortnight later. In a very low-scoring game, Eddie Gleeson's goal really counted as Sarsfields won by 1-4 to 1-0.

The Best of Times

John O'Grady, Tipperary minor hurling captain 1949, also known as 'Cúlbaire' (pictured), recalled the best of times:

So Thurles Sportsfield had its banks and terraces expanded considerably and the huge attendance poured in, borne by numerous rail excursions or in the square-backed motorcars of the period. It was still mostly Cork v Limerick. The Mackey-Power-Clohessy-Stokes-Ryan team bowed to age; Cork's four-in-a-row took over with Ring-Lynch-Condon-Lotty-Young-Thornhill and the rest of a powerful company.

The Sportsfield reached its zenith of attraction – I venture to say its golden period. How smartly it used to be prepared, with the white lines of almost Wimbledon sharpness, its sod noted to life and pace of the ground ball, then at its most fiery; and the old goal-posts with the netting supported by an amount of white painted timbering, like spars and struts.

How the flakes of white used cascade from the newly painted netting, when the bodies of inrushing attackers crashed headlong against it – no such thing then as the predictable free out to call a halt to hectic action near the inside of goals guarded by men like Scanlon, Mulcahy or Ware.

Tipperary Star, first published in *World of Gaelic Games*

CHAPTER 3

THURLES, THE MECCA OF THE GAEL

1946–1951

Cork, Munster Senior Hurling Champions 1946. Back row (l–r): Jim Young, Alan Lotty, Mossy O'Riordan, Gerry O'Riordan, Con Murphy (Valley Rovers), Con Murphy (Bride Rovers), Paddy O'Donovan, Jack Lynch, Jim Barry. Front row (l–r): Christy Ring (captain), Din Joe Buckley, Paddy Healy, Willie 'Long Puck' Murphy, Joe Kelly, Tom Mulcahy, Con Cottrell.

1946

Easy for the Rebels: Munster Senior Hurling Final

The 1946 Munster hurling final at Thurles Sportsfield on 14 July failed to live up to expectations and was really a disappointing day for the 39,000 attendance. The game lost interest midway through the first half. Mick Mackey was the only bright spot on a weak Limerick team, but on this occasion he was unable to cope with his fast marker, Din Joe Buckley. With Mackey held, the Limerick challenge collapsed, and Cork, captained by Christy Ring, were not unduly pressed to win by 3-8 to 1-3. The game proved that

Previous page: Mick Mackey and Christy Ring, Limerick and Cork captains, watching the toss of the coin at the 1946 Munster hurling final at Thurles Sportsfield. Referee, Willie O'Donnell, Tipperary, on left. Photo courtesy of the Irish Examiner *Archive.*

the experience and guile of the 'old hands' cannot stand up to youthful speed and dash. Mackey's sterling inter-county career was drawing to a close, and this year also saw his teammate Timmy Ryan effectively retired from inter-county hurling.

Cork Critical, but the *Star* Strikes Back

There was much criticism of the facilities at Thurles Sportsfield for the 1946 Munster final. 'Unless the catering in Thurles is improved, all such matches should be taken from it. The days when Thurles was famous are gone. Thousands of Cork supporters failed to get a bite to eat there and the stewarding was very bad,' said Rev Dr Connolly at a meeting of Cork County Board. 'The field arrangements,' said Mr S Long, Chairman of Cork County Board, 'were the worst I have seen in my experience.' Some of the thousands who came to the game failed to get into the Sportsfield and had to be content with listening to the radio broadcast downtown.

The comments of the Cork officials offended both the Sportsfield Committee and the people of Thurles. They acknowledged that the huge attendance put a strain on arrangements, but felt that Cork should be the last to criticise, recalling the debacle there in 1926, when the Munster final between Tipperary and Cork had to be abandoned due to crowd-control issues. The editor of the *Tipperary Star*, on 20 July, 1946, concluded,

> Thurles has catered magnificently during the last twenty years – since the call first came – and tributes have come countrywide. To pounce on it now, with food restrictions still in force, is, it seems to us, extremely ungracious and unworthy of the great Gaelic county of Cork.

No Room at the Inn but Dancing on the Streets

Many who had come the night before the 1946 Munster final on the mail train, hoping to be accommodated in Thurles, were disappointed, as every possible place was booked out. They were compelled to spend the night in the open, in some barn or outhouse. At three o'clock in the morning, a lively impromptu dance, to the music of an accordion, was held at the Westgate corner of Liberty Square, and at all hours people were moving up and down the streets.

Jim 'Tough' Barry

Jim Barry, known as 'Tough', was in charge of Cork's hurling teams for a period of forty years, 1926 to 1966. He was the trainer of twelve All-Ireland-winning Cork teams and assisted Limerick to the McCarthy Cup in 1934. In his youth, he was a successful amateur boxer and swimmer. A tailor by profession, Jim always dressed immaculately.

This photo was taken at half-time at Thurles Sportsfield during the 1946 Mun-

ster hurling final. With clenched fist, Jim 'Tough' Barry exhorts his players to better things. On the left, without jersey, is Cork hurler Con Murphy, who was GAA president from 1976 to 1979.

Jim 'Tough' Barry on Thurles: 'Anyone who couldn't hurl in Thurles shouldn't bother handling a stick.'

And on Cork hurlers: 'In Cork, hurlers come up overnight like mushrooms.'

Above left: A match programme for the 1947 Munster final, courtesy of the GAA Museum & Archive.
Above right: Limerick backs come under Cork pressure at Thurles in 1947.

Supporters in jovial mood, awaiting the hurling action.

1947

The Better Team Lost: Munster Senior Hurling Final

Limerick and Cork met again in the Munster final at Thurles Sportsfield on 20 July, 1947, and 34,000 spectators turned up. Special trains ran for the first time in seven years. Following the previous year's difficulties, accommodation in the field was increased by 6,500 with the construction of an embankment at the Killinan End. The press reported,

> If ever a better team lost, it was Limerick, who were dogged throughout by ill luck. They were magnificent in as dour a southern decider was ever played. Twelve months ago Limerick were completely blotted out by the exact same Cork fifteen but the boot was on the other foot on Sunday and it was a chastened Cork fifteen that left the arena winners by 2-6 to 2-3.

Séamus Ó Ceallaigh and Sean Murphy, *One Hundred Years of Glory* (1988)

Cork: Tom Mulcahy, Willie 'Long Puck' Murphy, Con Murphy, Din Joe Buckley, Paddy O'Donovan, Alan Lotty, Jim Young, Jack Lynch, Con Cottrill, Seán Condon (captain), Christy Ring, Con Murphy, Mossy O'Riordan, Gerry O'Riordan, Joe Kelly.

As late as the preceding Saturday, Cork were threatening not to come to the game, because of their failure to secure hotel accommodation in the town for their team. For the first time in twenty-one years, Munster final day was wet in Thurles. Because of the previous year's catering problems, many spectators decided to bring their own provisions, and as a result, several caterers in Thurles had large supplies of bread, etc., left on their hands on the Monday. There were also complaints of overcharging – four-penny bars were being sold openly for nine-pence!

Sportsfield Caretaker Paddy Brolan

Paddy Brolan, born in 1881, was a very promising hurler of the Tom Semple era. His usual position was at wing-forward, and he was a regular on Tipperary teams from 1906 until 1913. In that time he won four Tipperary senior hurling championships, four Munster titles – 1906, 1908, 1909 and 1913 – and All-Ireland medals in 1906 and 1908.

From 1944 to 1956, he was caretaker at Thurles Sportsfield. He was very particular about the field; it was hard to satisfy him. Even when the grass was cut, his son remembers having to pluck any long *tráineens* (long grasses) that escaped the mower. He remembered the embankments at the sportsfield being built with cinders from Thurles sugar factory. Paddy cared for 'the field' with loving hands, and even worked to a late hour there on the night preceding his death.

As a player and then a long-time caretaker, Paddy was in an ideal position to assess the evolution of the game of hurling. He commented,

Players nowadays don't hold their place on the field as we did. If they did, the game would be much more spectacular. In my day, you beat your man or he beat you. There was no cover up that you were helping out somewhere else. Your place was your place and it was your business to be there. In my time, I often saw the ball travel the length of the field half a dozen times in the air and no one marvelled at the spectacle, just accepted it as part of the game.

Ó Donnchú, Tom Semple and the Thurles Blues

Paddy Brolan died on 21 July, 1956, aged seventy-five years, on the eve of the Munster final.

Carrick Swan, Tipperary Senior Hurling Champions 1947. Back row (l–r): Jimmy Duggan, Mick Walsh, Paddy Kelly, Tom Wall, Jack Murphy, Michael O'Shea, Eddie O'Shea, Willie Wall (captain), John Barry. Middle row (l–r): Tom O'Shea, Willie Nugent, John Farrell, Paddy Madden, Mick Madden, Jimmy Hogan. Front row (l–r): Paddy Smyth, Paddy Fleming, Paddy Fahey, Michael Connolly, John Fleming, Steve Hogan.

1947
Carrick Swan Win Convincingly: Tipperary Senior Hurling Final

The Wall brothers formed the backbone of Carrick's victory over Borris/Ileigh, Willie at full-back and Tom at centre-back. Another star on show was Paddy Madden, whose hat trick of goals from full-forward stunned the Borris boys. At the long whistle Carrick Swan were champions for the first time: 5-4 to 2-2.

1948
Toscanini for the Music: Munster Senior Hurling Semi-Final

Over 40,000 supporters, possibly the largest to date, attended the Munster semi-final between Cork and Limerick at Thurles Sportsfield. The town was transformed into a miniature city for the day. Almost 17,000 people travelled on twenty special trains to Thurles. Cork won by 5-3 to 2-5, and at the end of the game the crush through the gates was unprecedented. At one stage, scores of people had perforce to 'back out' – swept along by the dense throng, they had given up their attempts to face around and at least see where they were going.

In *Tall Tales and Banter* (1998), the 'voice of the GAA' Seán Óg Ó Ceallacháin remembered:

> It was another of those heart-palpitating hurling contests in Thurles, between Cork and Tipperary. The atmosphere was electric and the exchanges flowed with frightening intensity. With time running out and Tipperary holding a slender lead, Ring saw his chance, grabbed possession, rounded his man and headed goalwards eluding tackles and smashing the ball to the Tipperary net. Up jumped an excited Cork supporter and proclaimed, 'Toscanini for the music, Katie Barry for the crubeens, but it's Ringey boy for the goals'.

1948
Ware Leads the Déise to Glory: Munster Senior Hurling Final

Waterford gave a magnificent display of do-or-die hurling, regaining the Munster title after an absence of ten years at Thurles Sportsfield on 1 August. It was a close affair with the minimum separating the sides at the long whistle. Cork were first down to business and looked like champions, but the Déise men settled and led 2-3 to 1-5 at the break. Waterford were gaining in confidence and went eight points ahead early in the second half, but the Cork men, true to their tradition, fought back. Great displays from veterans

Waterford, Munster Senior Hurling Champions 1948. Back row (l–r): John Keane, Willy Galvin, Christy Moylan, Eddie Carew, Mick Hayes, Seán Cusack, Kevin O'Connor and Tom Curran. Front row (l–r): Jackie Goode, Johnny O'Connor, Ned Daly, Jim Ware (captain), Andy Fleming, Jimmy Galvin and Vin Baston. Photo courtesy of Waterford Museum, Dungarvan.

Jim Ware in goal and centre-forward John Keane, giving leadership when it was really needed, not forgetting Vin Baston at centre-back and midfielders Johnny O'Connor and Ned Carew. The final score was Waterford 4-7, Cork 3-9.

For Waterford captain Jim Ware, Erin's Own, this would be his only Munster Championship medal. He came in for individual praise after making a number of spectacular saves. On 5 September, 1948, Ware became the first Waterford player and the oldest player to lift the Liam McCarthy Cup after a 7-6 to 2-4 defeat of Dublin in the All-Ireland final.

Entrepreneurial Spirit

An estimated £40,000 was spent in Thurles at the Munster semi-final. However, the publicans and caterers didn't make all the money. A vendor of soft drinks disposed of 120 dozen bottles in the Sportsfield at one shilling each, having bought them for two-and-a-half pence each. Three musicians had £26 after their day. A beggar-man changed £9 in coppers in a public house on the Square, while another merely held out his hat to the passing crowd near the field and found himself almost £5 to the good.

The Price to be Paid

Tomás Ó Cinnéide, nephew of Waterford centre-forward John Keane, recalls Thurles in 1948:

> I have a vivid memory of that game in Thurles and of walking back to the town from the field after the match, with John, who was still in his togs, and the multitudes of people cheering him and clapping him on the back. But the memory that made the most impression on me was the sight of his two hands covered in dried blood and his knuckles torn to shreds. It made me realise that hurling was a man's game and there was a price to be paid for all that cheering and back slapping.

David Smith, *The Unconquerable Keane* (2011)

Ó hEithir 'Excommunicates' Bishop

Commentator Mícheál Ó hEithir wrote in the Munster hurling final programme 1982:

In those sunny days of the [1940s], my commentary position was a seat on the sideline, with an open mike as distinct from the lip mike of modern times, an instrument that transmits only what is spoken directly into it.

Later a small wooden broadcasting box was built alongside what used to be the 'stand'. Space was at a premium and there was room for the radio technician and myself with the mike hanging out the open window to pick up all the noises and the commentary as well. Just as the ball was thrown in, a local official escorted a visiting bishop from far off lands and placed him in the box, making human sardines of us. I could not object … the game was on and there was no turning off.

However when he produced a cigar and proceeded to puff thickly around the place … it was too much, and silently, respectfully but firmly I turned from the game and 'excommunicated' the indignant cigar-smoking bishop from my little box and carried on in clearer air.

Young Holycross/Ballycahill Make History

The years 1948, 1951 and 1954 are etched in gold in the GAA annals of Holycross/ Ballycahill club. These glory years saw county hurling honours coming to the Abbeymen, as the club produced stalwarts of the hurling game including Pat Stakelum, Michael Maher and John Doyle. Lorrha/Dorrha fell to them in 1948 by 4-10 to 2-4, while Clonoulty were on the receiving end of a 5-15 to 1-4 result in 1951. In 1954, with the team strengthened by the inclusion of Toomevara native John Hough, they overcame the challenge of Roscrea in the county final by 6-5 to 2-3.

Holycross/Ballycahill, Tipperary Senior Hurling Champions 1948. Back row (l–r): Pake Hennessy, Paddy 'Sweeper' Ryan, Jack Ryan (A), Ned O'Gorman, Mick Stakelum, John Doyle, Jim Duggan, Danny O'Gorman, Tim Crowe, Phil Maher, Bob Stakelum, Tim Dwyer, Michael Ferncombe, Rev Michael Russell, Jimmy Kennedy, Willie Tuohy. Front row (l–r): Paddy Leahy, Pat Stakelum, Francis Maher (captain), Jack Dwyer, Jim Ryan (A), John Stakelum, John Byrnes, Francis Bannon, Rody Dwan.

1948

Doubling the Bank

In 1948, the Munster Council decided to spend £4,500 on improvements to Thurles Sportsfield. This sum would be matched by the local committee. The plan was to provide extra standing room for 14,000 patrons by doubling the long bank, and to add seated sideline accommodation for an extra 1,500 and a tunnelled entrance for teams. In the autumn, thousands of tons of filling were drawn from Thurles sugar factory to extend the existing embankments. Liam Skehan, contractor, had a bulldozer levelling the top of the 'banks', through which three concrete tunnels were being erected.

Tipperary GAA secretary Phil Purcell gives the players some advice during a break in training for the 1949 All–Ireland final.

1949

A Cunning Kenny Ruse

GAA historian Seamus J King remembers,

It has to be my earliest memory of Semple Stadium, October 2, 1949, the Mid-Tipperary final replay between Boherlahan and Borris/Ileigh. Two weeks before, the game ended in a draw, 4-1 to 1-10, Boherlahan scoring the goals and Borris/Ileigh the points. It had generated huge interest and the replay attracted even more, with 15,000 in attendance. The expectation was justified as the replay produced a spectacular game of hurling. The level of intensity was increased following a cunning ruse by the Kenny brothers ten minutes before half-time as Boherlahan led by 2-1 to 0-5. Borris/Ileigh were awarded a free about thirty yards out. It was too far from the goal for one of Paddy's lethal shots. As the Boherlahan backs lined the goals, Seán and Paddy Kenny appeared to have some argument as to who would take the free. First Paddy went towards the ball, then Seán and, as Paddy walked away, apparently disheartened, Seán lifted the ball but instead of striking hard just tipped it neatly to brother Paddy, who was unmarked, and he, catching the pass, slapped home a rasper, which Jimmy Maher hadn't a chance to save as it shot past his ear into the net. The game became even more intense and produced a terrific spell of wonder hurling, which followers of the game raved about for years afterwards.

The second half wasn't as good when the intense rivalry between the sides spilled over into rows and dangerous play, which referee Timmy Hammersley found difficult to control. He had already sent off Paddy Kenny and Philip Ryan at the end of the first half and Seán Kenny and Sonny Maher got their walking papers in the second half. The game ended in Borris/Ileigh's favour by 1-9 to 2-3 but the memories of the game and the ruse of the Kenny brothers will be remembered much longer than the result.

Borris/Ileigh, Tipperary Senior Hurling Champions 1949. Back row (l–r): Jim Costello, Joe Ryan (R), Ned Finn, Raphael Ryan, Donal Meagher, Rev John Ryan, Phil Crowley, Paddy Kenny, Billy Stapleton, Hugh Bourke. Middle row (l–r): Paddy Ryan Murray, Phibby Kenny, Jimmy Coffey, Mick Joe Dwyer, Ned Ryan, Johnson Hackett, Martin Ryan, Philly Ryan. Front row (l–r): Phil Maher, Tom Ryan Murray, Seán Kenny, Jimmy Finn.

Borris/Ileigh captain Seán Kenny leads his team in the pre-match parade at Thurles Sportsfield on 30 October, 1949. He is followed by Philly Ryan, Paddy Kenny, Hugh Bourke, Eddie Flynn and Mick Joe Dwyer.

1949

Borris on the Rise: Tipperary Senior Hurling Final

The county final was played at Thurles Sportsfield on 30 October, between Borris/Ileigh and Knockavilla Kickhams. Backboned by the three Kenny brothers, Seán, Paddy and Phibby, and upcoming hurling star Jimmy Finn, Borris/Ileigh were always in command and won by 4-6 to 2-1. Former Cork hurler and future GAA president Con Murphy refereed the contest. For Borris/Ileigh, this was their most successful period to date, winning their first senior county title and repeating the success in 1950 and 1953.

> At evening time in the old kiln field, you can see the boys so bold,
> 'Twould remind you of old Knocknagow, in Kickham's story told.
> To see them wield their camáns, so brave and manfully,
> There's many a Matt the Thrasher 'mongst the lads of Fair Ileigh.
>
> Pat Mahon, 'Lovely Fair Ileigh'

Sportsfield Stewards

These stewards were present at the county final: Larry Moloughney, Michael Connors, Dick Butler, Willie Butler, Michael Callanan, Andy Callanan, Jimmy Loughlan, Tommy Butler, Paddy Maher, Mickey Byrne, Denis Murphy, Ted Heffernan, Michael Butler, Paddy Power, Jack Ryan (G), Johnny Maher, Paddy Gleeson, Paddy Callanan, Danny Maher, Martin Troy, Jack Butler, John Ryan (B), Con Dwyer, Paddy O'Gorman, Mick Kennedy (Brittas).

Joe Campbell, Thurles Sarsfields, reported to the Mid Tipperary GAA board on his efforts to control spectators at the recent county football final, 'I tried to clear the field of spectators, but I got a few wallops and they had as much respect for me, as if I didn't exist.' Tommy Butler observed, 'There was a time when every steward at a match in Thurles Sportsfield had to carry an ash plant to protect himself.'

1949–1951
Tipperary's Three-in-a-Row

Tipperary's fortunes changed in 1949 when they broke Cork's stranglehold on the championship, beating them in a first-round replay by 2–8 to 1–9. In the Munster semi-final, Tipperary beat Clare 15–1 to 7–1, and Limerick fell to them in the provincial final by 1–16 to 2–10. The novel pairing of Tipperary and Laois met in the All-Ireland final. Laois kept in touch until half-time 1–5 to 0–3, but Tipperary finished strongly, winning by 3–11 to 0–3.

Below left: Pat Stakelum, Tipperary's 1949 captain, leads his team in the pre-match parade.
Below right: Pat Stakelum, Tipperary captain in 1949.

Tipperary hurlers training at Thurles Sportsfield for the 1950 All-Ireland final. From left to right: Jimmy Kennedy, Mickey Byrne, John Doyle and Paddy Kenny.

Tipperary, All-Ireland Hurling Champions 1949. Players: Flor Coffey, Seán Kenny, Tony Reddin, Phil Shanahan, John Doyle, Tom Dwyer, Sonny Maher, Seamus Bannon, Tony Brennan, Tommy Ryan, Mick Ryan, Mickey Byrne, Pat Stakelum (captain), Tommy Doyle, Jimmy Kennedy, Jack Ryan.

In the 1950 Munster semi-final against Limerick, Tipperary scraped past by three points to set up a meeting with Cork in the Munster final, which Tipperary won by 2–17 to 3–11. Having beaten Galway by seven points in the All-Ireland semi-final, it was a Tipperary/Kilkenny final. The game was tough, but Kilkenny looked to cause an upset, leading 0–7 to 0–5 at half-time. Tipperary recovered and led 0–9 to 0–8 in the final stages. Two goals were exchanged and Tipperary led 1–9 to 1–8 in the nervous last few minutes, but they held on to win.

Tipperary's opening Munster game in 1951 was against Waterford, and the Déise put up a mighty fight to lose only by a goal, 2-10 to 1-10. The semi-final against Limerick was much different, and Tipperary won easily, 3-8 to 1-6. It was a scorching day at the Gaelic Grounds, Limerick, when Cork stood between Tipperary and three Munster

Above left: Tipperary's captain Jimmy Finn leads his team in the pre-match parade before the 1951 All-Ireland final. He is followed by Tony Reddin, Tommy Doyle, Mickey Byrne, Seamus Bannon and Phil Shanahan.

Above right: Tipperary, All-Ireland Hurling Champions 1951. Back row (l–r): Phil Purcell, Seán Kenny, Jimmy Kennedy, John Walsh, John Hough, Tom Kevin, Tim Ryan, Dick Blake, Tony Reddin, Sonny Maher, Phil Shanahan, Tony Brennan, Connie Keane, Rev John Ryan, John Doyle, John Joe Hayes. Middle row (l–r): Paddy Leahy, Mick Ryan, Tommy Doyle, Jimmy Finn (captain), Mickey Byrne, Ned Ryan, Seamus Bannon, Paddy Fleming, Philly Ryan, Gerry Doyle. Front row (l–r): Paddy Kenny, John Purcell (mascot), Pat Stakelum.

titles in a row. Tipperary led 0–9 to 1–4 at half-time. The second half was hectic, with the lead exchanging and Christy Ring firing on all cylinders. An amazing Ring goal plus points set up Cork for a three-point lead with one quarter to go. Ned Ryan got a goal back for Tipperary and points were swapped as the game neared its end. Sonny Maher then put over the winning points for Tipperary's third Munster title in a row, by 2-11 to 2-9.

The All-Ireland final, which was seen by 70,000, saw Tipperary wearing Munster's blue and their opponents Wexford, Leinster's green. Wexford took an early five-point lead, but at half-time Tipperary had recovered to lead by a goal. The second half was all one-way traffic as Tipperary coasted to victory, by 7-7 to 3-9.

The flags are proudly waving and Croke Park is gold and blue,

And the haunting strains of Slievenamon would thrill you through and through.

We have won three titles in a row, forty-nine to fifty-one,

Let victory's cry be held on high and joy to everyone.

Jack Ryan, quoted in King, Ó Donnchú, Smyth, *Tipperary's GAA Ballads*

Jimmy's Playground

We all have our own way of practising … everyone has something they use to practise their accuracy. What I had was the scoreboard up on top of the town-end, at Thurles Sportsfield. There was a ventilation slit in the wall below that … I'd have three balls and I'd hit them on the run, at the slit in the wall. When the three balls had gone in the slit, I'd go up and collect the balls and come back out, then start again, over and over, all day long.

Diarmuid O'Flynn, *The Boy Wonder of Hurling:*
The Story of Jimmy Doyle Told in His Own Words (2015)

Jimmy Doyle and Patsy Dorney, juvenile hurlers with Bohernanave Street League team.

CHAPTER 4

WHEN RING WAS KING

THE 1950S

Christy Ring, with typical concentration and determination, prepares to strike. Photo courtesy of the Irish Examiner *Archive.*

Top left: Raymond Smith.
Action from the early 1950s: Top right: Tipperary great John Doyle bursting his way through a forest of sticks. Above: Despite the valiant efforts of Tipperary goalkeeper Tony Reddin, this Limerick shot sails over the bar. Limerick forward T Long awaits the outcome. The An Post GAA Hurling Team of the Millennium, chosen in 2000, included Reddin as goalkeeper.

The Scene is Set

Thurles native, author and journalist Raymond Smith experienced many a Munster final at Thurles Sportsfield. Writing in his book *Decades of Glory*, his vivid memories and images set the scene:

The turnstiles click merrily and the stands and embankments fill up – a shirt-sleeved crowd if the day is hot and colour everywhere. The crowd join in singing 'The Banks of My Own Lovely Lee' or 'Slievenamon'. There are certain songs as there are certain characters associated with the day and the occasion.

The players come out and walk up the sideline past the main stand. The crowd hums with expectation as the famous faces are recognised, the stars of the present and the great ones, now team mentors, who won renown on this ground in the past.

The teams are parading now and shrewd eyes look out calculatingly from under the lowered cap peaks of the knowing ones on the embankment – the men born and bred in Thurles, 'the cradle of the GAA'. These are the most exacting critics in the country and coldly dispassionate in their judgments of hurling men – even their own.

The cheers rise as the teams parade. They swing into the centre of the field and now they stand to attention as thousands of voices sing 'Faith of Our Fathers'. How stirring always the moment. You are standing there bare-headed as you look around the ground at the tight-packed crowd, the sea of faces; you feel the tradition built up down the years flowing through your veins. Silence now – the national anthem and then a surging roar as the ball is thrown in and the game is on …

I have seen the embankment become a sea of waving red as the Cork supporters gave vent to their feelings at some flashing individual feat by Christy Ring. Jimmy Doyle could make the hearts of Cork followers miss one big beat as he gained possession and weaved his way through, searching for an angle.

Nothing more thrilling or spine-tingling perhaps than the sight of John Doyle, an unruly lock of hair over his forehead, his socks down around the ankles, squaring his shoulders for the fray, a rock-like figure amidst the swinging ash, bursting his way through a forest of sticks, with almost contemptuous fearlessness to make a long relieving clearance.

Tipperary, Munster Junior Football Champions 1952. Back row (l–r): Richard McGrath, Pat Horgan, George Pyke, Dick Dunne (captain), Kevin O'Sullivan, Paddy Riordan, Percy Larkin, John McGrath. Front row (l–r): Theo English, Johnny Ryan, Jimmy McCarthy, Liam Barrett, Din Ryan, Billy Coffey, Bob Stakelum.

1952

Crown for Tipperary: Munster Junior Football Final

Tipperary's junior footballers drew the Munster final with Kerry at Fermoy, by 0-15 to 2-9. They had home advantage at Thurles Sportsfield in the replay. It was the first time for forty-five years that a Kerry football team played in Thurles. Things didn't look good at half-time, with the Kingdom ahead by 0-5 to nil, but Tipperary resumed with a completely different approach and had two points to spare at the long whistle, 0-8 to 0-6. However, Tipperary lost the All-Ireland semi-final to Leitrim two weeks later.

1953

From Thurles to Belfast

The new Casement Park, Belfast, was officially opened on 14 June, 1953, by John Francis Cardinal D'Alton. To coincide with the opening, a silver urn containing soil from Thurles Sportsfield, which had been dug by Tipperary captain Tommy Doyle, was carried to Belfast by a relay of runners. The soil would be spread on the new pitch, providing a symbolic link between it and the birthplace of the GAA.

Archbishop Jeremiah Kinane, patron of the GAA, blessed the soil and presented the urn to the first runner leaving Hayes's Hotel, Thurles. The relay of runners was organised by the

Above left: In June 1953, the urn is filled with soil from Thurles Sportsfield, destined for Casement Park in Belfast. Photograph shows, from left to right, Mickey Byrne, Pa Joe O'Brien, Phil Purcell (Tipperary GAA secretary) and Tommy Doyle.
Above right: The scene outside Hayes's Hotel as Jimmy Semple is the first of the relay runners to carry the urn. On Jimmy's right is Cormac Boomer, Corrigan AC, Belfast.

National Athletic and Cycling Association. Local athlete Jimmy Semple, Fianna Road, son of Tom Semple, carried the urn on the first leg of the journey, as far as Drish Bridge. Running beside Jimmy was Cormac Boomer of Corrigan AC, Belfast, who was one of twenty-seven Northern Irish athletes who had come to Thurles to provide an escort for the bearers. The relay continued to Croke Park, where soil was added to the urn from the spot on the pitch where Tipperary's Mick Hogan was killed on Bloody Sunday 1920. The relay continued through the night, arriving at Casement Park, Belfast, the following afternoon.

The 'Bould' Rubber Man

The Tipperary captain in 1953, Tommy Doyle, was winner of five All-Irelands in a career that spanned three decades. In one of the greatest clashes in hurling, Tommy, remembered as the 'Rubber Man', held Christy Ring scoreless for two Munster championship games plus extra time.

In nineteen forty-nine, Cork were held to a draw,

By a fine combination that had not a flaw.

'Twas a joyous occasion to be a Tipp fan

When Ring was held scoreless by the bould Rubber Man.

Paddy Power, Drangan, from King, Ó Donnchú, Smyth, Tipperary's GAA Ballads

1953

Borris/Ileigh v. Boherlahan: Tipperary Senior Hurling Final

Above is the scene at Thurles Sportsfield on 4 October, a sunny autumnal Sunday, as the pre-match parade of Borris/Ileigh and Boherlahan's best passes the main embankment. Tim Ryan captained this Borris team to victory by 4-8 to 4-4. A record attendance of 16,000 was present and saw brilliant performances from Paddy Delaney, Jimmy Finn and Paddy Kenny for Borris. Sonny Maher was best of the Boherlahan lads.

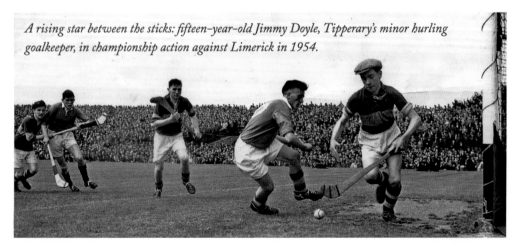

A rising star between the sticks: fifteen-year-old Jimmy Doyle, Tipperary's minor hurling goalkeeper, in championship action against Limerick in 1954.

Marching to glory at Thurles Sportsfield on county hurling final day, 3 October, 1954.

1954

Glamour and Pageantry: Tipperary Senior Hurling Final

An attendance of over 10,000 enjoyed a parade of clubs adding colour and pageantry to the occasion. As a club's name was called, a schoolboy wearing their colours and carrying his hurley joined the parade, headed by the Seán Treacy Pipe Band and three standard bearers carrying the papal, national and Tipperary flags, followed by the hurlers of Holycross/Ballycahill and Roscrea. Holycross/Ballycahill, captained by Francis Maher, defeated Roscrea, captained by Michael Butler, 6-5 to 2-3.

The Dunne Brothers: Hurling's Minstrels

As you walked from the Square in Thurles to the Sportsfield on big match days in the 1950s and early 1960s, the sound of fiddle and banjo could be heard on the breeze. There the Dunne brothers stood at the top of Parnell Street, playing lively selections of jigs and reels to entertain the crowds. An old coat would be spread on the ground in front of them to collect the coins thrown by good-humoured supporters.

Michael, Christy and Joseph Dunne got their interest in music from their father. Born in Cashel, they lived for some time in Gooldscross before settling in Cork. As they suffered from poor eyesight, they were occasionally referred to as the 'blind' Dunnes. They had gentle personalities, but their music was full of passion, heart and spirit, with a kind of wildness and beauty and freedom about it. They were very connected with their music and their instruments, of which they were technical masters, whether delivering soulful slow airs or infectious dance music. They played when traditional music was at a low ebb. Christy helped to pioneer the playing of the banjo in traditional music. He played the banjo with a thimble, while Joseph played both the fiddle and banjo, and Michael played fiddle. They preserved, in a living oral context, important aspects of our native culture.

They busked all over Ireland for many years, but whatever corner of the country they were in, they always made their way to Thurles for the Munster final. The Dunnes live on in the folk memory of many people who remember them with great affection.

1954
Delegates Relish Irish Culture

In July 1954, delegates from thirteen countries attended the conference of the International Institute of Sugar Beet Research at Hayes's Hotel, Thurles. While in town, they were guests at an exhibition hurling match and display of Irish dancing at Thurles Sportsfield. They were accompanied by Lieutenant General Michael J Costello, managing director of the Irish Sugar Company. This photograph also vividly recalls the covered stand and sideline, as it was at Thurles Sportsfield up to the mid-1960s.

Above left: Tipperary, Munster Minor Football Champions 1955. Back row (l–r): Philly Tobin, Gus Danagher, Pascal Buckley, Davy Stapleton, Jack Connors, Patrick Burke, Davy Fitzgerald, D Stapleton, Michael Ryan, Seán Condon, Gerry King. Front row (l–r): Paddy Nolan, John Brennan, Eddie Casey, Sean Connolly, Liam Boland (captain), Tom Walsh, Seán Moloney, John Ferris, Mick Moroney, Seán Ryan. Above right: A belated honour: Munster Council chairman Jerry O'Keeffe presents the Munster Cup to Tipperary minor football captain Liam Boland.

1955
Kingdom Falls to Tipperary: Munster Minor Football Final

Having beaten Cork in the Munster minor football semi-final by 2-6 to 1-2, Tipperary knew they had the potential to defeat Kerry in the Munster final, but it would need to be a tremendous performance. As it worked out, the forward play of the Tipperary boys stole the show in Killarney, and Kerry were very lucky to survive with a draw on 24 July, 0-9 to 1-6.

Three weeks later, on 21 August at Thurles Sportsfield, before an attendance of 5,000, Tipperary managed a deserving one-point win, 0-9 to 1-5. They had held Kerry scoreless in the first half, while scoring seven points themselves. Pat Tobin of Grangemockler, suffering from a broken collarbone sustained in the drawn match, was the hero of the hour.

The elated celebrations of the Tipperary footballers and supporters turned to confusion as they waited and waited for the Munster minor football cup to be presented to their captain, only to learn that there was no cup. Kerry, the reigning champions, had not brought it with them. It was an unfortunate oversight, they claimed, but many Tipperary supporters felt that Kerry were so sure of victory that they didn't bother to bring it along.

One week later, Tipperary defeated Mayo by 1-11 to 1-2 in the All-Ireland semi-final in Limerick, and they were presented with the Munster cup afterwards. They were well beaten by Dublin in the final by 5-4 to 2-7 in Croke Park.

Top left: Mickey 'The Rattler' Byrne, Thurles Sarsfields captain, receives the Dan Breen Cup from GAA patron Archbishop Jeremiah Kinane following the 1955 county hurling final. Also in this photograph is Dan Breen TD (left) and Phil Purcell, Tipperary GAA secretary (right).

Top right: Archbishop Jeremiah Kinane throws in the ball to start the final at Thurles Sportsfield. Pictured (l–r): Martin 'Musha' Maher (S), Mícheál McElgunn (S), Matty White (B), Tommy Barrett (S), Liam Devaney (B), Archbishop Kinane and Phil Purcell, Tipperary GAA secretary.

Above: Thurles Sarsfields, Tipperary Senior Hurling Champions 1955. Back row (l–r): Micil Callanan, Michael Craddock, Tommy Ryan, Paddy McCarthy, Tony Wall, P J O'Brien, Larry Keane, Mícheál McElgunn, Tommy Barrett. Front row (l–r): Martin 'Musha' Maher, John Kearns, Mickey Byrne (captain), Connie Keane, Michael 'Blackie' Keane, Michael Butler, Bobby Mockler, Gerry Doyle.

1955

'The Rattler' Leads the Blues: Tipperary Senior Hurling Final

The 1955 county final was played at Thurles Sportsfield on 2 October. Sarsfields completely outclassed Borris/Ileigh in soundness in defence and speed and accuracy in attack. Tommy Ryan was brilliant, seldom giving a better display. Larry Keane, at centre-forward, played a shrewd game, placing the ball nicely for corner-forwards Michael Butler and Tommy Barrett. Paddy McCarthy, the former Limerick player, had his best game to date at full-back. Final score: Thurles Sarsfields 4-10, Borris/Ileigh 0-6. This was the first in a five-in-a-row sequence of county successes for Sarsfields.

1955

Thurles Gaelic Sportsfield Society Officers and Committee

Chairman: Very Rev Philip Fogarty, Templemore. Vice chairman: James Maher, Parnell Street, Thurles. Treasurer: W J Dwan, Parnell Street, Thurles. Acting secretary: Joseph Campbell, Friar Street, Thurles. Committee: Ed Flynn, The Bridge, Thurles; William Leahy, Friar Street, Thurles; John Blake, West Gate, Thurles; John O'Keeffe, Fianna Road, Thurles; Thomas J Semple, Butler Avenue, Thurles; Sylvester Butler, Kavanagh Place, Thurles; Denis Ryan, Liberty Square, Thurles; John O'Brien, West Gate, Thurles; Patrick Leahy, Graiguenoe, Holycross (Central Council GAA); Philip Purcell, Árd na Croise, Thurles (Munster Council); Thomas Max, Butler Avenue, Thurles (Mid Tipperary GAA); Very Rev Christopher Lee, The Presbytery, Thurles (Thurles Sarsfields Club).

Above left: Clare, Munster Senior Hurling Finalists 1955. Back row (l–r): Mick Hayes, Willie Stritch, Jimmy Smyth, Dermot Sheedy, Des Dillon, Johnny Purcell, Noel Deasy. Front row (l–r): Jimmy Carney, Matt Nugent (captain), Gerry Ryan, Mick Leahy, Donal O'Grady, Jackie Greene, Dan McInerney, Haulie Donnellan. (Only players named.)

Above right: Jubilant Clare supporters shoulder goalkeeper Mick Hayes aloft.

Left: Munster championship 1955, first round official programme.

Below: Cork senior hurlers, 1955. Back row (l–r): Jack Barrett, Gerard Murphy, Joe Twomey, Derry Hayes, John Lyons, Liam McGrath, Dave Creedon, Mattie Fouhy, Jim 'Tough' Barry (trainer). Front row (l–r): Josie Hartnett, Christy Ring, Tony O'Shaughnessy, Johnny Clifford, Vincy Twomey, Willie John Daly, Seanie O'Brien, Mattie McAuliffe. Photo courtesy of the Irish Examiner.

1955

Clare Surprise Cork

Clare may have had a lot of talent, but they were pitted against the vast experience of Cork in the first round at Thurles Sportsfield on 5 June. Before a crowd of over 25,000, Clare had a dream start with a goal in the first minute by Jackie Greene, and another by Des Dillon later in the half. They were in a strong position at half-time, leading by seven points on a score line of 3-6 to 2-2. Early in the second half, Cork began to make inroads into the Clare defence. Particularly effective was Christy Ring, and, with ten minutes to go, the sides were level. It looked as if Cork had survived when Ring sent over from sixty yards to put Cork in front. But then, the Clare hero Jimmy Smyth rode to the rescue with two points to give Clare a winning score of 3-8 to 2-10.

Clare continued to surprise when they defeated Tipperary by 1-6 to 0-8 in the Munster semi-final at Limerick on 19 June, before being surprised themselves by Limerick, 2-16 to 2-6, in the Munster final on 10 July.

Jimmy Smyth scored Clare's final two points in the Cork game.

He ranks with Nicky Rackard or Jim Langton of great fame,
He ranks among the greatest men that ever played the game:
Neither Doyle from Tipperary nor the Rackards from Killane
Could hold that peerless Clareman, Jimmy Smyth from famed Ruan!

Séamus Mac Mathúna, Cooraclare, in Smyth, *Ballads of the Banner* (1998)

Jimmy Doyle had enormous regard for Smyth. In his biography, *The Boy Wonder of Hurling*, Doyle states:

Jimmy Smyth was a really great player. I always made out that if it hadn't been for Christy Ring, Jimmy Smyth would then have been Ring, if you follow me, he'd have been top of the tree.

1956

Ring Sparkles: Munster Senior Hurling Final

The Munster hurling final was back in Thurles on 22 July, for the first time since 1948. In anticipation of a huge attendance, seventy crush barriers had been erected on the embankments, ensuring greater comfort and safety for spectators. Twenty-seven special trains brought approximately 13,000 supporters, and the atmosphere in the town was typical old-time Munster final flavour. Almost 50,000 packed Thurles Sportsfield for the spectacle.

This was hurling of rare splendour and must rank with the best. It had intensity and excitement coupled with a multiplicity of incidents. Cork's aging team was pitted against

Far left: Crowds attended Mass in the Cathedral of the Assumption, Thurles, before the Munster hurling final.
Left: Image of match programme cover courtesy of the GAA Museum & Archive.
Below: Christy Ring leads the Cork team, while Tommy Casey captains Limerick.

Cork, Munster Hurling Champions 1956. Back row (l–r): Jack Twomey (selector), Mattie Fouhy, Eamon Goulding, Paddy Barry, Mick Regan, Josie Hartnett, Paddy Dowling, Terry Kelly, John Lyons and Paddy Fox Collins. Front row (l–r): Jack Barrett, Christy O'Shea, Willie John Daly, Mick Cashman, Tony O'Shaughnessy, Paddy Philpott, Christy Ring, Jimmy Brohan, Jim Barry (trainer).

Christy Ring was at the height of his powers in the mid-1950s. Photo courtesy of the Irish Examiner *Archive.*

a youthful Limerick side, whose speed appeared to be giving them the edge. If ever a match was won by one man, this was it. Entering the last quarter, Limerick led by 2-5 to 1-3, when Christy Ring unleashed a devastating display of hurling to score three goals in a four-minute spell. Taking a pass from Hartnett, Ring fought his way past the despairing tackles of two Limerick men and from a kneeling position, palmed the ball into the back of the net. A minute later, he did it again – a solo down the left wing for his second goal. The young Limerick team, shaken but undaunted, replied with a goal. But Ring wasn't finished, as he grabbed the sliotar from between the hurleys of two defenders and crashed home the goal that sealed Limerick's fate, 5-5 to 3-5.

> Tipperary, Limerick, Clare, all mighty hurlers there,
> But break they all upon the rock of Cloyne
> Where our darling hurler drove, deadly terror to his foes.
> Come here, pay your tribute to Christy Ring.
>
> 'Dear Old City by the Lee', author unknown

Mass before the Match!

Michael Hogan and Willie Boland left Kilbane in east Clare at eight o'clock on 17 June, 1956, for the Munster hurling semi-final between Clare and Limerick at Thurles, hoping for revenge for Clare's unexpected defeat in the previous year's final.

Their first stop was Birdhill, where they hoped to get Mass – a priority for the sixteen-year-olds – and also catch the train. However, when they saw a lot of supporters with bicycles at Mass, the two boys decided to join the others and cycle to Thurles instead, saving themselves the train fare.

The journey took them 1 hour 45 mins, which was good time but, as Willie remembers, it was mostly downhill from Newport. There was no joy in the result, with Limerick winning by 1-15 to 2-6. Immediately the game was over, they rushed out to make sure they got their bicycles and were back home by about eight o'clock. The rush had another purpose: There was a dance in Broadford that night, which they hoped to attend. Unfortunately, this was to be their second disappointment on the day. They weren't allowed to go because the parents told them they were out all day and had enough!

Canon Philip Fogarty

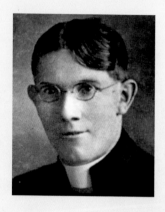

Born in Holycross in 1889, Philip Fogarty was ordained in 1915. He served as curate in Hospital, Newport, Moycarkey and Thurles before becoming Administrator at Thurles for a year prior to taking up his appointment as parish priest in Templemore in 1948. He was a life-long devotee of Gaelic games and a keen historian; his most famous work, *Tipperary's GAA Story*, was published in 1960. He succeeded Fr John Meagher as Tipperary GAA chairman in 1948. He remained in the position until 1970, when he retired and became the first president of the Tipperary GAA Board. He held the position of chairman of Semple Stadium through the 1950s and 1960s.

Thurles Sportsfield packed to the rafters.

1956
GAA Becomes Major Shareholder

In 1956, the Central Council of the GAA became the major shareholder of Thurles Gaelic Sportsfield Society Ltd. This facilitated investment in the development of the grounds. The non-stop succession of games had been putting considerable strain on the schedule at Croke Park, and the GAA authorities were anxious to develop a number-two arena. Thurles was the obvious choice, offering the most convenient venue in the southern half of the country and possessing ample space for any required expansion.

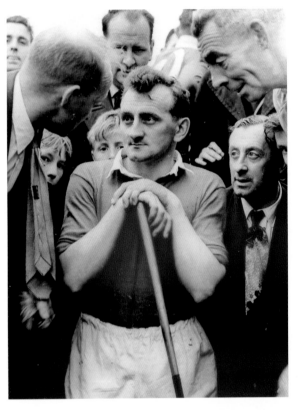

Above left: During half-time in the 1957 Munster hurling final, Paddy Barry (Cork) listens intently to advice from Mossy Dwyer and Christy Ring, who was sidelined through injury. On the right, leaning inwards, is Denis Conroy.

Above right: Image of the match programme courtesy of the GAA Museum & Archive.

1957

Déise v. Rebels: Munster Senior Hurling and Football Finals

For the second year in a row, Thurles Sportsfield was the venue for the Munster hurling final, on 14 July, with an attendance of 40,000. Waterford were at their best and their backs controlled the show against Cork. It was a spectacular final, and the Déise beat the Rebels by 1-11 to 1-6.

Waterford: Dick Roche, Tom Cunningham, Austin Flynn, John Barron, Michael O'Connor, Martin Óg Morrissey, Phil Grimes (captain), Johnny O'Connor, Mick Flannelly, Tom Cheasty, Frankie Walsh, Seamus Power, John Kiely, Larry Guinan, Donal Whelan. Substitutes: Mick Lacey, Ned Power.

On the following Sunday, 21 July, the Munster football final between Cork and Water-

Paddy Harrington with his son Pádraig, following the latter's success in the 1995 Irish Amateur Close Championship at Lahinch, just before he became a professional golfer.

ford was also staged at Thurles Sportsfield. This time Cork won by 0-16 to 1-2. It was Waterford's lack of experience that proved decisive, and Cork finished easy winners. The caterers of Thurles had a disappointing day, as only 11,000 attended and much stock was left unsold.

Cork: Liam Power, Paddy O'Driscoll, Donal O'Sullivan, Dan Murray, Paddy Harrington, Denis Bernard, Mick Gould, Seán Moore, Eric Ryan, Denis 'Toots' Kelleher, Niall Fitzgerald, Tom Furlong, Eamon Goulding, Nealie Duggan, J J Henchion. Substitutes played: Joe O'Sullivan, Eric Ryan.

Right half-back for Cork in the Munster football final at Thurles Sportsfield was Paddy Harrington, who hailed from Ardgroom in west Cork but spent many years in Dublin, where he worked as a Garda. In 1956, he played at half-back on the Cork team that defeated Meath in the National League final. Paddy represented Munster in the Railway Cup between 1958 and 1963. Paddy's son Pádraig is now a world-ranking professional golfer.

Far left: Image of match programme from the 1958 Munster hurling final courtesy of the GAA Museum & Archive.
Left: Tipperary's John Doyle.

Tipperary, All–Ireland Hurling Champions 1958. Back row (l–r): Noel Murphy, John McGrath, Michael Maher, Kieran Carey, Larry Keane, John Hough, Liam Devaney, John Doyle, Jimmy Finn, Mick Burns, Ray Reidy. Front row (l–r): Martin 'Musha' Maher, Liam Connolly, Jimmy Doyle, Tom Larkin, Theo English, Tony Wall (captain), John O'Grady, Mickey Byrne, Donie Nealon, Terry Moloney.

Left: Tipperary selector Paddy Leahy talks strategy with captain Tony Wall.
Above: Tony Wall receives the Munster Cup from Munster GAA chairman Frank Sheehy.

1958
Tipperary Rising: Munster Senior Hurling Final

The Munster final was at Thurles Sportsfield on 6 July, and it was described as one of the poorest finals for years. Forty-two thousand spectators attended and were thrilled with the scoring of two goals and a point within two minutes, but this early promise of a memorable decider was never fulfilled as Waterford wilted before Tipperary's superiority. The Tipperary forwards were on fire, particularly Larry Keane at corner-forward. John Doyle at wing-back gave a stirring display of defensive hurling. Tipperary were always in command, winning by 4-12 to 1-5.

The local Thurles caterers were reported to be disappointed that so many supporters brought their own supplies to the Munster final. Some even brought Primus stoves and made tea and snacks in the sportsfield.

Galway, Oireachtas Champions and All-Ireland Finalists 1958. Back row (l–r): Jim Fives, Mike Sweeney, Joe Young, P J Lawless, Pat Joe Lally, Tommy Kelly, Pakie Burke. Front row (l–r): Fintan Spillane, Joe Sammon, Jimmy Duggan, Seamus Cullinane (captain), Tim Sweeney, Fergus Benson, Tom Conway, Billy O'Neill.

1958
Galway Show their Mettle: Oireachtas Hurling Final

Hurling was on a high in Galway in 1958, but a lack of top-class inter-county matches was hindering the team from reaching their full potential. This was obvious in the All-Ireland final of that year, when Tipperary – with three decent championship games behind them – outclassed Galway by 4-9 to 2-5. Even though Galway were powered by quality hurlers such as Joe Sammon and Jimmy Duggan, the All-Ireland final was the Tribesmen's first championship match that year.

In those days, the Oireachtas tournament was held within weeks of the All-Ireland final. It was popular with supporters and genuinely contested by teams. In the final, played at Thurles Sportsfield on 19 October, Galway trounced Wexford by 5-16 to 2-4. Wexford were then halfway between their All-Ireland successes of 1956 and 1960 and a force to be reckoned with. Jim Fives, a native of Tourin, Waterford, then stationed at Renmore, was the Galway centre half-back. As Jimmy Duggan recalled, 'We beat Kilkenny and then played Wexford in Thurles in the final and won well, so that showed what we could have done if we'd had a bit more match practice going into the All-Ireland.'

Waterford, Munster and All-Ireland Hurling Champions 1959. Back row (l–r): Larry Guinan, Jackie Condon, Ned Power, John Kiely, John Barron, Mickey Lacey, Seamus Power and Phil Grimes. Front row (l–r): Tom Cheasty, Donal Whelan, Charlie Ware, Frankie Walsh, Austin Flynn, Martin Óg Morrissey and Joe Harney. Photo courtesy of the Waterford Museum, Dungarvan.

1959

Harney Stars in Déise Triumph: Munster Senior Hurling Final

Waterford scored an amazing sixteen goals in their two Munster championship games, on the way to the final against Cork at Thurles Sportsfield on 26 July. That day, a new record attendance was recorded at the venue, as 55,174 packed in. Twenty-seven special trains, a record number, brought 17,000 supporters. They were served up a treat of classic

Crowds leaving the stadium after the 1959 Munster final.

Munster hurling. Waterford, for whom Joe Harney emerged as the hero, repeated their 1957 success by 3-9 to 2-9.

Afterwards the crowd flows down like a great tidal wave over the railway bridge and back into town. The pubs spill over. The hotels and restaurants and the private houses with their 'Meat Teas' signs prominently displayed, quickly swallow up the hungry. Many of the spectators have been in the field since mid-day. Nowhere can they cater as they do in Thurles on big match days, for they have known these big occasions since 1926. There is hurling talk in the air and there is atmosphere – the atmosphere that Thurles alone can evoke on this day.

Smith, *Decades of Glory*

After the game, the throng packed the streets of the town. At West Gate, three parked cars caused an extraordinary scene as the tightly packed mass of people were unable to go backwards or forwards. There was the spectacle of men with their hands against plate glass-windows, trying to hold themselves from being pushed through. Women were terrified and children were crying. One shopkeeper helped to ease things by letting people in the front door and out the back into Wolfe Tone Place, West Gate.

In Ballyduff and Ballyurn, behold the bonfires burn
As they welcome home the victors from the fray.
In Dungarvan they're gone mad, in Abbeyside just as bad,
And in Cappoquin they're drinking more than 'tay'.

Pádraig S Ó Neachtain in Smyth, *In Praise of Heroes*

137

Above: Tipperary Senior Hurlers, Thurles
Sportsfield, 1960. Back row (l–r): Gerry Doyle,
Tony Wall (captain), Kieran Carey, John
Doyle, Seán McLoughlin, Michael Maher, Tom
Moloughney, Liam Connolly, Liam Devaney.
Front row (l–r): Jimmy Doyle, Terry Moloney,
Matt Hassett, Theo English, Tom Ryan, Mick
Burns, Billy Moloughney, Paddy Devaney. Donie
Nealon was selected instead of Billy Moloughney
on the Munster final team.
Right: Image of match programme from the 1960
Munster final courtesy of the GAA Museum &
Archive.

CHAPTER 5

ASH ON LEATHER

THE 1960s

1960
The Toughest Ever: Munster Senior Hurling Final

Cork really had to pull out all the stops to beat Clare in the Munster semi-final at Thurles Sportsfield on 12 June, but they advanced to the final by 2-12 to 1-11. Back they came to the same venue on 31 July to meet Tipperary, who had impressive victories behind them on their road to the final. The attendance was 49,705, and the crowd certainly got value for money as they witnessed a contest rated the toughest ever provincial decider. A thundershower during the minor game drenched the venue. The greasy underfoot conditions determined that it was not a day for classic hurling; nevertheless the spectacle gripped the attention of onlookers for the hour. This was a game that made one marvel at the durability of the human frame, as every man pursued the ball with a zeal that was breathtaking in its intensity and resolution. Both sets of backs were having a trying day which saw Tipperary ahead at the break by 3-4 to 2-4. In a game of many fine performances, that of Jimmy Doyle must stand out, scoring 1-8 in a gruelling contest. It was a veteran Cork side who made it difficult for Tipperary in a high-scoring final, with the home side ahead at the long whistle by just 4-13 to 4-11.

Marquess of Queensberry Rules OK

One of the flashpoints of the Munster final was when Cork's Paddy Barry (pictured above) and Tipperary's John Doyle decided to throw down their hurleys and fight it out like gentlemen.

Christy Ring: Biblical Studies

Christy Ring (left) had just delivered a stirring speech that had brought the blood of his teammates to a bubbling boil, but didn't overly impress the team's padre, Fr Cárthach McCarthy. 'You didn't find those words in the Bible, Christy,' said Fr McCarthy in as disapproving a tone as he could muster. Ring cast a jaundiced eye at the man of the cloth. 'No, Father. But the men who wrote the Bible never had to play Tipperary.'

John Harrington, *Doyle: The Greatest Hurling Story Ever Told* (2011)

Tipperary, All–Ireland Senior Hurling Champions 1961. Back row (l–r): Matt O'Gara, Tony Wall, Tom Moloughney, Kieran Carey, Liam Devaney, Michael Maher, John Doyle, Mick Burns, Liam Connolly, John Hough, Pat Ryan. Front row (l–r): Seán McLoughlin, Jimmy Doyle, Donie Nealon, Donal O'Brien, Matt Hassett (captain), Billy Moloughney, John 'Mackey' McKenna, Theo English, Tom Ryan, Roger Mounsey.

'Hell's Kitchen'

This was the term coined by sports journalist John D Hickey for the far-famed Tipperary full-back line of the early to mid-1960s. With Michael Maher at full-back flanked by John Doyle and Kieran Carey, they posed a formidable challenge to any forward line. They earned a well-deserved reputation for being one of the greatest full-back lines the game had ever seen, and as their nickname suggests, Maher, Doyle and Carey generated the sort of heat that suffocated most full-forward lines, who struggled to cope with their unique blend of physicality, hurling skill, and defensive know-how.

Tipperary, All–Ireland Hurling Champions 1962. Back row (l–r): Tom Ryan, Matt O'Gara, Ronnie Slevin, John Doyle, Tom Moloughney, Michael Maher, Kieran Carey, Tom Ryan, Liam Connolly, Matt Hassett, Michael Murphy. Front row (l–r): Mick Burns, Liam Devaney, Donal O'Brien, John 'Mackey' McKenna, Theo English, Donie Nealon, Jimmy Doyle (captain), Seán McLoughlin, Roger Mounsey, Christy Hartigan, Tony Wall.

1960s

'Die a Thousand Deaths'

You can die a thousand deaths in the last minute of a typical Munster final as the ball bobs about in the goalmouth and the dust flies in the clash of the ash. The tension becomes almost unbearable as time ebbs away and your team is desperately striving to hold on to a slender lead. And yet in those very moments of nerve-racking tension you live all that is great in our native pastime.

Those who have experienced it know what I mean; those especially, who come from the hurling strongholds of the south, and have been brought up to know that it is in the testing fires of Munster championship hurling that a Munster hurler must establish his reputation, if it is to be a lasting one. A Munster final etches incidents in the memory that never die. You can talk about them in the glow of the firelight for a lifetime …

Smith, *Decades of Glory*

Toomevara, Tipperary Senior Hurling Champions 1960. Back row (l–r): Jim Delaney, Jimmy Donovan, Neil Williams, Dominic Ryan, J J McCormack, Con Ryan, Tom Ryan, Phil Shanahan, Roger Mounsey, Gerry Hough. Front row (l–r): John Hough, Jim McDonnell, Frankie Ryan, Matt O'Gara, Billy Donovan (captain), Tom Shanahan, Matt Hassett.

Photograph taken outside Shamrock bus office, Liberty Square, courtesy of the Keane family, Kincora Terrace, Thurles. Left to right: Martin Drew, Micil Callanan, Con Lucy, Mikey Treacy, Jack O'Keeffe, Joe McLoughney, Jack Costello, John Joe Callanan, Danny Keane, Kevin O'Connor, Patsy Ryan. Danny Keane had a stall under the Old Stand at Thurles Sportsfield for many years, selling sweets, chocolate, fruit and soft drinks. Many an exhausted player was forever thankful for Danny's refreshments.

1960s
Aficionados of the School around the Corner

When the hurling was over and the dust had settled on the square at Thurles Sportsfield, the trains had pulled out and the car parks had emptied, twilight lengthened into darkness on Liberty Square, but the hurling talk was only getting going. No place better for this than in the shadow of the Dr Croke Memorial, near Hogan's bus office and Mockler's Chemists, where the knowing ones gathered and hurled it all over again. They had seen it all, from Semple's time, and expounded with the authority of their years. Success here was a treasured accolade.

1960
Toomevara End Sarsfields Run: Tipperary Senior Hurling Final

The county final was played on 16 October before an attendance of 10,681. Thurles Sarsfields were going for their sixth title in a row but were comprehensively beaten by a more determined Toomevara team, by 3-15 to 2-8. On the day Toome, captained by Billy Donovan, were more enthusiastic and hungrier for the fray. They led 2-6 to 1-5 at half-time. They got the best start possible with two goals and held the advantage for the hour.

1961

Ring's Scoring Spree: Munster Senior Hurling Semi-Final

Cork and Waterford attracted a record attendance of 42,824 to the Munster semi-final at Thurles Sportsfield on 9 July. The game proved a rip-roaring contest which was balanced on a knife edge. An injury that forced Waterford's full-back, Austin Flynn, to retire unsettled their backline thereafter. Christy Ring capitalised on the situation, embarking on a scoring spree, registering 3-4. Ring lifted the Rebels and they withstood huge Waterford pressure to win by 5-7 to 2-7.

Tipperary, Munster Intermediate Hurling Champions 1961: Back row (l–r): Paddy O'Meara, Tommy O'Brien, Sean McGovern, Jim McGrath, John McGrath, John O'Dwyer, Pat Kearns, Dick Callanan, Christy Hartigan, Tom Flynn. Front row (l–r): Micky Lonergan, Pete O'Dwyer, Eddie Maher, Donal Ryan, Sean Cullagh, Pat Ryan, Babs Keating, Billy Ryan, Liam Tierney (captain), Tom Larkin.

1961

Tipperary Win Inaugural Munster Intermediate Title

In a thrilling Munster Intermediate hurling final at Thurles Sportsfield, Tipperary defeated Cork by 3-10 to 2-12. Tipperary later lost the replayed All-Ireland final to Wexford by 4-11 to 3-9.

1961
A Thurles Wonderland

Broadcaster and musician Pat Costello remembers:

The excursion from Josie Fitzgerald's yard to the field on the Sunday of a big match was without doubt a voyage of discovery for a young nipper of twelve years of age. The meanderings of Fawcett on the Amazon or Napoleon's tribulations on the Nile did not reveal as much spectacle and frivolity as that short journey through Thurles on a warm championship Sunday.

My father parked the bicycle, a formidable machine, post office issue with the demeanour of an armoured car. Bicycle clips removed and the folded top coat removed from the carrier which now provided custody for the sandwiches. A bottle of Dwans lemonade would later complete the aperitif. All this was carried out in the company of a fine gathering of patrons all seeking a safe sanctuary for their three-speed Raleigh or Rudge in Fitzgerald's yard.

Arriving in the Square was like stumbling into a Shakespearean spectacle. People moving in every direction with vigorous determination, solitary figures poring over a folded newspaper or standing, hands cupped to light a cigarette, others in elegant defiance of the chaos sipped tea from a flask and sampled the sandwiches. Like a distant call to prayer the voices rang out, *apples, pears and bananas, lovely ripe bananas,* challenged by, *hats and colours 'a the match, get your hats and colours.* The wearer of one of these brightly coloured fedoras passed by and a combination of Brylcreem and the heat of the day conspired to dissolve the colour which ran and gave his expression a war-like demeanour as he moved, eyes fixed, towards Parnell Street, strengthened in his resolve by a couple of bottles of stout.

A tall, slightly built man stood with his back to the market house. A solitary button restrained a threadbare coat and across his breast he embraced a battered single row melodeon. The voice was strong and eyes closed he sang of The Old Turf Fire. His name was Paddy 'Shan', I found out many years later, from the Kilkenny direction, an unlit Afton or Woodbine dangled from the corner of his mouth and danced erratically in time to the music.

Then almost without warning, that sea of humanity, like a flock of starlings, swept towards Parnell Street and the sportsfield. Past the stainless steel wonder of the milk bar, beneath a sign offering Plain Teas and Meat Teas, heads, hats and caps bobbing in the effort at the final ascent of the railway bridge. The crowds seemed quieter in those days, soon the strains of more music drifted across the bobbing heads and then, there they were, the Dunnes, heads inclined over their instruments, the fiddle and banjo, sprinkling the air with notes that jostled with each other for attention, a hint of the excitement to come, 'The Swallow's Tail', 'The Bird in the Bush', the music poured from these two mysterious and dignified men. Slowly they faded as a new and more familial sound filled my bewildered ears. Big men, strong men wearing skirts and moving effortlessly across the green sward, the pipes singing on their shoulders, the Moycarkey band led out the two reluctant lines of warriors, impatient for the fray. One final hurdle, the National Anthem, a curious mixture of pathos, patriotism and religious fervour. Although brief it still tests the patience of the crowd, the final verse submerged beneath the swelling roar of forty thousand voices, the band scampers from the field, the referee takes a few steps backwards blows the whistle and gratefully disposes of the ball in the direction of the jostling players. The timber flashes, the crowd roars with increasing vigour, the ancient prophecy is fulfilled and another Championship Sunday begins.

Munster Championship programme, May 2016

Sportsfield Caretaker John Joe Callanan

For a period in the 1960s, John Joe Callanan was caretaker and groundsman at Thurles Sportsfield. A noted hurler with Thurles Sarsfields and Tipperary, John Joe captained the county to All-Ireland success in 1930, the Treble Crown year, and the following year he led Tipperary on a tour of the USA.

As a student in Dublin, John Joe was active in the War of Independence in the city, notably as a courier for Michael Collins. On Bloody Sunday, 21 November, 1920, he and Bob Mockler, Horse and Jockey, were umpires at the Tipperary/Dublin football match in Croke Park. While in Dublin (1919–1925), John Joe hurled with Faughs, who won the Dublin hurling championship in 1920. The same year, he was on the Dublin senior hurling team that won the All-Ireland.

On his return to Thurles in the mid-1920s, he resumed his hurling with his colleagues of old and was a vital cog in the breakthrough of 1929. John Joe was on the Munster Railway Cup team that defeated Leinster, 2-2 to 1-2, on St Patrick's Day, 1928, at Croke Park.

Remembered as a skilful forward, he continued to line-out for Sarsfields into the mid-1930s, and when his playing days were over, he was a successful county senior hurling selector in the 1940s and 1950s. In 1940, John Joe refereed the All-Ireland hurling final between Limerick and Kilkenny.

Thurles Sarsfields, Tipperary Senior Hurling Champions 1962. Back row (l–r): Joss Connors, Noel Murphy, Larry Keane, Seán McLoughlin, Tim Walsh, Tony Wall, Benny Maher, Michael Murphy, Gerry Doyle. Front row (l–r): Mickey Byrne, Kevin Houlihan, Patsy Dorney, Paddy Doyle, Martin 'Musha' Maher, Mícheál McElgunn (captain), Michael 'Blackie' Keane, Bobby Mockler.

1962

Sarsfields Triumph in Titanic Struggle: Tipperary Senior Hurling Final

Thurles Sportsfield hosted the county final on 14 October before a crowd of nearly 10,000. Moycarkey/Borris almost caused a major upset but were beaten by 1-7 to 1-6. The losers had most of the play, throwing everything into attack over the hour, but they didn't capitalise on it. This was where Sarsfields had the extra polish and sheer accuracy that gave them the scores from fewer opportunities. At half-time Sarsfields were ahead by 0-5 to 0-2. Point by point, Moycarkey hauled back the lead, and they went ahead when a long, high ball from Paddy Coman dropped into the Sarsfields net. The Blues were worried and drafted Jimmy Doyle into attack. Sarsfields' only goal was scored by Musha Maher, who pounced on a half-cleared ball as two Moycarkey backs collided and put it past John O'Grady. Moycarkey had a late, last chance to draw the game, but Donal Ryan's free drifted wide. Outstanding for Sarsfields was Tony Wall at centre-back.

Goalmouth action in Thurles during the 1962 Munster semi-final between Cork and Waterford. Ned Power saves despite the close attention of Christy Ring. Also in the picture, Tom Cunningham (W), Austin Flynn (W) and Liam Dowling (C). The scene is brilliantly captured by photographer Louis MacMonagle. Photo courtesy of the Irish Examiner *Archive.*

1962

Ring's Last Hurrah: Munster Senior Hurling Semi-Final

It was appropriate that Christy Ring would play his last Munster championship game for his beloved Cork at Thurles Sportsfield; a semi-final against Waterford on 8 July. Thurles was the place that, for over two decades, he adorned the ancient game with his unique and exceptional talent. He had amazing natural ability to deal with a ball no matter what way it came. As he said himself, 'I had fierce determination to win, I challenged for every ball, I was a great competitor, always out to win the ball'. Off the field, Christy is remembered as a shy man who

John Doyle signs an autograph.

gave very few interviews. He famously commented: 'All my talking was done on the field with a hurley.' But this was Waterford's day, winning by 4-10 to 1-16. Tipperary's John Doyle recalled Ring:

> Christy Ring was by far the best hurler I ever saw. He had unbelievable skill and could do anything with a ball. If he got a score he'd dance a little jig to annoy his opponent and straight away won the psychological battle. He was also a very tough hurler, a true perfectionist. He was always trying to perfect and practise his skills. The interesting thing was that unlike most players, the older he got the better he performed.
>
> John Scally, *The GAA Immortals: 100 Gaelic Games Legends* (2018)

1962
Match Day Catering: Not What It Used to Be!

Many local caterers were disappointed with the ever-growing trend of supporters bringing their own eatables and only purchasing a cup of tea in Thurles. The advent of fish and chip vans was also damaging their trade. The *Tipperary Star* reported,

> The great rise in the cost of ham, which is now around eight shillings per pound and butter 4/7. At one time a good meal of tea, ham, bread and butter could be got for 2/6. A Plain Tea is now three shillings. The increased cost of paid help coupled with the uncertainty of the size of the crowd must also be considered. All in all, 'the game is scarcely worth the candle', nowadays. The great catering tradition of the 'cradle' town is on the way out.

The report also mentioned the growing menace of drunkenness on such occasions and added, 'Unfortunately, the heavy drinking is not now restricted to the male sex only'.

1963–1964
Thurles in Line for Major Upgrade

In 1963, Bord na bPáirc recommended to GAA Central Council that Thurles be developed as a major venue for hosting games. The GAA by then was the major shareholder

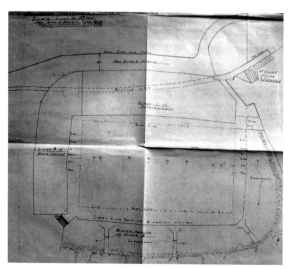

in Thurles Gaelic Sportsfield Society Ltd., and this facilitated access to major development funding.

At the Munster Convention on 7 March, 1964, a joint proposal relating to investment in Thurles Sportsfield by Bord na bPáirc and Munster Council was approved. It was agreed that an investment of £90,000 be made and funded as follows: £45,000 from Central Council, £30,000 from Munster Council and £15,000 from Tipperary County Board. The Ciste na Banban GAA pools were used by Tipperary GAA as a major fundraiser for the development.

The main purpose of the investment was to upgrade the seating accommodation and to improve the assembling and dispersal arrangements. The southern side would be first developed with a new stand, capable of holding 16,000, some of which would be covered. New dressing rooms with hot and cold showers would be installed as well as modern facilities for press, radio, TV and public address. To facilitate the development, land was purchased from two neighbouring farmers.

Agreement was also reached between Thurles Urban Council and Thurles Sportsfield Committee for the laying of a new road, along by the rear of the stand, from Boher-nanave to Garryvicleheen. Thurles Sportsfield agreed to pay £600 towards the cost of the tarmacadam road.

1964

The Keys to the Kingdom: Munster Senior Football Championship

Tipperary beat Clare in the first round of the Munster football championship at the Gaelic Grounds, Limerick. Conditions were poor but Tipperary got through by 2-5 to 1-7. Kerry were their opponents in the provincial semi-final at Thurles Sportsfield on 28 June. While the final score was 1-14 to 1-7 in the Kingdom's favour, Tipperary were reasonably pleased with their performance. Petty fouling and missed chances told the tale. Patsy Dawson was excellent at centre-back, as was Brian O'Callaghan at full-forward.

Tipperary: Connie Cleere, John Fleming, Mick Egan, Tom Walsh, Paddy Doyle, Patsy Dawson, Liam Connolly, Stephen McCormack, Patsy Conway, John Keating, Gus Danagher, John O'Donoghue, Liam Boland, Brian O'Callaghan, Michael 'Babs' Keating.

Michael 'Babs' Keating, Ardfinnan, a stalwart of Tipperary football.

151

Photographs courtesy of Donal Sammon, Thurles.

The Dressing Rooms

The old dressing rooms, shown in the first photograph above, were very different from those now hidden from view down the tunnel. The old ones were much more public. Knots of camp-followers stood around outside the door, watching the preliminaries. Small boys would put their eyes to the broken diamond-shaped panes of the windows, hoping for a closer look at the warriors. Well-wishers would crowd into the already inadequate space inside, asking the traditional, 'How's the form?' The air was pungent with the fumes of wintergreen and embrocation. Coming near the deadline, the door would be firmly shut and through the rising tension, urgent words of pep-talk would drop into the heavy hush, ending with a spatter of hand-claps, an abrupt opening of the door and the emergence of set-faced hurlers to do their duty.

The second picture shows how the stand at Thurles Sportsfield looked from the 1920s until its demolition in 1965. The dressing rooms were under the stand, and the small construction beside it housed the commentator, usually Mícheál Ó hEithir, on big match days. A great view of the old Thurles sideline is also seen.

When Mícheál wasn't functioning, the broadcasting box became a sort of private prie-dieu for attending clerics of importance. Several archbishops of Cashel and Emly climbed the access ladder in their time, keeping their dignity as best they could.

1965

Construction of Stand Begins

After months of planning and detailed preparation, the major development, costing £90,000, announced during the previous year, began in May with the building of a new stand. Initially, one-third of this stand was covered, but it was intended that the remainder would be covered as soon as possible. The pitch was closed during the period of construction. The stand when complete was expected to have seating capacity for 16,000. The contractors were Malachy Burke Ltd., Galway. This firm was also in the process of completing the extensive new wing at St Patrick's College in the town.

Hurling Skill, My Greatest Strength

Tipperary great Jimmy Doyle recalls:

From the first time I picked up a hurley, I was working on the skills and that became my greatest strength. I don't mean anything fancy, I mean the basic skills – hitting a ball left and right, being able to run onto a ball at speed and pick it without breaking stride, being able to strike with accuracy on the run and of course the ground stroke.

O'Flynn, *The Boy Wonder of Hurling: The Story of Jimmy Doyle*

Above left: Tommy Max, the new secretary of Thurles Sportsfield Committee.
Above right: Carrick Davins, Tipperary Senior Hurling Champions 1966. Back row (l–r): Jackie Walsh, Con Broderick, Noel Walsh, Tom Arrigan, Billy Mackey, Brian Kenny, Patsy Arrigan, Mick Roche. Front row (l–r): P J Ryan, Seamus Kenny, Richie Walsh (captain), Tom Waters, Tommy Ryan, Michael Hassett, Jimmy Ryan.

1966

A Crown for Carrick Davins: Tipperary Senior Hurling Final

The sixth of November was a fine but cold day at Thurles Sportsfield, where Carrick Davins made history by winning their first senior county title. Before an attendance of 7,500 they comprehensively overwhelmed Lorrha/Dorrha, winning by 2-12 to 1-3. Carrick had aces in their pack with Mick Roche in sparkling form at midfield, ably assisted by P J Ryan. Roche was also top scorer, notching 1-5. The following year the Carrick lads, captained by Mick Roche, showed that this victory was no flash in the pan by retaining the Dan Breen Cup, accounting for an up-and-coming Roscrea side by 2-10 to 2-7 in the final.

1967

Remembering Jack Russell, Thurles Sportsfield Secretary

Jack Russell was secretary of the Thurles Sportsfield Committee from 1953 to the time of his death in 1967. He was captain of the Tipperary minor hurling team that won the All-Ireland in 1930, Treble Crown year. Jack resided at Liberty Square, Thurles, where he ran a successful drapery and licenced premises. He played a leading role in the development and expansion of Thurles Sportsfield.

The Plain or Meat Tea

Up to the mid-1960s, supporters going to big games in Thurles would find cardboard notices in the windows of houses in the vicinity of the Sportsfield advertising 'Plain Teas' or 'Meat Teas' at 3s 6p, 4s 6p, or whatever the going rate was. The Meat Tea consisted of a plate of ham with as much buttered white bread and tea as you wanted. The Plain Tea was the above without the meat.

At that time few people patronised hotels except for a wedding or other major social occasion, as they would be considered too posh, and there weren't many restaurants in operation. Economic prosperity in the 1960s, an increase in the car population, better roads and improved lifestyles, plus the introduction of the Thermos flask, put an end to the Plain and Meat Tea!

1967
John Doyle Leaves the Arena

Having played for nineteen consecutive years on the Tipperary senior hurling team, 1949 to 1967, the legendary Holycross colossus retired from inter-county hurling. He had represented Tipperary in all six defensive positions and is remembered as a rollicking, charismatic, physical, fair and skilled hurler, who gave extraordinary and faithful service to his club, county and to hurling.

He is tall and slim and loose of limb
And strong as Cashel's tower

He knows no fear – just see him clear

As men before him cower.

When bodies crash and hurleys clash

Around the enemy square,

Where stand the brave their goal to save?

John Doyle is always there.

Joseph Perkins, from King, Ó Donnchú, Smyth, *Tipperary's GAA Ballads*

ᵹᴇᴀᴛᴀ '84

I ᵹcuimne ᴀʀ óunú

Ċumᴀnn Lúᴛċleᴀs ᵹᴀel

I nᴅúʀlᴀs éile

Lá Sᴀmnᴀ 1884

Contractors Malachy Burke Ltd., Galway, undertook the construction of the new stand. As it was nearing completion, the go-ahead was given for the covering of the centre third of the stand.
Bottom right: This memorial stone at the entrance to the new stand commemorates the foundation of the Gaelic Athletic Association at Hayes's Hotel, Thurles, on 1 November, 1884.

1968
Opening of the Kinane Stand

The new stand was named Ardán Uí Chuinneáin in memory of GAA patron Archbishop Jeremiah Kinane. It had seated accommodation for 16,000 spectators and was the longest single-structure concrete stand in Europe.

The official opening of Thurles Sportsfield took place on 9 June, 1968. The ceremony was performed by GAA patron Most Rev Dr Thomas Morris. The total cost exceeded the original £90,000 by £17,000. Central Council agreed to pay half of the extra, with the other half shared between the Munster Council and Tipperary GAA Board.

'Cúlbaire', in his column in the *Tipperary Star,* wasn't impressed with the new stand:

The whole thing has to be written down as a tremendous disappointment. The money spent is far more impressive than the product … All in all this expensive structure is a bleak and comfortless colossus of concrete which has brought little visible benefit to us in our local games and wrecked the homeliness of the old layout at the same time.

Irish Press journalist Norman Freeman gave a colourful description of the new facilities:

The scene at the special entry in Thurles at the Munster final was typical. There is a door and a gate for cars and wheelchairs. Beside there is a limestone plaque commemorating the foundation of the GAA in 1884, so that the spot is referred to as Geata '84. Outside Geata '84, we watched men being handed circular badges, bearing the inscription 'maor'. These badges transformed their wearers into men of stature and authority. They rapped at the door confidently and were instantly admitted. Occasionally following close behind them, almost holding their coat-tails, were badgeless individuals. Sometimes they managed to squeeze in before the door was closed. Other times they were repelled and went away uttering dark obscenities.

The St John's Ambulance men and women in their lightly grey uniforms entered in dribs and drabs. One was followed by a man clutching what appeared to be a bulging black bag. He had the concerned demeanour of a doctor who may be called on to exercise his skills. Later on, we saw him safely ensconced on the sideline, his bearing now that of an eager spectator, while he took a flask and sandwiches from the black bag.

A person in a wheelchair was pushed towards the gate – pushed by no less than six people, each with a hand on the wheelchair frame to establish their authenticity. The gate was pulled across and after some hesitation all six were allowed in.

The Man behind the Stand

In many ways the GAA and Archbishop Jeremiah Kinane were inseparable. He was born at Gortnahulla, Upperchurch, County Tipperary, on 15 November, 1884, a fortnight after the founding of the GAA.

He had a passionate love for hurling, which he played with zest in his youth. On the field of play, he was fearless and he had little regard for any player that showed a trace of cowardice. Recalling his hurling days, he stated, 'I can almost say I was born with a hurley in my hand, and for many years the clash of the camán was sweet music in my ears'.

Jeremiah Kinane was ordained to the priesthood in Rome on 24 April, 1910. He was appointed Archbishop of Cashel and Emly on 11 September, 1946. He died in office on 18 February, 1959, aged 74. Ardán Uí Chuinneáin at Semple Stadium honours his memory.

1968

Oireachtas Victory Restores Tipperary's Pride

The defeat by Wexford in the All-Ireland final was a major disappointment to Tipperary. It was the second year in a row that the county had fallen at the final hurdle. The Oireachtas tournament was an opportunity to redeem lost status, and their semi-final victory over Kilkenny at Croke Park, by 5-9 to 4-9, augured well. The newly refurbished Thurles Sportsfield hosted the final against Cork on 27 October. This was a rip-roaring contest in the true Tipp/Cork tradition and the best for years. The shackles of championship hurling were thrown to the wind, and the hurlers as free spirits relished the freedom. Even though the pitch was sodden and it was late October, the contest was low-scoring and waged with intensity and pride, with the crowd on their toes. Tipperary were lucky enough to win, by 1-9 to 1-6, but hurling was the real victor. The home team had a star in goal, John O'Donoghue, who had possibly his best performance in a Tipp jersey.

Tipperary: John O'Donoghue, John Costigan, John Kelly, John Gleeson, Tadhg O'Connor, Noel O'Gorman, Matt Stapleton, P J Ryan, Mick Roche (captain), Jimmy Ryan, Noel O'Dwyer, Francis Loughnane, Liam Devaney, Phil Lowry, Michael 'Babs' Keating.

Below: John Dillon leads the Roscrea team in the 1968 pre-match parade.

Bottom: Roscrea, Tipperary Senior Hurling Champions 1968. Back row (l–r): J J Maher, Pat Dynan, Seamus Moloney, Liam Spooner, Willie Stapleton, Liam Brussels, Paddy Landy, Kieran Carey, Jackie Hannon, John Dillon (captain), Mick Minogue, Harry Loughnane, J Moloney, M Loughnane. Front row (l–r): Liam Bourke, M Moloney, Joe Tynan, Mick Nolan, Brendan Maher, Mick Hogan, Barney Hogan, Tadhg O'Connor, Patsy Rowland, Tadhg Murphy, Francis Regan, Francis Loughnane.

1968–1970

Roscrea Three in a Row: Tipperary Senior Hurling Championship

In 1968, Thurles Sarsfields were outclassed by a hungrier and fitter Roscrea side, who won by 2-11 to 3-4. John Dillon was the first Roscrea captain to receive the Dan Breen Cup. A year later, captained by Mick Hogan, they overwhelmed Carrick Davins, by 4-13 to 0-5, to retain the title in a disappointing final. The following year, 1970, as Roscrea aimed for a third title, they had to overcome a great Thurles Sarsfields rally in a hectic final five minutes. A goal separated the sides with one minute remaining, and Sarsfields got one last chance to level, when a Jimmy Doyle free went screaming over the bar. Roscrea, captained by Patsy Rowland, had their three in a row, by 3-11 to 2-12.

Throughout the three campaigns, Roscrea were well served by goalkeeper Tadhg Murphy. Their defenders: Brendan Maher, Kieran Carey, Tadhg O'Connor and Jimmy Crampton. Francis Loughnane was vital to the successes, assisted in the mid-field area by Mick Minogue, while Donie Moloney, Jackie Hannon and the youthful Joe Tynan caused havoc to many a back-line.

> On the thirteenth of October in the year of sixty-eight,
> The story of a hurling game to you I'll now relate.
> It was the county final and all hurling hearts were gay
> When fifteen gallant hurlers brought the title to Roscrea.
>
> Pat Joe Whelan, from King, Ó Donnchú, Smyth, *Tipperary's GAA Ballads*

A Bohernanave Lad Remembers

In the 'Opening of Semple Stadium' souvenir brochure, 31 May, 1984, local man Jimmy Duggan reminisced about growing up in the shadow of the stadium:

> Come championship time, Bohernanave, that collection of terraced houses along the Sportsfield wall, was the place to live. Expectations mounted steadily as the team trained and by Thursday night the excitement began to grip. At the 'pitch and toss' school at the corner of the high wall, Joe Ryan, who worked on the railway, was heard to remark that there were fifteen 'specials' due from Cork alone. Mary Breen was charging a tanner a

bike and my Uncle Pat spent all day Friday stencilling 'Plain and Meat Teas' signs in the ramshackle shed beside the railway track. All the houses on our terrace did Plain and Meat teas. My father was never there when the Cork crowd arrived. Like most of the men he was working on a stile. Anyway we could have done with him around the house when those Cork people with strange names and a funny ways of talking began to terrify the heart of a young lad with the 'magic of Ringy' and the way they tossed out names like Barry, Brohan, Cashman with consummate ease.

All day Saturday the hammer blows echoed from the Sportsfield as Tommy Max and his willing helpers fitted the stiles one by one and repaired all doors and gates. Inside Jack O'Keeffe lovingly lined the twenty-one yard line. Tomorrow, with any luck, the Cork net would bulge from the same twenty-one and the crowd on wooden sleepers on the sideline would rise as one man and cheer their heroes. As dusk falls, all is in readiness.

At twelve o'clock the first special rolls in. The crowds cascade from the green carriages dressed uniformly in dark suits and white shirts. Their features are bronzed by the June sun and their hair is closely cropped. All are cleanly shaved. Most carry a gabardine coat on the arm or slung over the shoulder, its pockets bulging with sandwiches. They walk at an even pace and speak a strange language but reply good humouredly to our taunts, laughing derisively at the blue and gold flags that adorn almost every window on the street. One 'special' follows another and by one o'clock the trickle of humanity has become a flood.

As the teams parade behind the pipe band, I slip inside the gate at the bottom of the open stand and flop down on my stomach on the grass. The crowd rises to the first swirling notes of the National Anthem and as the tension rises, all the inherited hate and bitterness wells up inside, a sea of red dances before me and as the last notes are lost in a mighty roar, I cry with everything that's in me 'C'mon Tipp'!

Tipperary, All-Ireland Hurling Champions 1971. Back row (l–r): Michael 'Babs' Keating, Roger Ryan, John Flanagan, Liam King, John Kelly, Seamus Hogan, Mick Roche, Noel O'Dwyer. Front row (l–r): John Gleeson, Francis Loughnane, Dinny Ryan, Tadhg O'Connor (captain), Len Gaynor, P J Ryan, Peter O'Sullivan.

CHAPTER 6

FROM THURLES SPORTSFIELD TO SEMPLE STADIUM

THE 1970s

1970
Neither Side Spared the Ash: Oireachtas Hurling Final

Tipperary and Cork met before 20,000 spectators in the Oireachtas final at Thurles Sportsfield on 13 December. Played in glorious sunshine, the game is remembered for outstanding goalkeeping by Peter O'Sullivan and teak-tough performances from the Tipperary backline. The victory, by 1-12 to 0-8, was a vital one, restoring Tipperary's pride and paving the way for All-Ireland success the following year.

Tipperary: Peter O'Sullivan, Noel Lane, John Kelly, John Gleeson, Tadhg O'Connor, Liam King, Len Gaynor, P J Ryan, Mick Jones, Francis Loughnane, John Flanagan, Noel O'Dwyer, Pat O'Neill, Jimmy Doyle, Mick Roche.

Sportsfield Caretaker Jack O'Keeffe

Jack O'Keeffe, Fianna Road, Thurles, was caretaker at Thurles Sportsfield during the 1960s and early 1970s. Jack was a member of the far-famed O'Keeffe family of the Horse and Jockey, renowned in GAA annals. His cousins Jim, Joe and Dick were winners of seven All-Ireland senior medals with Tubberadora, Horse and Jockey, Two-Mile-Borris and Thurles. Jack's cousin, Denis O'Keeffe, was among the local Thurles group that in 1910 purchased Thurles Showgrounds, which in time became Thurles Sportsfield, where Jack was caretaker. No wonder he had a special grá for the venue.

1971

Thurles Sportsfield is named Semple Stadium

At the annual convention of Thurles Sarsfields club, held in December 1970, it was decided to submit a motion to Tipperary county convention requesting that Thurles Sportsfield be renamed in honour of the famed captain of the Thurles Blues.

This motion was proposed by Thurles Sarsfields chairman Fr James Feehan CC: 'That Thurles Sportsfield be named Semple Park to perpetuate the memory of the late Tom Semple.' The motion was seconded by Boherlahan/Dualla delegate Philly O'Dwyer,

N T Gaile, who suggested that Semple Stadium would sound more attractive than Semple Park. This was agreed and the motion was carried unanimously.

Tom Semple (pictured) was a native of Drombane, some fourteen kilometres from Thurles, where he moved as a young man and gained employment with the Great Southern and Western Railway Company. Tom revitalised the fortunes of hurling at Thurles Sarsfields, also known as the Thurles Blues. He won his first All-Ireland with the Two-Mile-Borris selection in 1900 and captained the Blues selection to All-Ireland successes for Tipperary in 1906 and 1908. His fame as a leader of men gained iconic status, and he was recognised far and wide for turning the tide of hurling glory back to Tipperary in the first decade of the twentieth century.

Following the purchase of Thurles Sportsfield in 1910, Tom played a hands-on role in the early development of the venue and is credited with building its reputation as Munster's premier location for major games. During the War of Independence, Tom Semple played a vital role as one of Michael Collins's most trusted railway couriers.

His biography, *Tom Semple and the Thurles Blues*, by this author, was published in 2015.

Above: Féile na nGael founder members Tomás Ó Baróid, Séamus Ó Riain and Éamon de Stafort.
Right: Official programme for the first Féile na nGael.

1971
The First Féile

The main aim of Féile na nGael was to foster a love of hurling among the youth of Ireland. The idea was developed by Tomás Ó Baróid, Tipperary GAA secretary, Séamus Ó Riain, Tipperary GAA chairman, and Éamon de Stafort, Shannonside Tourism, and the playwright Bryan MacMahon, Listowel, suggested the title.

Counties throughout Ireland held competitions for Under 14 hurlers and sent the winning teams to Thurles – thirty-one in all – on the weekend of 18–20 July. These teams were received by thirty-one clubs in Tipperary, who hosted them for the weekend. Teams were graded into four divisions and games were played on Saturday, with the finals on Sunday at Semple Stadium. Before the finals, almost 2,000 participants paraded in the team colours through the streets of Thurles to Semple Stadium. The first Féile na nGael winners were Blackrock (Cork), Comeda (Antrim), Dungiven (Derry) and Portroe (Tipperary).

Carraig Dubh (Blackrock, Cork), first winners of Division 1, Féile na nGael 1971. Panel: Tom Cashman, Ger Kenny, Sean Mintern, Mick McCabe, John Garvan, Finbarr Delaney (captain), Joe Kelly, Ferghie O'Neill, Pierce Power, Danny Buckley, Joe O'Leary, Pat O'Sullivan, Kieran Lyons, Tom Lyons, William Ahern, Ger Downey, Sean Horgan, Kieran Murphy.

Like Father, Like Son

Tom Cashman was following in his father's footsteps as he stood in goals at Semple Stadium in the first Féile na nGael final. It was a position that his father, Mick, the legendary hurling goalkeeper with Blackrock and Cork during the 1950s and 1960s, had held. As Tom matured as a hurler, he played for the Cork senior hurling team for twelve years. Equally comfortable as a half-back or at midfield, Cashman is regarded as one of the most skilful players of all time. Recalling that day in 1971, Declan Hassett wrote,

> The final was played before a fine attendance who thrilled to the splendid goalkeeping of Tom Cashman, whose display was equal to anything ever given by his famous father, and to Danny Buckley's electrifying runs which had the crowd buzzing with excitement.
>
> Paddy Madden and Declan Hassett, Blackrock's Centenary Year publication
> *The Rockies* (1984)

A Living Tradition

GAA president Pat Fanning (pictured) announced in his address at the first Féile:

> Here in Tipperary you have seen the living tradition that is hurling. You have perhaps for the first time savoured the strength and the glory of hurling as you lived with the people of Tipperary over these past two days ... And I know you now realise how much a part of the lives of the people of Tipperary is this game of which you are the custodians.
>
> RTÉ *Sport in Action* report, 22 July, 1971

Top: Rest of Ireland stars of the past, 1971. Front row (l–r): Jimmy Duggan, Frankie Walsh, Jimmy Smyth, Colm Corless, Paddy Barry (Cork Sarsfields), Joe Sammon, Willie John Daly, Josie Hartnett. Back row (l–r): Matt Nugent, Jimmy Brohan, Mick Cashman, Denis Murphy, Tom Cheasty, Kevin Long, Dermot Kelly, Timmy Maher, official unknown.

Above: Tipperary stars of the past, 1971. Back row (l–r): Phil Shanahan, Billy Hayes, Billy Moloughney, Tom Moloughney, Seán McLoughlin, Michael Maher, John Doyle, Kieran Carey, Gerry Doyle. Front row (l–r): Tom Larkin, Pat Ryan, Donie Nealon, Theo English, John 'Mackey' McKenna, Paddy Kenny, Pat Stakelum.

Veteran Hurlers Show How It's Done

In conjunction with Féile na nGael, an exhibition hurling match was played at Semple Stadium on July 18, 1971, between former star hurlers from Tipperary and the rest of Ireland. Tipperary won by 4-9 to 3-8.

Moyne/Templetuohy, Tipperary Senior Hurling Champions 1971. Back row (l–r): Martin O'Grady, Tom Russell, Mick Coen, Bill O'Grady, Tom O'Grady, Tom Quinlan, Michael O'Grady. Front row (l–r): Willie Fogarty, Martin Esmonde, Martin Troy, Tom Fogarty, Jim Fogarty (captain), Paddy Sweeney, Jim Fogarty, Tom Egan.

1971

Sensational Victory for Moyne: Tipperary Senior Hurling Final

From the throw-in, the Mid men took control of the game and never allowed the star-studded Roscrea team settle. The score was close enough until the final quarter, when Murty Troy and Martin O'Grady shook the Roscrea net with vital goals. Moyne also had stars in Tom Russell, Martin Esmonde, Mick Coen and Tom Fogarty. It was Moyne/Templetuohy's first senior title, winning by 2-8 to 0-6. Their captain, Jim Fogarty, accepted the Dan Breen Cup from Tipperary GAA chairman Séamus Ó Riain.

> The bold Roscrea had held firm sway three seasons in a row,
>
> And now the fourth was booked for North, on the latest betting show;
>
> The punters brash, produced their cash and laid it on the line
>
> At threes and more for a winning score against the lads of Moyne.
>
> John O'Grady ('Cúlbaire'), *Tipperary Star*, December 1971

1972

Norberg Captains 'Rebels' to League Success

Cork won the National Hurling League final at Semple Stadium on 7 May, beating Limerick by 3-14 to 2-14, before an attendance of 30,000. Their scores came from Donie Collins (1-2), Seánie O'Leary (1-2), Charlie McCarthy (0-5), Con Roche (1-0), Mick Malone (0-2), Justin McCarthy (0-2) and Ray Cummins (0-1). Limerick's scorers were Richie Bennis (1-6), Éamonn Cregan (1-2), Éamonn Grimes (0-3), Willie Moore (0-1), Bernie Hartigan (0-1), Frankie Nolan (0-1).

1970s

Eddie Flynn, Chairman

Eddie Flynn succeeded Canon Philip Fogarty as chairman of Thurles Sportsfield Committee, a position he held for much of the 1970s. Eddie was a member of a long-established Thurles family, who ran a successful drapery business on Liberty Square. At Semple Stadium, he was to the forefront in the development and modernisation of the grounds. Eddie was also keenly involved in the fortunes of Thurles Golf Club.

The Thurles Silver Band performed at the Munster final at Semple Stadium in July 1972. This photograph includes Charlie Harkin, who is seated in the centre of the front row. Billy Bowe is standing on the right, while bandmaster Joe Ryan is on the extreme left of the front row.

1972
Rebel Forwards Run Riot: Munster Senior Hurling Final

Clare in 1972 had a resounding victory over neighbours Limerick in the Munster semi-final, by 3-11 to 2-10, and hopes were high as they faced Cork in the Munster final at Thurles Sportsfield on 30 July. It was the sides' first meeting in forty years in a provincial final, although Cork had a more arduous route there, beating Waterford, then a draw and replay with Tipperary, progressing by 3-10 to 2-7. The final was a disappointing affair, in which Clare failed to reveal their true form and were well beaten. The brilliant Cork inside-forward line of Charlie McCarthy, Ray Cummins and Seánie O'Leary ran riot. It was Clare's heaviest defeat in a Munster decider since 1918. The final score was Cork 6-18, Clare 2-8. Referee: Seán O'Grady, Limerick.

Cork: Paddy Barry, Tony Maher, Pat McDonnell, Brian Murphy, Frank Norberg (captain), Seamus Looney, Con Roche, Justin McCarthy, Denis Coughlan, Gerald McCarthy, Mick Malone, Pat Hegarty, Charlie McCarthy, Ray Cummins, Seánie O'Leary. Substitute: Ted O'Brien.

Tipperary Host Féile na nGael

The scene from the stand at Semple Stadium during the massed gathering of 1,280 boys from every county in Ireland for the 1972 Féile na nGael.

Roscrea, Tipperary Senior Hurling Champions 1972. Back row (l–r): Thomas O'Reilly, Seamus O'Doherty, Luke Carroll, John Joe Maher, Jimmy Crampton, Tom Tynan, Jody Spooner, Willie Stapleton, Jackie Hannon (captain), Tadhg Murphy, Mick Minogue, Martin Loughnane. Front row (l–r): Willie O'Reilly, Francis Loughnane, Joe Cunningham, Mick Hogan, Donie Moloney, Patsy Rowland, Brendan Maher, Joe Tynan, Tadhg O'Connor.

1972
Roscrea Too Crafty for Borris: Tipperary Senior Hurling Final

The county hurling final was played in a downpour at Semple Stadium on 12 November, before one of the smallest attendances ever of just 3,000. Roscrea were in goal-scoring form and had three by half-time from Joe Tynan, Donie Moloney and Jody Spooner, to give them a 3-5 to 1-2 advantage at the break. Noel O'Dwyer had scored the Borris/Ileigh goal from a free. In fairness to Borris, they made a great recovery in the second period and came within a goal of the champions. But Roscrea struck back with two goals from Joe Cunningham and Francis Loughnane to put the issue beyond any doubt. Jackie Hannon accepted the new Dan Breen Cup. They had won their fourth senior county title, by 5-8 to 3-6.

Top left: Match programme for the Munster final, 1973.

Top right: Limerick's Frankie Nolan scores an early goal against Tipperary at Semple Stadium.

Above: Limerick, Munster and All-Ireland Hurling Champions 1973. Back row (l–r): Richie Bennis, Liam O'Donoghue, Jim O'Brien, Pat Hartigan, Joe McKenna, Éamonn Cregan, Willie Moore, Ned Rea. Front row (l–r): Seán Foley, Mossy Dowling, Bernie Hartigan, Éamonn Grimes, Phil Bennis, Frankie Nolan, Séamus Horgan.

Above right: Tipperary's Jimmy Doyle.

1973

The Point That Was or Was Not: Munster Senior Hurling Final

The stage was set for a classic Tipperary/Limerick see-saw battle at a sunny Semple Stadium on 29 July. Limerick's brilliant point-scoring was matched by goal-hungry Tipperary forwards. A draw looked the likely outcome when John Flanagan levelled the sides with a long-range point from all of seventy yards. The final seconds ticked down and Éamonn Grimes won a disputed seventy for the Shannonsiders. Referee Mick Slattery of Clare informed Richie Bennis that he must score direct. Richie's nerve held and the ball headed goalwards. The umpire raised the white flag, even though there were many who claimed that it had veered wide at the last moment. Limerick had won their first title in eighteen years, 6-7 to 2-18. The attendance was 41,723.

Jimmy Doyle later recalled:

People often wonder about that ball, was it inside the post or outside. I'm telling you now, I saw it and that ball was wide – 'twas a foot wide.

A few weeks later I was driving the ambulance for the hospital, was above in Limerick waiting for me patient to come out and who walked past only Richie Bennis.

'Come over here, I want to have a word with you.'

He got into the ambulance beside me and I asked him – 'Was it or wasn't it a point? In my books it wasn't – I was almost under the post, looking up at it, and it was at least a foot wide.'

'Well,' he says, 'we got it anyway!'

'I know ye got it, and ye went on to win the All-Ireland and fair play to ye, I'm delighted for ye, but in my books it was a foot to a foot-and-a-half wide.'

Richie wasn't giving in though, and fair dues to him. That was a very good Limerick team – Ned Rea went to town on us that day, scored three goals, so I'm glad I wasn't in the goals! It was the beginning of the end of Tipperary for a long time, that day; it was also my last day in that jersey.

O'Flynn, *The Boy Wonder of Hurling: The Story of Jimmy Doyle*

Above left: Image of match programme courtesy of the GAA Museum & Archive.
Above right: Limerick, Munster Senior Hurling Champions 1974. Back row (l–r): Richie Bennis,
Bernie Hartigan, Pat Hartigan, Jim O'Brien, Joe McKenna, Tom Ryan, Eamonn Rea, Willie Moore,
Éamonn Cregan. Front row (l–r): Éamonn Grimes, Frankie Nolan, Seán Foley (captain), Liam
O'Donoghue, Matt Ruth, Séamus Horgan.

1974

Limerick Retain Their Crown: Munster Senior Hurling Final

A crowd of 36,446 witnessed the final between Limerick and Clare at Semple Stadium
on 28 July. Limerick had little difficulty as Clare failed to perform to expectations. Final
score: Limerick 6-14, Clare 3-9. Referee: John Moloney, Tipperary.

Opposite bottom: Kilkenny, All-Ireland Under 21 Champions 1974. Back row (l–r): Tom McCormack, Malachy Hogan, John Dowling, Mick Tierney, Ger Henderson, Brian Cody, Kevin Fennelly, Shem Brophy. Front row (l–r): Ger Woodcock, Tony Teehan, Pat Kearney, Ger Fennelly (captain), Nickey Brennan, Billy Fitzpatrick, Jimmy Dunne.

1974
A First for Kilkenny: All-Ireland Under 21 Hurling Final

Seven minutes from the end of this thrilling contest, Waterford were ahead by 3-7 to 2-5. Goals by Ger Woodcock and substitute Bobby Sweeney and points from Ger Fennelly, Bobby Sweeney and Billy Fitzpatrick turned what looked like inescapable defeat into a resounding victory, by 3-8 to 3-7.

Waterford: Willie Ryan, Frank McCarthy, Micheál Flynn, Kieran Ryan, Liam O'Brien, John Galvin, Eamonn Ryan, Pat Egan, Pat McGrath (captain), Tom Casey, Liam Power, Patsy O'Keeffe, Brendan Mansfield, Mossie McNamara, Paul Moore.

Semple Stadium Caretaker Miley Troy

Miley Troy was a native of Castletown, Moyne, Thurles. In his hurling days, he played for Moyne for many years and also for Killmallock, Limerick. While at Kilmallock, Miley won a Limerick junior championship in 1943, Kilmallock's only adult team at that time. He was later employed at Thurles Sugar Factory as a gardener before replacing Jack O'Keeffe as caretaker at Semple Stadium. He worked at the stadium from 1973 to 1978, when Jim Hickey took over. Miley continued to help out at the stadium for major occasions such as the GAA centenary All-Ireland in 1984 and the 1987 Munster final. Replacing the sodding on the squares was his speciality. In 1961, Miley and his cousin Mick Troy trained and selected the first Moyne-Templetuohy team to win a county hurling championship, the Tipperary No 1 Junior.

1974

Doyle Leads Sarsfields to Glory: Tipperary Senior Hurling Final

In the county hurling final at Semple Stadium on 13 October, Thurles Sarsfields, captained by veteran Jimmy Doyle, regained the county title after a lapse of nine years. The final score was 3-6 to 1-10, and the attendance of 10,500 experienced an exciting contest between the Blues and Silvermines, particularly near the finish.

Sarsfields got off to the perfect start with a goal by Johnny Bourke after two minutes, and another by Johnny Dwyer on the stroke of half-time gave them a flattering 2-3 to 0-5 interval lead. Johnny Bourke added another goal for Sarsfields while Pat Quinlan converted a close-in free for Silvermines to leave the tie delicately poised going into the final stages.

Silvermines played their best hurling at this stage, throwing caution to the wind and exerting the utmost pressure on the Thurles goal. Jim Ryan (A) and Pat Leane weren't found wanting in the full line; neither was Jimmy Duggan, whose saves in the final minutes kept Sarsfields ahead at the long whistle.

Roscrea, so bold, had long controlled the trophy of Dan Breen,

But the 'Blues' revived their former pride to dominate the scene;

A comeback planned by the master hand, the soul of craft and guile,

In a year when youth, in every truth, bowed low to Jimmy Doyle.

John O'Grady ('Cúlbaire'), *Tipperary Star*, 28 December, 1974

Opposite: Thurles Sarsfields, Tipperary Senior Hurling Champions 1974. Back row (l–r): Seán Maher, Tony Ryan, Jimmy Duggan, Martin Byrne, Michael Dundon, Denis Curtis, Johnny Bourke, Michael Grogan, Liam Ó Donnchú, Jimmy Doyle, Tossie Hayes, Seán Hussey, Pat Stakelum, Michael Gleeson, Pat McCormack. Front row (l–r): Paul Byrne, Jim Ryan (A), Jackie Cooke, Paddy Doyle, Johnny O'Dwyer, Jimmy Doyle (captain), Pat Leane, Francis Murphy, Brendan O'Neill, Seán McLoughlin, Tom Barry, Paddy McCormack, Eddie Clancy. Aidan Murphy (mascot).

1976

From Generation to Generation

Jim Max (pictured) succeeded his father, Tommy, as secretary of Thurles Sportsfield Committee. The Max family have been associated with the venue since the early days. Jim was closely involved with the running of big match days, where he worked with stewards, gatemen and stiles-men to ensure the smooth and safe operation of events.

1976

Leahy Seals Village Victory: All-Ireland Club Hurling Final

The final was contested at Semple Stadium on 14 May by James Stephens (Kilkenny) and Blackrock (Cork).

On a very wet day, the Rockies got off to a great start as Éamonn O'Donoghue scored a goal inside the first minute. A goal from a Pat Moylan penalty in the sixteenth minute gave Blackrock a lead of 2-1 with James Stephens yet to score. By half-time James Stephens had cut the lead to five points as they trailed by 2-2 to 0-3.

A draw looked likely as the game entered the final stage, however a last-minute Mick Leahy goal put the game beyond doubt as James Stephens claimed a 2-10 to 2-4 victory.

Scores for James Stephens: Liam O'Brien 1-4 (3f), Mick Leahy 1-0, John McCormack 0-3, Mick Crotty 0-1, M Taylor 0-1, J O'Brien 0-1; Blackrock: Pat Moylan 1-3, Éamonn O'Donoghue 1-0, D Collins 0-1.

Some points in the difference, some minutes to go

Chunky had a goal that rattled the foe

We were in front and the seal was set

As Mick Leahy lashed another to the back of the net.

Poem by Jim Rhattigan

1976
Preparing for the GAA Centenary

A deputation representing Thurles Sportsfield Committee presented development plans to Munster Council and requested grant aid of £50,000. The estimated cost of the development was £280,000, and it was to provide for the terracing of the embankments, which would be completely walled off. The line of the existing pitch would be slightly altered to ensure an unhindered view of the pitch from all angles. The work would result in a comfortable capacity of 50,000 at the venue, and it was hoped to finish well before 1984, when the centenary of the foundation of the GAA in Thurles would be celebrated.

In order to initiate fundraising and see the plans to fruition, Tipperary County Board decided to appoint the full county board en bloc onto the existing Thurles Sportsfield Committee. Michael Frawley, Emly, was appointed as chairman of this group, to be known as County Tipperary GAA Centenary Commemoration and Development Committee.

Moneygall, Tipperary Senior Hurling Champions 1976. Back row (l–r): Séamus Ryan, John Gleeson, Billy Fanning, Pat Sheedy, Philip Ryan, Michael 'Spike' Nolan, Donal Kennedy, Seán Doughan. Front row (l–r): John Ivors, Jim Guilfoyle, Jack Ryan, Bobby Jones, Mick Doherty (captain), Eugene Ryan, Philip Fanning, Noel Whyte.

1976

Moneygall Retain Dan Breen: Tipperary Senior Hurling Final

In the 1975 county final in Semple Stadium on 12 October, Moneygall, captained by Pat Sheedy, drew, 3-9 each, with Kilruane MacDonagh. In the replay two weeks later at the same venue, Kilruane slumped to a heavy defeat, 3-13 to 0-5, and Moneygall celebrated their first senior county title. The following year, Moneygall, led by Mick Doherty, won their way to the final at Semple Stadium on 12 September, before a 10,000 attendance. Facing their great rivals, Roscrea, they confounded all the critics and with skill, determination and resilience, retained the title, by 1-9 to 2-5.

1976

Kilkenny Master Clare in Replay: National Hurling League Final

Kilkenny and Clare drew 0-16 to 2-10 in the 1975/1976 National Hurling League final at Semple Stadium on 9 May, 1976. The Cats won the replay at the same venue on 20 June, 6-14 to 1-14.

Kilkenny: Noel Skehan, Phil 'Fan' Larkin (captain), Nicky Orr, Brian Cody, Pat Lawlor, Pat Henderson, Ger Henderson, Liam O'Brien, Frank Cummins, Mick Crotty, Matt Ruth, Billy Fitzpatrick, Mick Brennan, Pat Delaney, Eddie Keher.

Séamus Durack, Clare's star goalkeeper.
Photo by Ray McManus, Sportsfile.

179

Clare, National Hurling League Champions 1978. Back row (l–r): Enda O'Connor, Ger Loughnane,
Noel Casey, Martin McHeogh, Jim Power, Jackie O'Gorman, Seán Hehir, Michael Moroney, Johnny
Callanan. Front row (l–r): Johnny McMahon, Seán Stack (captain), Séamus Durack, Pat O'Connor,
Colm Honan, Jimmy McNamara.

1977–1978
Clare Take the Crown: National Hurling League 1976/1977 and 1977/1978

Clare, captained by Jimmy McNamara, shocked the hurling world by beating Kilkenny, 2-8 to 0-9, in the National League final at Semple Stadium on 24 April, 1977. It was their second league title overall and their first since 1945/1946. They got off to a dream start with an opening goal by Jimmy McNamara in the second minute of play. Tom Crowe got the second goal. The following year, led by Seán Stack, Clare were defending league champions and showed great resilience, retaining the title. Back at Semple Stadium on 30 April, Kilkenny were at the receiving end of a Clare victory by 3-10 to 1-10.

The Clare players involved in these successes were: Jimmy McNamara, Seán Stack, Séamus Durack, Jackie O'Gorman, Jim Power, Johnny McMahon, Ger Loughnane, Seán Hehir, Gus Lohan, Michael Moroney, Colm Honan, Enda O'Connor, Tom Crowe, Noel Casey, Johnny Callinan, Pat O'Connor, Martin McKeogh, Timmy Ryan, Tom Glynn, D J Meehan, Con Woods, Michael O'Connor (Tubber), Michael O'Connor (Parteen), Michael Murphy, Gerry Nugent, Pat Morey, Tommy Keane, Leo Quinlan, Con McGuinness, Brendan Gilligan, Flann McInerney, Noel Burke, Jimmy Puddin Cullinan.

1977
A Second for the Glen: All-Ireland Club Hurling Final

Cork's Glen Rovers bounced back in 1976, with Martin O'Doherty leading the club

Glen Rovers, Cork County Champions 1976. Back row (l–r): Patsy Harte, Jerry O'Sullivan, Tom Collins, Pat Horgan, Martin O'Doherty, Paddy O'Doherty, Frank O'Sullivan, Denis Coughlan. Front row (l–r): Joe Joe O'Neill, Vincie Marshall, Red Crowley, Donal Clifford, Paddy Barry (captain), Teddy O'Brien, Finbarr O'Neill.

to a 2–7 to 0–10 victory over Blackrock in the county final. In the Munster final, the Cork champs were pitted against Limerick side South Liberties. After an entertaining hour of hurling, the Glen had their third Munster club title, winning by 2–8 to 2–4. They sailed through the All-Ireland quarter- and semi-finals, then faced Camross in the decider at Semple Stadium. Nine survivors from the 1973 All-Ireland victory powered the Glen to a 2–12 to 0–8 win over the Laois champions, who were inspired by the Cuddy family. It was the Glen's second All-Ireland club title.

1977

The Rebels March On: Munster Senior Hurling Final

The Munster final at Semple Stadium on 10 July attracted an attendance of 44,586, including President Patrick Hillery and newly appointed taoiseach Jack Lynch. Inexperience cost Clare dearly, and when they were reduced to fourteen players just

Top left: Cork star forward Jimmy Barry-Murphy celebrates their win. Photo by Ray McManus of Sportsfile.

Top right: Cork, Munster Senior Hurling Champions 1978. Front row (l–r): Tom Cashman, Dermot McCurtain, Seán O'Leary, Charlie McCarthy (captain), Martin Coleman, Brian Murphy, Gerald McCarthy. Back row (l–r): Fr Bertie Troy (coach), Jimmy Barry-Murphy, John Crowley, Tim Crowley, Ray Cummins, Martin O'Doherty, Pat Moylan, John Horgan, Denis Coughlan. Photo: Connolly Collection, Sportsfile.

Left: Image of match programme courtesy of the GAA Museum & Archive.

before half-time with the sending off of full-back Jim Power, the task proved too great for them. Although there were only two points between the teams at that stage, Cork 3-5, Clare 2-6, the Bannermen never recovered, but they played well and finished just five points in arrears, 4-15 to 4-10. Jackie O'Gorman was a star for Clare at right full-back, while others to shine were Séamus Durack, Johnny McMahon, Ger Loughnane, Seán Hehir, Mick Moroney, Johnny Callanan and Noel Casey.

While this Munster final day is remembered for Cork's victory, it was somewhat overshadowed by the discovery that in the course of the second half, armed raiders got away with £24,579, more than half of the gate receipts. It was an audacious move, since there was unprecedented security at the stadium for the attendance at the game of Uachtarán na hÉireann, An Taoiseach and several other members of the cabinet.

1977

Stadium Planning

Much of the year was spent finalising development plans which included the terracing of all three embankments, the provision of spacious toilets, and improving access and exiting. This was seen as the first phase of development leading to the 1984 centenary celebrations, and work commenced in the spring of 1978. As Michael Frawley was the incoming Munster Council chairman, he stepped down from his position as chairman of the Centenary Commemoration and Development Committee. Fr Pierce Duggan (pictured top), C.C. Upperchurch/Drombane, a native of Two-Mile-Borris, took up the position, with Liam Ryan of Holycross as secretary and John Lanigan, Thurles Sarsfields (pictured bottom), as treasurer. In 1979, Liam resigned his position as he entered St Patrick's College to study for the priesthood and was replaced by Tom O'Hara.

Above right: Kilkenny, All-Ireland Under 21 Champions 1977. Back row (l–r): Joe Hennessy, Murty Kennedy, Ger Tyrrell, Dick O'Hara, Richie Reid, Richie Power, Paddy Prendergast, John Henderson. Front row (l–r): Eddie Mahon, Jimmy Lennon, Brendan Fennelly, Brian Waldron, Michael Lyng (captain), Paudie Lennon, Joe Wall.

1977

Kilkenny Win the Double

Kilkenny won their third All-Ireland Under 21 title at Semple Stadium on 12 October. Captained by Mickey Lyng, their scorers were Brendan Fennelly (1-2), Brian Waldron (0-5), Richie Power (1-0), Kieran Brennan (0-1) and Paudie Lennon (0-1). Cork's sharpshooters were Tom Lyons (1-1), Tadhg Murphy (0-3), Tom Cashman (0-2), Richie McDonnell (0-1), Pat Horgan (0-1) and John Crowley (0-1). Final score: Kilkenny 2-9, Cork 1-9. Referee: Jimmy Rankin of Laois.

On the same day at Semple Stadium, Kilkenny won the All-Ireland minor hurling final replay, beating Cork by 1-8 to 0-9.

Kilkenny minors: Lester Ryan, Canice Mackey, Michael Meagher, Bill O'Hara, Tom Lennon (0-2), Seán Fennelly (captain), Dominic Connolly, Gordon Ryan, John Mulcahy (0-1), Eugene Deegan (0-2), Richard Murphy (0-1), Eddie Crowley (0-1), Michael Nash, Eddie Wallace, William McEvoy (1-1). Substitute played: Jimmy Heffernan, J Waters.

1978

A Radical Change of Course

In late January, gale-force winds lifted part of the roof off Ardán Uí Chuinneáin (the Old Stand) and sent jagged pieces of asbestos flying in the direction of Childers Park. Houses were damaged and windows were broken by the flying debris. Some years later, Fr Pierce Duggan, chairman of Semple Stadium, would remark that the storm 'was a blessing in disguise'. It was after the storm that the centenary committee took a radical look at Semple Stadium and decided on a completely new development, one which seemed overambitious to some observers.

Towards the end of the year, the Centenary and Development Committee presented plans and a scale model of the proposed stadium to the press. A new covered stand on the northern terrace, with a capacity of 11,000, was planned, with the provision of concrete on the Killinan and Town terraces, giving a total ground capacity of between 55,000 and 60,000. There would be new access routes to the Nenagh and Holycross

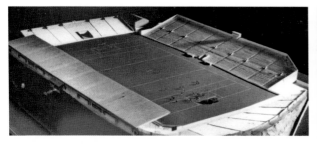

The scale model of the new-look Semple Stadium, 1978.

roads. The committee announced that they hoped to raise £250,000 from the sale of 2,500 ten-year tickets, which would guarantee holders a central position in the new stand for a variety of games. Total expenditure was expected to be in the order of £500,000.

This aerial photograph (below) of Semple Stadium, taken in 1978, illustrates the condition of the venue at the time. Only the Old Stand side of the grounds had been developed, and the storm damage to the roof is obvious. The embankments seen here had not been changed in decades. The stadium was expected to host the GAA centenary All-Ireland hurling final in 1984; the task facing the recently formed County Tipperary GAA Centenary Commemoration and Development Committee was awesome.

Semple Stadium Caretaker Jim Hickey

Jim Hickey, a native of Kilcommon parish, became head groundsman at Semple Stadium in 1978. He took over from Miley Troy and would hold the position until after the centenary All-Ireland hurling final in 1984. Jim's period at the stadium was a busy one, coinciding with major renovations and redevelopment as well as the centenary celebrations. For Jim, a quiet and unassuming man, the pitch was his top priority. Over the years, the quality of his work was plain to be seen, and he received many plaudits.

St Finbarrs, All-Ireland Club Hurling Champions 1978. Back row (l–r): Brendan O'Shaughnessy, Bertie O'Brien, John Foster, Jerry O'Shea, Jim Power, Christy Ryan, Brendan Manley, Malachy Kennedy, Charlie Barrett, Donal O'Grady, Con Roche. Front row (l–r): Seamus Gillen, Tony Butler, Jimmy Barry-Murphy, John Allen, Denis Burns, Gerald McCarthy, Charlie McCarthy, Éamonn Fitzpatrick, Gerry Murphy, Barry Wiley, John Cremin, Tony Maher.

1978

Second Triumph for the Barrs: All-Ireland Club Hurling Final

At Semple Stadium on 27 March, a gale-force wind hindered the St Finbarr's challenge in the opening half of the All-Ireland club final, allowing Rathnure to take an 0-8 to 0-1 interval lead. Ten minutes from the full-time whistle, Barry Wiley scored an equaliser that gave the Barrs an increased impetus. A Jimmy Barry-Murphy goal from a rebound settled the game as St Finbarr's claimed a four-point victory. The final score was St Finbarr's 2-7, Rathnure 0-9.

The scorers for St Finbarr's were Charlie McCarthy (0-4, 4f), Éamonn Fitzpatrick (1-0), Jimmy Barry-Murphy (1-0) and Barry Wiley (0-3); and for Rathnure, J Holohan (0-3), J Murphy (0-2), D Quigley (0-2), M Quigley (0-1) and J Quigley (0-1).

> The Rockies thought that they were stars,
> 'Till they met the Saint Finbarr's
> Here's up 'em all
> Say the boys of Fair Hill.
>
> Seán O'Callaghan, Blackpool, Cork, 'The Boys of Fair Hill'

1978
Cork Triumph without a Goal: Munster Senior Hurling Final

Clare had clear victories over Tipperary and Limerick in the run-up to the Munster final, and coupled with their National Hurling success, their supporters had good reason to hope that the Bannermen would win their first Munster title for forty-six years. Cork, meanwhile, were going for their fourth Munster title in a row and their third successive All-Ireland.

Such was the crowd at Semple Stadium on 30 July that the gates were locked an hour before the start, leaving many disappointed patrons outside. The attendance of 54,181 was the largest since 1961 and included An Taoiseach Jack Lynch and President Paddy Hillery.

They got great value for money, and Cork, captained by Charlie McCarthy, playing with the breeze, had a lead of 0-5 to 0-3 at the break. This didn't seem nearly enough for victory – Clare had the wind to come, and their supporters were humming happily – but Cork rearranged their forces and began to dominate midfield, frustrating all Clare attempts to draw level. The final point of the game came from Clare's wing-back Ger Loughnane, whose long-range effort was intended to land in the square but was carried over the bar by the strong breeze. Cork's superb defence saw them through to their fourth Munster crown on the trot.

Top left: Image of match programme courtesy of the GAA Museum & Archive.

Top right: Left wing-back Dermot McCurtain of Blackrock, Cork, clears his lines in the 1978 Munster final against Clare at Semple Stadium.

Above: Making the announcements: this author, Liam Ó Donnchú, Thurles Sarsfields, with sound technician Paddy Prior, Dovea and Borrisoleigh.

Final score: Cork 0-13, Clare 0-11. Referee: John Moloney, Galtee Rovers GAA, Tipperary.

Cork: Martin Coleman, Denis Burns, Martin O'Doherty, John Horgan, Dermot McCurtain, John Crowley, Denis Coughlan, Tom Cashman, Tim Crowley, Gerald McCarthy, Jimmy Barry-Murphy, Pat Moylan, Charlie McCarthy (captain), Ray Cummins, Mick Malone. Substitutes: Éamonn O'Donoghue, Pat Horgan.

Our aim was to win an All-Ireland. You may think inside this dressing room that aim is kind of forgotten now. But I can tell you it is not forgotten … We were beaten before and I am telling you we are going to be back again.

Ger Loughnane interviewed by RTÉ's Doireann Ní Bhriain, 30 July, 1978

When the game was over, Loughnane slumped to the ground in frustration, and as he thumped his hurley off the turf, one could imagine his feelings and those of the many other Clare people in the ground. It was a sad setback for a hopeful team and one that may take some time to get over.

Paddy Downey, *The Irish Times*, 31 July, 1978

Five Year Ticket Scheme

The Five Year Stand Ticket Scheme was one of the main fundraising ideas to offset the development costs. Tickets costing £100 entitled the holder to a seat in a prime viewing location in the Kinane Stand for a five-year period.

Stadium Centenary Logo

The new Semple Stadium centenary logo was launched at the end of 1978. It depicted GAA patron Archbishop Thomas Croke, GAA founder Michael Cusack and GAA founder and first president Maurice Davin.

1979
'Fan' Larkin Leads Leinster to Victory: Railway Cup Hurling Final

The Railway Cup Interprovincial hurling final was played at Semple Stadium on 1 April. Leinster, captained by Kilkenny's Phil 'Fan' Larkin, defeated Connacht by 1-13 to 1-9. A goal from Tony Doran in the fiftieth minute sealed the verdict. It was Tony's seventh Railway Cup success, having also captained Leinster to victory in 1971 and 1977.

Leinster: Noel Skehan (Kilkenny), Phil Larkin (Kilkenny, captain), Willie Murphy

(Wexford), Jimmy Prendergast (Wexford), Joe Hennessy (Kilkenny), Peadar Carton (Dublin), Colm Doran (Wexford), Ger Henderson (Kilkenny), Paddy Quirke (Carlow), Joachim Kelly (Offaly), Mick Holden (Dublin), Mick Walsh (Laois), Billy Fitzpatrick (Kilkenny), Tony Doran (Wexford), Ned Buggy (Wexford). Substitutes: Damien Martin (Offaly), Paddy Prendergast (Kilkenny), Michael Kennedy (Offaly), Frank Cummins (Kilkenny), Pat Delaney (Offaly), Paddy Kirwan (Offaly), Pat Carroll (Offaly), Frank Keenan (Laois).

Tony Doran of Wexford and Leinster. Photo by Ray McManus, Sportsfile.

1979
Goals Galore for the Rockies:
All-Ireland Club Hurling Final

Blackrock, Cork, won their third All-Ireland club hurling final at Semple Stadium on 25 March, 1979, beating Kilkenny's Ballyhale Shamrocks, who were hoping to claim their first. Blackrock appeared to have the game wrapped up when Tom Lyons whipped through a goal to leave them fourteen points ahead with just a quarter of an hour left to play. Ger Fennelly pointed a free to reduce the deficit for Ballyhale, before Pat Holden, Kevin Fennelly and Liam Fennelly scored three goals without reply. Moylan pointed to reinforce the lead for Blackrock, however a long shot from out the field landed in the Blackrock square before Brendan Fennelly got the final touch to send it over the line. This left the Shamrocks trailing by two points, and they ran out of time. Final score: Blackrock 5-7, Ballyhale Shamrocks 5-5. The referee was Seán Purcell of Galway.

I met an old hurler, now sixty and six,

Who played centre-forward and under the sticks,

He played with the Islands, The Redmonds and Barrs,

He had medals to prove it with old battle scars,

He could play don't forget although an old crock.

But the best men he met were the boys of Blackrock.

'The Boys of Blackrock', traditional Cork song, author unknown

Above left: Munster final 1979 match programme. Above right: Limerick's Jim O'Brien, Bruree, keeps a close eye on Cork full-forward Ray Cummins in the 1979 Munster final at Semple Stadium.

1979

Cork Five in a Row: Munster Senior Hurling Final

An attendance of 47,849 thronged Semple Stadium on 8 July for what materialised as a disappointing Munster final. Limerick were without Pat Hartigan, and his loss was sorely felt as the Shannonsiders lacked the same fire and drive of their earlier games. Cork, a mature, consistent and experienced side, won easily. The final score was Cork 2-14, Limerick 0-9. The referee was George Ryan, Lattin/Cullen GAA, Tipperary.

A Munster final fiercely fought,

Will set our hearts aglow,

Where there's speed and dash and clashing ash

And memories of long ago.

Br Joseph Perkins, Tales of the Gaels, *Tipperary Star*

Cork, Munster Senior Hurling Champions 1979. Back row (l–r): Tim Crowley, John Crowley, Jimmy Barry-Murphy, Martin O'Doherty, Ray Cummins, Brian Murphy, Denis Coughlan. Front row (l–r): Charlie McCarthy, Dermot McCurtain, Seán O'Leary, John Horgan (captain), Pat Moylan, Gerald McCarthy, Martin Coleman, John Fenton.

1979

Kilruane MacDonagh Three in a Row: Tipperary Senior Hurling Final

Eight thousand spectators were at Semple Stadium on 7 October, 1979, to witness Kilruane MacDonagh receive the Dan Breen Cup for the third year in succession. The north men led from the start and were in a commanding position over Thurles Sarsfields at half-time, ahead by 1-10 to 0-4.

The third quarter saw Kilruane assert their superiority as they raced into a fourteen-point lead. It was then that Sarsfields realised they were in a county final and pulled out all the stops with a three-goal blitz from Johnny Bourke, Paul Byrne and Tom Barry. Following a goalmouth melee, substitute Johnny Dwyer grabbed the ball and shot low, but Tony Sheppard saved for Kilruane. However Sarsfields couldn't sustain the onslaught, and a further Kilruane goal ended their hopes. Paddy Williams received the Man of the Match award for an outstanding performance. The final score was Kilruane MacDonagh 2-18, Thurles Sarsfields 3-6.

Kilruane MacDonagh Tipperary Senior Hurling Champions 1979: Tony Sheppard,

Kilruane MacDonagh, Tipperary Senior Hurling Champions 1978. Back row (l–r): Paddy Williams, Mackey Keogh, Enda Hogan, Billy O'Shea, Tony Sheppard, Dinny O'Meara, Éamonn O'Shea, Seán O'Meara. Front row (l–r): Dinny Cahill, Seán Hyland, Jim Williams (captain), Gilbert Williams, Jim O'Meara, Séamus Hennessy, Dinny Whelan.

Seán Hyland, Denis O'Meara, Enda Hogan, Jim O'Meara, Paddy Williams, Dinny Cahill, Séamus 'Mackey' Keogh, Séamus Hennessy, Éamonn O'Shea, Liam O'Shea (captain), Gilbert Williams, Jim Williams, Seán O'Meara, Séamus Waters. Substitute: John Quinlan. Kilruane MacDonagh winning captains: 1977, Dinny Cahill; 1978, Jim Williams; 1979, Liam O'Shea.

O God bless the great MacDonaghs, may their name and fame live on,

Cloughjordan and Ardcroney and dear old Kilruane.

Hand in hand we march together on to victory again –

Give three cheers for Dinny Cahill and his bold MacDonagh men.

Con Heffernan, Ardcroney, from King, Ó Donnchú, Smyth, *Tipperary's GAA Ballads*

1979

Christy Ring RIP

In March, the unexpected death of Christy Ring brought sadness to all lovers of hurling. Rated by many as the greatest hurler of all time, Semple Stadium was the scene of many of his triumphs as he so often stood between Tipperary and victory. His tussles with Tipperary backmen such as Tommy Doyle and Mickey 'The Rattler' Byrne were the stuff of legend.

Tommy Doyle commented, 'Ring had something no other player had. He was strong, fast, fiercely determined and a hurling brain second to none.' Mickey Byrne added, 'To me Christy Ring was the complete hurler. He had everything – skill, guts, and a terrific will to win. It is hard to believe that a man so ruthless on the field could be so shy and reserved off it.'

His former teammate and the taoiseach at the time, Jack Lynch, delivered a heartfelt graveside oration that included these words:

As a hurler he had no peer. As long as young men will match their hurling skills against each other on Ireland's green fields, as long as young boys bring their camáns for the sheer thrill of the tingle on their fingers of the impact of ash with leather, as long as hurling is played, the story of Christy Ring will be told – and that will be forever.

Photo courtesy of the Irish Examiner *Archive.*

The covered section of Ardán Uí Chuinneáin (Old Stand) was re-roofed in 1980.

CHAPTER 7

GAA CENTENARY CELEBRATED

THE 1980S

1980
Ardán Ó Riain Completed

The cost of the development was now reaching £700,000. The new covered stand on the northern side of the ground, Ardán Ó Riain, was completed in time for the Munster hurling semi-final on 22 June, 1980. The covered section of Ardán Uí Chuinneáin (the Old Stand) was re-roofed, the Town End was terraced to accommodate 15,000, and new toilet complexes, modern shopping areas and a radio/TV media facility were added. Duggan Bros., Templemore, were the building contractors, with Horgan & Lynch as architects.

The new stand was named in memory of Michael Kennedy Ryan (Lacken), born at Knockfune, Newport, Tipperary on 29 September, 1868. He studied for the priesthood at St Patrick's College, Thurles, and at Maynooth, where he was ordained on 25 June, 1893. He became a professor at St Patrick's College in 1901. Canon M K Ryan was part of the deputation of local Thurles Gaels that negotiated the purchase of Thurles Sportsfield from the Thurles Agricultural Show Committee in 1910, and chairman of Tipperary GAA from 1917 until 1924.

Above left: Match programme from the Munster hurling final 1980.
Above right: Limerick full-back Leonard Enright. Photo by Ray McManus, Sportsfile.

1980

Limerick Show True Courage: Munster Senior Hurling Final

Cork had beaten a spiritless Tipperary in the semi-final but were surprised by a Limerick ambush in the Munster final at Semple Stadium on 20 July. The game was close – the best for years – and kept the 43,090 spectators on their toes. An early Limerick goal by Éamonn Cregan set the Shannonsiders on their way, and they led by 1-7 to 1-4 at the interval. Goals from Éamonn O'Donoghue and Seánie O'Leary kept the Rebels in contention, but the vital score was Ollie O'Connor's goal from a Donal Murray pass. Cork had lost their captain, Dermot McCurtain, through injury midway through the second half. For all its fire and fury, this was an exemplary exhibition of all-out sporting endeavour. The final score was Limerick 2-14, Cork 2-10.

Opposite bottom left: Match programme from the Tipperary county hurling final 1980.
Opposite bottom right: Roscrea, Tipperary Senior Hurling Champions 1980. Back row (l–r): John Stone, Kevin O'Connor, Ger O'Connor, Joe Rowland, Philip Ward, Jody Spooner, Brendan Maher, Liam Spooner, Willie O'Reilly. Front row (l–r): Tadhg O'Connor, Peadar Queally, Michael 'Jackie' Shanahan, Kevin Brady (captain), Joe Butler, Joe Tynan, Francis Loughnane.

1980
A Last Gasp for Roscrea: Tipperary Senior Hurling Final

It took a last-minute goal by inter-county veteran Roger Ryan to secure Roscrea's first Tipperary title since 1973. Goals from Francis Loughnane and John Stone had them ahead by 2-8 to 2-6 at the break, while both of Kilruane's goals came from Éamonn O'Shea. Close exchanges, goalmouth thrills and determined hurling kept the spectators enthralled. Kilruane fought back, levelled and went ahead by four points. However three from Loughnane had Ros well in the shakeup when Tynan passed to substitute Roger Ryan for the killer blow. The final score was Roscrea 3-11, Kilruane MacDonaghs 2-13.

1981
Centenary All-Ireland for Semple Stadium

At the annual GAA Congress, held in the Gleneagle Hotel, Killarney, on 29 March, a motion calling for the amendment of the appropriate rule to allow the 1984 All-Ireland hurling final to be played at Semple Stadium, Thurles, was unanimously adopted.

1981
O'Grady Captains Rebels to Glory: National Hurling League Final

Cork, captained by Donal O'Grady, defeated Offaly in the 1980/1981 National Hurling League final at Semple Stadium on 3 May. The final score was Cork 3-11, Offaly 2-8.

The scorers for Cork were Jimmy Barry-Murphy (2-1), Tim Crowley (1-0), Padraig Crowley (0-4), Éamonn O'Donoghue (0-2), John Horgan (0-2), Seánie O'Leary (0-1) and Dermot McCurtain (0-1); and for Offaly, Padraig Horan (1-2), Mark Corrigan (1-1), Pat Delaney (0-2), Brendan Bermingham (0-1), Danny Owens (0-1) and Pat Carroll (0-1).

Above left: Match programme for the National Hurling League Final 1981.
Above right: Cork's long-serving goalkeeper Ger Cunningham. Photo by Ray McManus, Sportsfile.

Their Elysian Field

Cork's Kevin Cashman recalled the atmosphere in Thurles on match days:

Thurles is the capital of hurling. Drinking your pint on a Thurles pavement after a lively match on a sunny Sunday, the doings of Mackey, Clohessy, the Doyles, John Keane, Jimmy Smyth, Seán Óg and Ring become as real and immediate as what you've just witnessed. If you sat quietly on the remains of the old bank at twilight you could picture Ring or Tommy Daly or Ted Sullivan or Purcell or Mackey or many another limbering up below you, maybe noting the changes or having a joust or two for old times' sake. This is their Elysian field and the turf and the grass and even the steel and concrete of this place are the keepers of their youth and the youth of all of us, who shaped them.

The pubs of Thurles on a big match day have something that no other pubs can give. It has been called 'atmosphere', 'bond', 'fraternity' and much more – it's magic in the air.

Kevin Cashman, *Magill*, July 1981 (Munster Hurling Final programme 1982)

Ballyhale Shamrocks, All-Ireland Club Champions 1981. Back row (l–r): Kevin Fennelly, Frank Holohan, Seán Walsh, Pat Holden, Seán Fennelly, Maurice Mason, Michael Fennelly, Liam Dalton. Front row (l–r): Liam Fennelly, Ger Fennelly, Declan Connolly, Richie Reid (captain), Mick Kelly, Brendan Fennelly, Wattie Phelan.

1981
A First for Ballyhale: All-Ireland Club Hurling Final

May 17 is a day well remembered in south Kilkenny, as on that day Ballyhale Shamrocks, captained by Richie Reid, won their first All-Ireland club final against Cork and Munster champions St Finbarr's in Semple Stadium. All their scoring came from the Fennelly brothers, Brendan (0-11), Liam (1-1) and Ger (0-3). The final score was Ballyhale Shamrocks (Kilkenny) 1-15, St Finbarr's (Cork) 1-11.

Limerick's star goalkeeper Tommy Quaid. Photo by Sportsfile.

1981
McKenna Hat Trick Sinks Banner: Munster Senior Hurling Final

Clare had beaten Waterford and highly rated league champions Cork to earn a place in the Munster final at Semple Stadium on 5 July. Their opponents Limerick, meanwhile, had accounted for Tipperary in a replayed semi-final. This was an absorbing and excellent game before an attendance of 40,205. Star of the show was Limerick's full-forward Joe McKenna, whose hat trick of goals ensured that the title stayed Shannonside for another year. The final score was Limerick 3-12, Clare 2-9.

Limerick: Tommy Quaid, Paudie Fitzmaurice (captain), Leonard Enright, Pat Herbert, Liam O'Donoghue, Sean Foley, Dom Punch, Mike Grimes, Jimmy Carroll, Paddy Kelly, John Flanagan, Brian Carroll, Ollie O'Connor, Joe McKenna, Éamonn Cregan. Substitute played: Willie Fitzmaurice.

1981
Borris Back from the Cold: Tipperary Senior Hurling Final

Noel O'Dwyer gave a brilliant display for Borris/Ileigh, ably assisted by Bobby Ryan, Owen Walsh and T F Stapleton, as they captured the Dan Breen Cup after twenty-eight barren years at Semple Stadium on 25 October. Roscrea got off to a poor start, conceding a soft goal, and they were behind at the interval, 1-9 to 0-5. Roscrea had fine performances from Brendan Maher and Joe Tynan, but it was Borris/Ileigh's day as they extended their lead, finishing ahead by 1-14 to 0-12.

Seamus J King, in the 2009 Tipperary hurling final progamme, wrote about the origins of the Borris mascot, a bantam cock:

Borris/Ileigh's lucky mascot, seen here in the care of Paddy Dolan at the Tipperary county final.

The cock is synonymous with the Borris/Ileigh club and occupies a prominent place on the club crest. There are a number of stories as to its origin. One is that on achieving unity in 1948 the Borris and Ileigh players were so proud that they would strut confidently, regardless of the opposition, onto the playing field like bantam cocks. Others point to a much older origin to the days of the faction fights. In the glory days of the early fifties Paddy D'Arcy of Ileigh used to sell the team colours on match days and he used to have as his 'assistant' the cock, resplendently dressed up in the club colours.

1982
Double Your Money

The County Tipperary GAA Centenary Commemoration and Development Committee announced details of Double Your Money, a major fundraising initiative for the completion of Semple Stadium. Investors would put forward £100 and receive back double at any time within a ten-year period, depending on the luck of the draw. The committee sought 5,000 investment units to clear the debt and enable completion of Phase 2. These units would be repaid over ten years: 250 per year for the first four years, then 500 annually for a further four years, and 1,000 per year for the final two years.

Present at the launch of the Double Your Money investment scheme were Séamus Ó Riain (former GAA Uachtarán), John Lanigan (treasurer, Semple Stadium), Fr Pierce Duggan (chairman, Semple Stadium), Tomás Ó Baróid (Tipperary GAA secretary) and Liz Howard (PRO, Tipperary GAA).

The County Tipperary GAA Centenary Commemoration and Development Committee and guests pictured at Semple Stadium in 1981. Back row (l–r): John Dowling, Séamus O'Riain, Gerry Long, Tom Kirby, Tim Maher, Phil O'Shea, Tom O'Hara, Tommy Murphy, ---. Third row (l–r): Tommy Barrett, Seán Mockler, Martin O'Connor, Mick Maguire, George Ryan, John Fleming, John Ryan, John Kehoe. Second row (l–r): P J Ryan, Liz Howard, Donal Whelan, Padraig Mac Floinn (GAA president), Donal O'Sullivan (Munster Council), Liam Mulvihill (GAA director general), Fr Pierce Duggan, Michael Maher. Front row (l–r): Liam O'Dwyer, James O'Leary, Paddy Maher, Noel Morris.

1982
So Easy for the Rebels: Munster Senior Hurling Final

The Déise accounted for Munster champions Limerick in the semi-final, and, for the first time since 1966, were back in a Munster final. But their opponents, Cork, with Jimmy Barry-Murphy at the helm, gave a classic exhibition of hurling which completely outclassed Waterford at Semple Stadium on 18 July. Munster Council collected a record gate of £135,038 from an attendance of 38,558. The final score was Cork 5-31, Waterford 3-6.

1982
Farewell to Mick Mackey

Mick Mackey of Ahane and Limerick, who died on 13 September, 1982, is seen by many as the greatest centre-forward of all time. Born in Castleconnell, Mick played for Limerick from 1930 until 1947, winning three senior All-Ireland medals and a host of other honours. He combined skill and strength perfectly, and his famous solo runs from centre-forward were devastating, tearing defences to ribbons.

Mackey's many tussles with John Maher of Thurles Sarsfields and Tipperary, whether at club or county level, were the stuff of legend. Recalling Mackey's hurling prowess, John said,

Mick had a great side-step. Once he took possession, he was fast on his feet; he'd run in a crouched position; you couldn't shift him with a tackle. If the occasion required, then he was prepared to take you on, go straight for you. He was the toughest centre-forward of all to keep in check. I put him before Christy Ring. I would regard him as a much more dangerous player altogether.

Ah, bitter death, our hero you have claimed,
And rent the heart of every hurling man
With savage grief. But still the glorious name
Of Mackey will defy your rapacious hand!
Br Dáithí Fitzgerald, Doon,
from Smyth, *In Praise of Heroes*

1983

League Title Stays Noreside: National Hurling League Final

The final score at Semple Stadium on 24 April, 1983, was Kilkenny 2-14, Limerick 2-12, making the Cats National Hurling League champions 1982/1983. Back row (l–r): Dick O'Hara, Frank Cummins, Christy Heffernan, Paddy Prendergast, Seán Fennelly, Billy Fitzpatrick, John Henderson. Front row (l–r): Ger Fennelly, Paddy Neary, Noel Skehan, Ger Henderson, Liam Fennelly (captain), Harry Ryan, Richie Power, Nickey Brennan.

1983

Stadium Gets Green Light

After months of controversy and doubt, GAA president Paddy Buggy finally gave the green light to the completion of Phase 2 of the development of Semple Stadium at the Tipperary county convention in Clonmel on 30 January. The Double Your Money fund-raising campaign was proving successful, with the sum of £400,000 collected by September.

In December, it was agreed that the Town End terrace would be named the Davin Terrace, in memory of Maurice Davin, Deerpark, Carrick-on-Suir, a GAA founder and its first president.

Staging the Centenary

Six sub-committees were set up to plan the facilities and events of centenary year. Their chairmen were: Press and Communications, Liam Ó Donnchú; Accommodation, Martin O'Connor; Museum, William Corbett; All-Ireland Festival, Michael Maher/ Tomás Ó Baróid; Traffic and Transport, Michael Lowry; Stewarding, Matt Hassett.

A fine aerial view of Semple Stadium, taken in 1983.

Manning the GAA centenary celebrations. Back row (l–r): Liam Ó Donnchú, Tom O'Hara (secretary), Martin O'Connor, William Corbett, Tomás Ó Baróid. Front row (l–r): Michael Lowry, Fr Pierce Duggan, Michael Maher.

GAA patron Archbishop Thomas Morris blessing Semple Stadium prior to its official opening. Also included are Declan O'Rourke (altar server), Brendan Vaughan (Munster Council chairman), Fr Pierce Duggan (chairman, Centenary and Development Committee), Liam Ó Maolmhichíl (Árd-Sriúrtheoir, CLG).

1984
Reopening Semple

The new-look Semple Stadium was officially opened on 31 May. The Killinan End was now terraced, as was the Town End (Davin Terrace), and the sideline capacity was now 3,000; altogether, the stadium could accommodate 65,000 spectators. Following the improvements to the stadium, the local development committee was left with an outstanding debt of over £1.28 million.

Above right: Dean Christopher Lee blesses a plaque to the memory of Maurice Davin (above left) at Semple Stadium on 30 May 1984. Also present were Pádraic Dundon (altar server), Séamus Ó Riain (former GAA president), Tom O'Hara (secretary), John Lanigan (treasurer) and Pat Buckeridge.

Cúl Ó Daimhín

The founder and first president of the GAA, Maurice Davin, was honoured during centenary year with the naming of the Town End of the grounds as Cúl Ó Daimhín.

Right: This plaque at the Nenagh Road entrance to Semple Stadium, completed in 1984, notes major dates in the development of the stadium and bears the GAA centenary crest and a mural of the four provinces.

1984

Kelly Superb for Shannonsiders: National Hurling League Final

Wexford failed to match the pace, power and punch of this Limerick side, who led from the start at Semple Stadium on 8 April. Half-forward Paddy Kelly displayed superb accuracy, notching twelve points. The final score was Limerick 3-16, Wexford 1-9. Attendance at Semple Stadium on the day was 19,436.

Right: Liam O'Donoghue of Limerick.
Photo by Ray McManus, Sportsfile.

1984

Carnival Atmosphere

Mícheál Ó hEithir recalls the atmosphere at Semple Stadium on the day of the centenary Munster final:

I'll never forget the unbelievable atmosphere in the revamped Semple Stadium for the Cork/Tipperary Munster hurling final. It was the first meeting of these two great rivals in a final for fourteen years and they hadn't clashed in a Thurles final since 1960. Added excitement came from Tipperary's burning desire to win this very special final because of the year that was in it and because here it was being played in the town that likes to be known as the cradle of the GAA.

Next there was the extraordinary staging of the All-Ireland final at Semple Stadium against the wishes of many people

including, at one period, leading officials of the Association. That was an exhilarating week-end of carnival atmosphere in the town of Thurles.

It was a triumph in particular for Tipperary GAA and all the locals associated with it, and in general for the GAA itself, who put so much energy into the whole weekend once the irrevocable decision that the match should go to Thurles was made.

Michael O'Hehir, *My Life and Times* (1996)

Above left: Match programme for the Munster hurling final 1984.
Above right: Tipperary, Munster Senior Hurling Finalists 1984. Back row (l–r): Donie O'Connell, Michael Doyle, Pat Fitzelle, Pat Sheedy, Jack Bergin, Noel O'Dwyer, Jim Keogh, John McIntyre. Front row (l–r): Ralph Callaghan, Dinny Cahill, Philip Kennedy, Bobby Ryan (captain), Seamus Power, Liam Maher, Nicky English.
Left: Tipperary captain Bobby Ryan.

1984

The Agony and the Ecstasy: Munster Senior Hurling Final

Over 50,000 thronged into Semple Stadium for the Munster final between Tipperary and Cork on 15 July. The gate receipts of £186,647 set an all-time record. Tipperary supporters were in the majority, and they arrived with confidence of success. The hurling was superb, the atmosphere electric, the sportsmanship excellent – all in all, the occasion was comparable to anything ever seen at this level.

In the end the expectation, the preparation, the hoping and the wishing weren't enough for Tipperary, and the ecstatic supporters saw a four-point lead astonishingly transformed into a four-point deficit in the final minutes of a tantalising contest. The final score was Cork 4-15, Tipperary 3-14. Raymond Smith, writing in the *Tipperary GAA Centenary Yearbook*, recalled,

> It burned into the very marrow of our bones. And without ever having to play the video of those last dramatic final minutes over again, they will remain etched in my mind – as I remember the way Munster battles in the fifties were lost against Cork and Christy Ring by the break of a ball or the cruel operation of the advantage rule.

In an interview for *Hogan Stand* many years later, captain Bobby Ryan said:

> Until the day I die I'll never forget the whole day. I was captain at twenty-three, the final was in Thurles, it was the GAA's centenary year and I had the world at my feet. Cork were red-hot favourites, but we hurled magnificently on the day until we were caught at the end. We should have won. It was such a bizarre defeat and a dreadful disappointment.

Tipperary's John McIntyre (pictured) had plenty of other things on his mind:

> It's the single greatest regret of my hurling life and it gets worse as time goes on. It seems mad now but I went out that evening and played a challenge for my club against Holycross. Then I made a

dash home to watch the match on *The Sunday Game*. And the next morning I was up at seven o clock to draw in hay. Whatever about the Munster final, the bales still had to be brought into the hayshed. I got no special dispensation.

Éamonn Sweeney, 'Motivated by memories of failure', *Irish Independent*, 27 June, 2004

Eudie Coughlan, the Oldest Living Captain

As part of the centenary celebrations, all living former All-Ireland winning captains were given a special introduction prior to the hurling final on 2 September. Spectators took to their feet as they witnessed some of the greatest hurlers in the history of the game take to the field. Among these was the oldest surviving captain, Eudie Coughlan of Cork. In this photograph, he receives a special presentation from GAA president Paddy Buggy. Veteran match commentator Mícheál Ó hEithir is in the background.

In the *Tipperary GAA Centenary Yearbook*, Séamus Leahy described the scene:

When Eudie raised his hand in acknowledgement of the applause, I thought of *Oisín i ndiaidh na Féinne*, and in my mind's eye, I saw comrades and opponents of his. If the ghost of Tom Semple was keeping an eye on the crowd, then the ghosts of Seán Óg Murphy and of Jim Hurley, of Lory Meagher and Matty Power, of Martin Kennedy and Mick Darcy and hosts of others in red and white, and black and amber, and blue and gold, were there with the old Rockie, acknowledging the applause with him, nodding with pleasure to see that Thurles is as it was – the home of hurling men.

Top: Aerial view of Semple Stadium during the 1984 centenary All-Ireland hurling final.
Above: Cork, All-Ireland Senior Hurling Champions 1984. Panel: Donal O'Grady, Tomás Mulcahy,
Tim Crowley, Kevin Hennessy, Ger Cunningham, Jimmy Barry-Murphy, John Crowley, Tony
O'Sullivan, Denis Mulcahy, Dermot McCurtain, Tom Cashman, John Fenton (captain), John Hodgins,
Pat Hartnett, Seánie O'Leary, Ger Power, John Blake, Pat Horgan, John Buckley, Denis Walsh, Bertie
Óg Murphy, John Harnett. Photo by Ray McManus, Sportsfile.

Top: Cork captain John Fenton holds the Liam McCarthy Cup, having received it from GAA president Paddy Buggy. Photo by Ray McManus, Sportsfile.

Above left: Match programme for the day's events.

Above right: Mícheál Ó hEithir signing autographs.

1984

Minors Hectic but Seniors an Anti-Climax: All-Ireland Hurling Finals

A dream came to fruition with the playing of the GAA centenary All-Ireland hurling finals at a packed Semple Stadium on 2 September, 1984. The minor match between Limerick and Kilkenny ended in a draw, 1-14 to 3-8. With less than a minute remaining, Kilkenny scored a goal to put them one point ahead. The final seconds were hectic, with Limerick barely having time to equalise. But equalise they did, and they went on to win the replay at the same venue, by 2-5 to 2-4, in another classic game. Paddy Downey, in *The Irish Times*, summed up the general feeling when he wrote, 'It is probably true to say that there never has been a better minor All-Ireland final.'

The senior final between Cork and Offaly, meanwhile, turned out to be an anti-climax largely because Cork were so dominant. The first half saw the Rebels slow to settle, leading by just two points at the break. But they found their form after the resumption and coasted to victory. Captained by John Fenton, they won by 3-16 to 1-12. The attendance on the day was 59,814. The legendary broadcaster of Gaelic games, Mícheál Ó hEithir, in his book *My Life and Times*, commented,

This was a stirring occasion, superbly and efficiently organised despite the doubting Thomases, who had predicted chaos. It was a great day to be in Semple Stadium.

Finest Hurling Pitch in the GAA

Here we see stadium groundsman Jim Hickey checking the nets prior to the centenary All-Ireland finals. The pitch at Semple Stadium was in pristine condition for all the major matches played during centenary year. The groundstaff of Hickey, Tommy Max and Bobby Mockler were lavishly praised. There was praise too for the organisers of the centenary celebrations led by Fr Pierce Duggan (chairman), Tom O'Hara (secretary) and John Lanigan (treasurer), and the countless volunteer workers who had undertaken such a mammoth task.

1984
New Handball Court Opened

The official opening of the new handball court at Semple Stadium was performed by Tommy O'Brien, President of the Irish Handball Council. The new complex – which cost £50,000 and was equipped with a 60 × 30 court, spacious dressing rooms and all the expected modern facilities – was blessed by Most Rev Dr Thomas Morris, Archbishop of Cashel and Emly. Two years previously, Thurles Handball Club had been revived under Paddy Barry as chairman, Joe Fitzgerald as secretary, Willie Kelly as treasurer, and Pat McKenna, Childers Park, as PRO.

1984
Moycarkey/Borris, Centenary Champions: Tipperary Senior Hurling Final

Lorrha/Dorrha made all the early running in the county final at Semple Stadium on 21 October and led by 0-6 to 0-4 at the interval. As the game entered the final quarter, Lorrha were still ahead, but two goals in the space of four minutes tipped the scales in Moycarkey's favour. Ned Slattery got the first, and veteran John Flanagan notched the second. These decisive scores gave the Mid men, captained by Jack Bergin, victory by 2-8 to 0-9.

Above left: Match programme for the Tipperary hurling final 1984.
Above right: Moycarkey/Borris, Tipperary Senior Hurling Champions 1984. Back row (l–r): Willie Ryan, Jim Bergin, Jim Flanagan, Tommy Quigley, Tom Mullins, Jimmy Leahy, Ned Slattery, John Hackett, Tom Doran, Robert Hayes, Liam Dempsey, John McCormack, Liam Hackett, Mícheál Clohessy, Matty Bourke, Michael Fanning. Front row (l–r): Michael McKenna, Declan Kirwan, Liam Bergin, Timmy Cullagh, Jack Bergin (captain), Robert Doran (mascot), John Flanagan, Eamon Darmody, Dick Quigley, Tommy Noonan, Billy Fogarty, David Fogarty.

They'll hear of how in eighty-four
We won the 'county' yet once more,
With Bergin leading from centre-back
And Tobin throwing away his cap.

'The Jockey' by Liam Ó Donnchú,
from King, Ó Donnchú, Smyth, *Tipperary's GAA Ballads*

1984

A First for Sixmilebridge: Munster Senior Club Hurling Final

Sixmilebridge showed good form right through the championship, especially in the Munster final, where they had a convincing ten-point victory over Limerick's Patrickswell. The final score was Sixmilebridge 4-10, Patrickswell 2-6.

1984

Semple Stadium Caretaker Jimmy Purcell

Following the centenary All-Ireland hurling final, Jim Hickey retired from his position as groundsman at Semple Stadium. Jimmy Purcell, a native of Loughmore/Castleiney, was appointed in his place. Jimmy (pictured top) set a high standard in field management; working with Bobby Mockler and with guidance from pitch advisor Mick Carroll, Semple Stadium held its place as hurling's best playing surface.

In the bottom photograph, Bobby Mockler, former full-back with Thurles Sarsfields, keeps a close eye on his well-manicured stadium. A quiet-spoken, thoughtful man, he never spared himself when it came to his work. His much quoted saying was, 'The field should look down on the stadium'. Bobby believed that if the pitch was in perfect condition, other things were of secondary importance.

Nicky English in top form. Photo by Sportsfile.

1985
English Goals Herald Munster Glory: Railway Cup Hurling Final

The Railway Cup Interprovincial hurling final was played at Semple Stadium on 18 March. The game only came to life in the final quarter. At that stage, Connacht had stretched their lead to ten points, but two goals from Nicky English heralded a Munster rally. Tomás Mulcahy's goal levelled matters with five minutes remaining, and Kevin Hennessy added the winning point. Munster, captained by Cork's Ger Cunningham, defeated Connacht by 3-6 to 1-11.

Munster: Ger Cunningham (Cork, captain), Seán Hehir (Clare), Leonard Enright (Limerick), Pat Herbert (Limerick), Tom Cashman (Cork), Seán Stack (Clare), Dermot McCurtain (Cork), Jimmy Carroll (Limerick), Pat Hartnett (Cork), Nicky English (Tipperary), Donie O'Connell (Tipperary), John Fenton (Cork), Tomás Mulcahy (Cork), Kevin Hennessy (Cork), Tony O'Sullivan (Cork). Substitutes: John Callinan (Clare), Seamus Power (Tipperary), Bobby Ryan (Tipperary), Pat Ryan (Waterford), Paddy Kelly (Limerick), Gerry McInerney (Clare), Tommy Quaid (Limerick), Ollie O'Connor (Limerick), Denis Mulcahy (Cork), D J Leahy (Kerry).

1985

Limerick, National League Champions Again

Limerick achieved a second league title in a row when Leonard Enright (pictured) led them to a decisive 3-12 to 1-7 victory over neighbours Clare on 14 April.

Above left: Match programme for the county hurling final 1985.
Above right: Kilruane MacDonaghs, Tipperary Senior Hurling Champions 1985. Back row (l–r):
Ed Fogarty (masseur), Paddy Williams, Séamus Gibson, John Cahill, Enda Hogan, Dinny O'Meara,
Éamonn O'Shea, Jim Williams. Front row (l–r): Dinny Cahill, Gilbert Williams, Jim O'Meara,
Michael Hogan, Tony Sheppard (captain), Séamus Hennessy, Gerry Williams, Philip Quinlan.

1985

MacDonaghs on the Rise: Tipperary Senior Hurling Final

Over 10,000 attended the county hurling final at Semple Stadium on 13 October. It was an all north Tipperary affair as Kilruane MacDonaghs defeated Roscrea by 2-11 to 0-10. Roscrea dictated the trend of play in the first period and led at the break by 0-8 to 0-4, but MacDonaghs thundered into the game after the interval, taking the bit between their teeth. Emotions ran high as Pat Quinlan shot them into the lead with a goal in the fifty-first minute. Two minutes later, Éamonn O'Shea added another, and the title was on its way back to Cloughjordan. This team went on to win Munster and All-Ireland titles.

1985
Lowry Foresees Féile

Following the development of the stadium, Tipperary GAA were left with a crippling debt. Chairman Michael Lowry, in his address to the county convention, stated,

We must accept that in these difficult economic times, our traditional supporter is hard pressed. We have to realise that the young people of today are the ones with excess money to spend. The power of music and show-business is mighty …We must set aside our conservatism, move with the times without sacrificing our principles. We should organise a major annual event to attract and entertain the youth of the nation.

1986
Holohan Captains 'Cats' to Success: Ford National Hurling League Final

The final score at Semple Stadium on 11 May was Kilkenny 2-10, Galway 2-6, making Kilkenny the National Hurling League Champions 1985/1986. Back row (l–r): Paddy Prendergast, Christy Heffernan, Joe O'Hara, Richie Power, Ger Henderson, Seán Fennelly, John Henderson, Kevin Fennelly. Front row (l–r): Lester Ryan, Kieran Brennan, Pat Walsh, Joe Hennessy, Ger Fennelly, Frank Holohan (captain), Liam Fennelly.

1986
The Tribesmen Book Croke Park Spot:
All-Ireland Senior Hurling Semi-Final

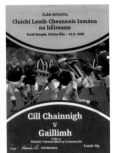

Galway were convincing winners over Kilkenny at Semple Stadium on 10 August. Goals win matches, and Galway got four. Two goals from Joe Cooney and one each by Anthony Cunninghan and Noel Lane made all the difference. Final score: Galway 4-12, Kilkenny 0-13.

1986
The Title Goes West: Under 21 All-Ireland Hurling Final

On 14 September, Galway, captained by Anthony Cunningham, won the championship following a 0-14 to 2-5 defeat of Wexford in the final at Semple Stadium. This was their fourth All-Ireland title in the Under 21 grade.

Galway star forward Joe Cooney. Photo by Ray McManus, Sportsfile.

Galway, All-Ireland Under 21 Champions 1986. Back row (l–r): Pat Higgins, Michael Helebert, Patrick Dervan, Michael Connolly, John Commins, Martin Kelly, Declan Jennings, Pat Nolan. Front row (l–r): Aodh Davoren, Michael Flaherty, Joe Cooney, Pat Malone, Anthony Cunningham, Gerry McInerney, Tom Monaghan.

1986

Cork Take Three in a Row: All-Ireland Under 21 Football Final

On 14 September at Semple Stadium, Cork won the Under 21 football championship following a 3-16 to 0-12 defeat of Offaly in the final. This was their seventh All-Ireland title overall and their third in successive seasons.

Cork: Jerome O'Mahony, Kevin Scanlon, John Murphy, Denis Walsh, Michael Slocum (captain), Brendan Stack, Tony Griffin, Paddy Hayes, Teddy McCarthy, Con O'Connell, Michael McCarthy, Barry Coffey, Paddy Harrington, John O'Driscoll, Paul McGrath.

1987

Croke Cup Crosses the Shannon: National Hurling League Final

On 3 May, 1987, Galway, captained by Conor Hayes, won the National Hurling League title following a 3-12 to 3-10 win over Clare in the final at Semple Stadium. The scorers for Galway were Joe Cooney (2-6), Anthony Cunningham (1-1), Eanna Ryan (0-2), Brendan Lynskey (0-1), Martin Naughton (0-1) and Michael McGrath (0-1); and for Clare, Cyril Lyons (0-7), Tommy Guilfoyle (1-0), Gerry McInerney (1-0), Syl Dolan (1-0) and Michael Guilfoyle (0-3).

Galway: Peter Murphy, Sylvie Linnane, Conor Hayes (captain), Pearse Piggott, Ollie Kilkenny, Tony Keady, Tony Kilkenny, Michael Coleman, Steve Mahon, Michael McGrath,

Conor Hayes, Galway captain and full-back.
Photo by Sportsfile.

Joe Cooney, Michael Naughton, Eanna Ryan, Brendan Lynskey, Anthony Cunningham. Substitutes played: Noel Lane, Michael Coen.

1987
Fenton's Wonder Goal:
Munster Senior Hurling Semi-Final

Semple Stadium on 28 June was the venue for the replayed Munster semi-final between Cork and Limerick. The sides had played a fairly thrilling 3-11 apiece draw at the same venue two weeks earlier. Cork ran out easy winners in the replay, 3-14 to 0-10, but it was one goal – one moment of sheer hurling magic – that caused this game to live on in memory. A loose ball around midfield was won by Tomás Mulcahy, and he sent it in the general direction of Cork midfielder John Fenton. The Midleton man flicked the ball forward to open space, sized it up and absolutely hammered it to the net past Tommy Quaid, some fifty metres away. It is rated by many as the goal of the century.

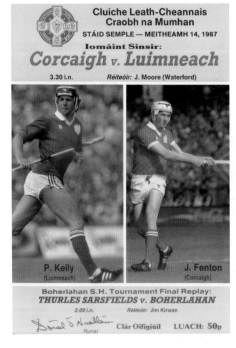

Cluiche Leath-Cheannais
Craobh na Mumhan
STÁID SEMPLE — MEITHEAMH 14, 1987
Iomáint Sinsir:
Corcaigh v. Luimneach
3.30 i.n.   Réiteóir: J. Moore (Waterford)

P. Kelly
(Luimneach)
J. Fenton
(Corcaigh)

Boherlahan S.H. Tournament Final Replay:
THURLES SARSFIELDS v. BOHERLAHAN
2.00 i.n.   Réiteóir: Jim Kirwan
Rúnaí   Clár Oifigiúil   LUACH: **50p**

1987
Nicky's Moment of Genius: Munster Senior Hurling Final

The Munster final between Tipperary and Cork was at Semple Stadium on 12 July. This was seen as D-Day for Tipperary hurling, as Cork were heading for six in a row in Munster. The official attendance was 56,005 – several thousand more gained free admission. By the time referee Terence Murray threw in the ball, there were possibly over 60,000 packed in. Liberty Square that morning was the place to be, as thousands arrived and savoured the banter and good-humoured atmosphere typical of Thurles on

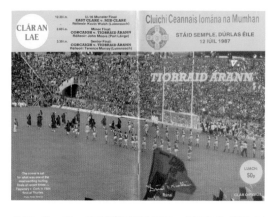

big match days. This game had everything for the hurling enthusiast, and Tipperary displayed their superiority, leading by 0-11 to 0-7 at the interval. The remaining half was a classic, ending 1-18 aside. Two late Pat Fox points grabbed a draw for Tipperary, but all agreed that Nicky English's kicked goal was the highlight of the classic contest. As he described it himself,

Well Joe Hayes's pass from midfield carried a lot further than either myself or Richard Browne (Cork) anticipated. As the ball came over our heads, I realised that – if he missed it – I'd have a big advantage on him. And that's exactly what happened. Richard failed to reach the ball and, in a split second, I was clean through behind the full-back line with only Ger Cunningham to beat.

Just one snag. I arrived in there without my hurley. 'Jesus, I thought. The one good ball I get all day and I have no hurley. What in the name of God am I going to do here?'

As I closed in on Cunningham's goal, the sliothar at my feet, I honestly hadn't a clue what I was going to do next … Cunningham had started to advance a little bit. So effectively, I was left with no real option but to have a go. 'I'll just have to try to flick it past him', I thought.

To this day, I still can't believe what the ball did. It actually swerved around him, just like you would kick a soccer ball from left to right.

'The Maradona goal' – as they called it – was down to luck.

Beyond the Tunnel: The Nicky English Story with Vincent Hogan (1996)

The replay at Fitzgerald Stadium, Killarney, saw Tipperary take the Munster title 4-22 to Cork's 1-22. On accepting the cup at the end of the game, Tipperary captain Richard Stakelum gave his famous 'The famine is over' speech.

Opposite page: Match programme for the Munster final 1987.
Top right: Nicky English awaits the next ball in the 1987 Munster final.
Middle left: Aerial action from the Munster final as Cork's Teddy McCarthy reaches highest. Also included are Joe Hayes, John Kennedy and Colm Bonnar (Tipperary). Photo courtesy of the Irish Examiner *Archive.*
Bottom right: Nicky English. Photo by Sportsfile.
Bottom left: The agony and the ecstasy following Nicky English's 'Maradona goal'.

Cappawhite, Tipperary Senior Hurling Champions 1987. Back row (l–r): Noel Buckley, Ger O'Neill, Tom Coughlan, Simon Ryan (L), Johnny Ryan (P), Conor Ryan (H), Ger Ryan (B), Danny O'Neill, Michael Ryan (L), Anthony O'Neill, John Barry. Front row (l–r): Austin Buckley, Paul Buckley, Pa O'Neill, Michael Buckley, John O'Neill, Martin McDermott, Mylie Coughlan, Deasún Hennessy, Dan Ryan (P), Eamon Ryan (B), Dick Quirke.

1987
Cappawhite Thriller: Tipperary Senior Hurling Final

The centenary county hurling final took place at Semple Stadium on 1 November. Neither side had ever won a title before. In the last ten minutes of the first half, a Martin McDermott goal gave Cappawhite a much-needed boost, and by half-time the score stood at Loughmore/Castleiney 1-8, Cappawhite 1-6. As the game entered the final quarter, only one point separated the teams. Loughmore added two further points to go a goal up. The West men surged back for three points without reply, to level the game with eight minutes to play. Loughmore edged in front again, but Pa O'Neill levelled. Ger O'Neill collected a Mike Buckley clearance and progressed down the right wing. Austin Buckley raced to shadow him and linked up for the vital pass, which he shot straight and true to put Cappawhite in the lead. They were champions for the first time ever, in the hundreth county final.

Arise, arise, your hurleys take,

The west's awake, the west's awake,

Rejoice, rejoice, your banners shake,

Sing loud and long for Cappa's sake.

Br Joseph Perkins, from King, Ó Donnchú, Smyth, *Tipperary's GAA Ballads*

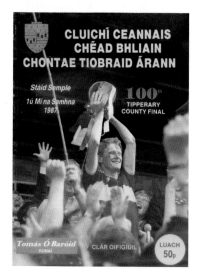

1987

One Hundred County Finals

On the day of the centenary final, the first ever county final, in 1887, was recalled. In that game, Thurles easily defeated North Tipperary. Now one hundred years later, John Hassett, a native of Ballytarsna and a Thurles resident, drove a horse and trap from Hayes's Hotel to the stadium. The pony's name was Tubberadora, and the trap dated from the 1880s. His passengers were John Walshe of Tubberadora, son of the famous Johnny; Michael Wallace of Ardmayle; and John Maher of Killinan, son of Dinny Maher, who captained the county champions a century before. Michael Lowry, Tipperary GAA chairman, also travelled in the trap.

1988
Personnel Changes at Semple Stadium

Changes on the board of Semple Stadium Development Committee were the order of the day at the 1988 annual general meeting, as chairman Fr Pierce Duggan and secretary Tom O'Hara did not seek re-election. Both had served the committee with dedication and distinction, and their leadership in the redevelopment of Semple Stadium and the organisation of the centenary All-Irelands was unequalled. The tireless work of John Lanigan, who continued as treasurer, was equal to that of his two retiring colleagues. The newly elected chairman was Michael Lowry of Holycross/Ballycahill (pictured), who had recently completed his term as Tipperary GAA chairman. Tackling the huge debt on the stadium was given top priority, and the possibility of using the facility as a concert venue was gaining support.

Opposite page, bottom: Loughmore/Castleiney, Tipperary Senior Hurling Champions 1988. Back row (l–r): Jackie Walsh (coach), Ned Ryan, Jim Maher, Pat Cormack, Pat McGrath, John Cormack, Peter Brennan, Pat Treacy. Front row (l–r): Tom McGrath, Frankie McGrath, Liam Cormack, Eamon Sweeney, Michael McGrath, Eamon Brennan, Seamus Bohan, Tom Larkin.

1988
A Thrilling End for Loughmore: Tipperary Senior Hurling Final

In damp conditions, on 2 October at Semple Stadium, this final between Loughmore/Castleiney and Borris/Ileigh developed into an intense but scrappy encounter. The first half was undistinguished except for a great goal by Seamus Bohan two minutes from half-time, which gave Loughmore/Castleiney a 1-3 to 0-3 lead at the interval. Borris/Ileigh played their best hurling in the third quarter and went into the lead. Loughmore came back into the game and went two points ahead, but points by Noel O'Dwyer and Conor Stakelum brought the sides level with six minutes to go, and that's how it finished: 1-6 to 0-9. The replay was fixed for six days later, 8 October.

The replay will be remembered for its sensational ending. With two minutes to go, Borris/Ileigh seemed a certainty; they were two points up and set for victory. But Loughmore/Castleiney kept plugging away. The ball was making its tortuous progress along the Kinane Stand side of the field. At the far side, Pat McGrath was following its progress and staying parallel. When Liam Cormack's shot was blocked out by Noelie Maher, McGrath was present to slap home an all-important goal. Michael McGrath shot another point from the puck-out, and a devastated Borris/Ileigh were left without time to redress the situation.

Young boys were seen in red and green and cheered with sheer delight;

And ladies fair, without a care, danced 'round the fires that night.

But old men wept as they homewards crept and thought of days of yore,

Of many a son, who played and won, with Castleiney and Loughmore.

Br Joseph Perkins, from King, Ó Donnchú, Smyth, *Tipperary's GAA Ballads*

1988

First Title for 'The Well': Munster Senior Club Hurling Final

Patrickswell of Limerick took their first ever Munster club title at Semple Stadium on 4 December, 1988, after defeating Waterford's Mount Sion. The final score was Patrickswell 3-13, Mount Sion 2-13.

Patrickswell: Joe Murphy, Philip Foley, Leonard Enright, Paul Foley, Dave Punch, Pa Carey, Pa Foley, Anthony Carmody, David Punch, Ciarán Carey, Gary Kirby, Seamus Kirby, Ger Hayes, Sean Foley, Frankie Nolan. Substitute: Gerard Burke.

1989

Stadium Committee

Semple Stadium and Tipperary Board officers on a fundraising mission to Dublin in 1989. Back row (l-r): Liam Ó Donnchú, Semple Stadium PRO; Noel Morris, Tipperary GAA chairman; John Doyle, Central Council rep. Front row (l-r): Martina Ryan, Semple Stadium secretary; Michael Lowry, Semple Stadium chairman; Tomás Ó Baróid, Tipperary GAA secretary and Semple Stadium treasurer.

1989

Tipperary Homecoming

After Tipperary's 4-24 to 3-9 win over Antrim in the All-Ireland final in Croke Park on 3 September, the homecoming celebrations were held in Semple Stadium rather than the traditional locations of Liberty Square or on the Cathedral steps. The team management, in conjunction with Semple Stadium management, decided to hold a

The crowd enjoying the homecoming concert at Semple Stadium.

concert and reception for the team in the stadium, in part because of safety concerns for the huge crowd expected. Almost 30,000 attended and were entertained by Comhaltas and Scór groups followed by the Wolfe Tones and Joe Dolan. It was a great success and progressed the idea of establishing Semple as a venue for future concerts.

Tommy Barrett, Treasurer

At the Semple Stadium annual general meeting 1989, Tipperary GAA secretary Tommy Barrett succeeded the late John Lanigan as treasurer. The debt on the stadium, now standing at £1.1 million approximately, was a major headache for the committee.

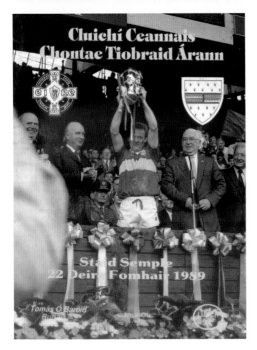

Top: Clonoulty/Rossmore, Tipperary Senior Hurling Champions 1989. Back row (l–r): John Kennedy, Dan Quirke, Joe Hayes, Peter Hayes, Cecil Ryan, Declan Ryan, Noel Keane, David Ryan (H). Front row (l–r): Seamus Hammersley, Kevin Ryan, Micheal Heffernan, Tommy Kennedy, T J Ryan (captain), Andrew Fryday, Phil Shanahan. Thomas Ryan (mascot).
Above: A fine view of Ardán Úi Chuinneáin and Cúl Ó Daimhín at Semple Stadium.

1989

Clonoulty/Rossmore End the Decade with Glory:
Tipperary Senior Hurling Final

Over 20,000 spectators flocked to Semple Stadium on 22 October to watch the men of Holycross/Ballycahill and Clonoulty/Rossmore in the county hurling final. Clonoulty had marginally the better of affairs and led by three points, 0-8 to 0-5, at the interval.

Nine minutes into the second half came a crucial score when Peter Hayes swept the ball to the Holycross net. A pointed penalty by Kevin Ryan soon had Clonoulty six points up and heading for victory. However, Holycross came back, and when substitute Donal Ryan goaled to leave just a point between the sides, there were still two minutes to play. The last word came from outstanding centre-back John Kennedy, who pointed a sixty-five to secure Clonoulty's win by 1-11 to 1-9 amid unrestrained euphoria.

CHAPTER 8

WHEN SEMPLE ROCKED TO FÉILE

THE 1990S

1990

Féile na nGael Homecoming

Féile na nGael returned to Tipperary in 1990 and 1991 after an absence of nineteen years, having been inaugurated in the county in 1971. It was a wonderful spectacle of youth, hurling, camogie and handball. President Patrick Hillery, in his address to the assembled participants at Semple Stadium on 24 June, 1990, stated,

> The GAA has always proclaimed its faith in youth, promoted pride in place, encouraged togetherness in the community, inspired love of our heritage and of everything that as Irish men and women we should cherish.

1990

'Donkeys Don't Win Derbies': Munster Senior Hurling Final

This famous clash in Semple Stadium on 15 July saw Cork fired up by the pre-match taunt of 'Donkeys don't win derbies' by then Tipperary manager Michael 'Babs' Keating.

Above right: Cork's Ger Fitzgerald in action against Tipperary's Bobby Ryan in the 1990 Munster hurling final. Photo by Sportsfile.

Even though Tipperary, as All-Ireland champions, were hot favourites to retain their Munster title, Cork looked sharper and more focused in the opening half. Jim Cashman was a dominant figure at centre-back, while Tony O'Sullivan was hugely influential at wing-forward. Goals by Mark Foley late in that half and an early one by John Fitzgibbon after the interval kept them in control. Both players added further goals in the second half, and at the final whistle Cork were deservedly ahead by eight points. They had stopped Tipperary from recording their first ever Munster four in a row. The final score was Cork 4-16, Tipperary 2-14.

Féile '90: The Trip to Tipp

A sub-committee formed the previous year to explore the possibility of staging a major concert at Semple Stadium reported positively on its economic potential. Concert promoters MCD were approached, and the musical extravaganza Féile '90 – or The Trip to Tipp – became a reality on 3, 4 and 5 August 1990. It was an unprecedented money-spinner for Thurles and its environs, and the biggest and most innovative concert of its kind ever staged in Ireland. A crowd of close to 60,000, mostly teenagers and young adults, attended and enjoyed a fabulous musical festival over a relatively incident-free weekend.

Meatloaf, Big Country and No Sweat topped the bill on Friday night, while Something Happens, The 4 of Us and Hothouse Flowers brought a crowning glory to Saturday.

With the Féile '90 stage under construction in the background, event plans are finalised. Left to right: Liam Ó Donnchú, Semple Stadium PRO; Michael Maher, Semple Stadium vice-chairman; Michael Lowry, Semple Stadium chairman; Eamon McCann of concert promoters MCD; Tommy Barrett, Tipperary GAA secretary.

Sunday was labelled as the 'Family Day', and Christy Moore, Deacon Blue and The Saw Doctors thrilled the crowds, while later that evening Van Morrison was the highlight.

While Féile '90 took a good slice off the debt on the stadium, there is little doubt that it ruffled the feathers of some traditionalists. Cúlbaire struck the right note in his *Ballad of 1990*:

> There was rock 'n' roll and 'crack' and ól to while the hours away,
> No place 'twas clear for the pioneer if the project was to pay;
> We had Hothouse Flowers till the early hours, the Moving Hearts were there,
> And Dr Croke nearly got a stroke on his perch atop the Square!

John O'Grady ('Cúlbaire'), *Tipperary Star*, 30 December, 1990

Top left: Match programme from the county hurling final 1990.

Top right: Holycross/Ballycahill, Tipperary Senior Hurling Champions 1990. Back row (l–r): Criostóir Croke, Tony Lanigan, Tom Dwyer, Tony Stakelum, Johnny Doyle, Stephen Dwan, Pat Slattery, Declan Carr (captain), Phil Dwyer, Michael McGrath, Ciaran Carroll, Benjy Browne, Tommy Lanigan, Jim Ryan, Gerry Fennessy. Front row (l–r): Donal Ryan, Pat Cahill, Paul Maher, Paul Slattery, Phil Cahill, Paddy Dwan, Michael Doyle, P J Lanigan, Rory Dwan, Robert Stakelum, Michael Fleming.

1990

Number Four for Holycross: Tipperary Senior Hurling Final

The county final at Semple Stadium on 14 October was a closely contested affair, in which defences dominated and the greater experience of Holycross/Ballycahill won out in the end. There were two points between the sides at half-time, with Holycross ahead by 0-6 to 0-4, and when Cashel drew level with eight minutes to go, it seemed as though they had the initiative. But Holycross threw in a sparkling finish with three brilliant points by Tony Lanigan. The final score was Holycross/Ballycahill 0-13, Cashel King Cormacs 0-10.

> A game of true grit it was plain to be seen,
>
> Three cheers for our heroes, that gallant fifteen;
>
> We dream of Tipperary and her hurlers supreme,
>
> Holycross/Ballycahill is part of this dream.
>
> Johnny Dwyer, from King, Ó Donnchú, Smyth, *Tipperary's GAA Ballads*

A determined Ciarán Carey, Limerick, in possession against Michael Cleary, Tipperary, in the Munster semi-final at Semple Stadium on 9 June. Tipperary won by 2-18 to 0-10.

The First Song of the Cuckoo

The Munster hurling championship is one of the great institutions of Irish sport. Its commencement each year is like the first song of the cuckoo; it lifts the heart in hope of brighter, warmer days and epic games in Thurles town or as Bryan McMahon wrote, by the Shannon's race.

Paddy Downey, *The Irish Times*, Munster Hurling Final programme 1982

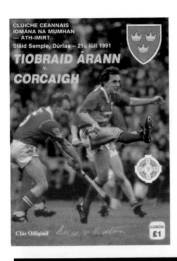

Opposite top left: Match programme for the Munster final 1991.
Opposite top right: Bearing down on the Cork goal at the Killinan End, Aidan Ryan fired the sliotar low past Ger Cunningham's left, pumped his fist in the air, in joy, in relief, then was engulfed by a throng of jubilant Tipperary supporters surging with their flags, hats and rosettes onto the Semple sod.
Opposite bottom: Declan Carr of Tipperary lifts the Munster Cup following the replay between Tipperary and Cork at Semple Stadium. Also included is Michael Maher, Munster Council chairman. Photo by Ray McManus, Sportsfile.

1991

A Burst of Blue and Gold Brilliance: Munster Senior Hurling Final

The Munster final was played at Páirc Uí Chaoimh on 7 July. Cork had the better of the early exchanges and led by four points at the interval. First-half goals by John Fitzgibbon and Ger Fitzgerald had Cork in a strong position, but a young John Leahy kept Tipperary clinging on for dear life. Even though Nicky English had a goal disallowed, it fell to a late Pat Fox leveller to save Tipp's bacon, Cork 4-10, Tipperary 2-16.

Close to 60,000 attended the replay at Semple Stadium on 21 July and witnessed a tumultuous encounter that saw Tipperary come from nine points down to win. A memorable pitch invasion from the Killinan End was sparked by a superb goal, late on, from Tipperary's Aidan Ryan. Before that Cork led by 3-13 to 1-10 with just a quarter of the game remaining. But the Premier lads kept plugging away, and goals from Pat Fox and captain Declan Carr hauled them back level. They surged into a two-point lead, and the scene was set for Ryan to gallop through and crown a magnificent win. Cork goal machine Fitzgibbon responded with the side's fourth goal, but Tipp held out, 4-19 to 4-15.

1991

Féile na nGael Comes of Age

It was fitting that the twenty-first Féile na nGael was hosted by Tipperary. In his address, GAA Uachtarán Peadar Ó Cuinn stated,

Féile na nGael was conceived twenty-one years ago from a deep sense of commitment to our youth and hurling by men who

Munster Council chairman Michael Maher raises the Féile flag accompanied by Michael Maguire, Tipperary GAA chairman, and Donal Shanahan, Tipperary Féile na nGael chairman.

had a vision and a dream ... Each year it has gone from strength to strength. It gives underage hurling countrywide a focus and an impetus. It integrates every county into a great national effort in the promotion of hurling, and it introduces young players from every part of the country to the camaraderie and the extended family that is Cumann Lúthchleas Gael.

1991

The Centre of the Universe

Thurles is to hurling as Milan is to Grand Opera and Nashville is to Country and Western music. The Munster hurling final in Thurles is deemed by many as one of the greatest days in the GAA's calendar. Thurles is also one of the last bastions of a rather piquant aspect of our culture: that is the Meat Tea, pronounced the 'Mate Tay'. The passing stranger might

Journalist Con Houlihan.
Photo by Ray McManus, Sportsfile.

think that the Meat Tea was a meal fit for a king – in fact, it usually suggests that the country is suffering from a scarcity of bread and butter and beef. The great crowds come to the games and the local economy benefits. Its centre, Liberty Square, seems like the centre of Ireland on days of big games – it is a great place for buskers and other musicians and for that mysterious entity known as the craic. The people of Thurles and the surrounding countryside are noted for their passionate love of sport – hurling, the racehorse and the greyhound play a great part in their culture.

I love Thurles, especially on the days of big games – then in Bowe's pub down by the railway station you feel that you are at the centre of the universe.

Con Houlihan, *Irish Independent*, 23 March, 2013

Féile '91: Europe's Greatest Rock Festival

It was estimated that Féile was worth some £5 million to the local economy, and it had grown to be the greatest collage of rock on the continent of Europe. The attendance at Féile '91 was around 70,000, surpassing the previous year.

Cashel King Cormacs, Tipperary Senior Hurling Champions 1991. Back row (l–r): Justin Irwin, Tony Slattery, Michael Perdue, Ger Slattery, Don Higgins, Peter Fitzelle, Declan McGrath, John Grogan, Pat O'Donoghue, Tommy Grogan, Seán Rodgers. Middle row (l–r): Timmy Moloney, Jamsie O'Donoghue, Willie Fitzelle, Cormac Bonnar, John Ryan, Pat Fitzelle, T J Connolly, Conal Bonnar, Seánie O'Donoghue, Seánie Barron, Liam Devitt. Front row (l–r): Brendan Bonnar, Justin McCarthy (coach), Ailbe Bonnar, Seánie Morrissey, Seán Slattery, Seamus J King (chairman), Colm Bonnar (captain), Joe Minogue, Ramie Ryan, John Darmody, Aengus Ryan. Absent from photograph: Joe O'Leary.

1991

Cashel King Cormacs Make History: Tipperary Senior Hurling Final

An estimated attendance of 12,000 was present at Semple Stadium on 10 November as Holycross/Ballycahill strove to keep their title against west champions Cashel King Cormacs, who were seeking their first. Little separated the teams in the first half except for a lucky Holycross goal by Pat Cahill, which left the holders ahead at the break by 1-4 to 0-4. It took the full third quarter for Cashel to draw level, but the turning point came in the sixteenth minute when Tommy Grogan netted to put Cashel two points ahead. Michael Doyle replied with a point, the only score by Holycross in the half. Even though Cashel were dominant, the only reward they got was a point in the forty-seventh minute by T J Connolly. However, five minutes from time, Cormac Bonnar clinched the title for King Cormacs with a superb goal. Cashel celebrated their first county final victory, by 2-8 to 1-5.

Kiltormer Man of the Match Fionán Curley, left, and captain Aidan Staunton with the Tommy Moore Cup after the 1992 All-Ireland club hurling final at Semple Stadium. Photo by Ray McManus, Sportsfile.

1992

Kiltormer Keep the West Awake: All-Ireland Senior Club Hurling Final

Played at Semple Stadium on 29 March, Kiltormer emerged victors over Birr by 0-15 to 1-8, before an attendance of 13,855. Kiltormer stalwarts Ollie Kilkenny and Brendan Dervan were ruled out of the final through injury after a three-game saga with Tipperary and Munster champions Cashel King Cormacs in the semi-final. The final failed to top that excitement.

Kiltormer: Seán McCague, Brian McManus, Conor Hayes (scored 0-2), Kevin Tierney, Fionán Curley, Pakie Dervan, Gerry Kelly, Tony Larkin, Aidan Staunton (captain, 0-1), Justin Campbell (0-3), Tony Kilkenny (0-1), Damien Curley (0-7), Dermot Fox, Martin Staunton, Seán Kelly. Substitutes: Tony Furey (0-1), Tomás Hanrahan.

Féile '92: Breaking Records

At the Tipperary convention on 2 February, Semple Stadium chairman Michael Lowry reported that the debt on the stadium had been reduced from some £1.2 million to £420,000 in three years. For Féile '92, the entertainment in Semple Stadium was the finest in Europe. International stars such as Bryan Adams, Simply Red, David Byrne and The Wonder Stuff mixed with such home-grown talent as Sharon Shannon, Christy Moore, The Sawdoctors and The Stunning. An estimated 120,000 music fans flooded through the stiles over the three days. The atmosphere in the stadium was particularly noticeable – rarely could such an aura of camaraderie and friendship be witnessed in such a thronging mass of people.

1993
Third Time Lucky for Cork:
Royal Liver National Hurling League Final

Cork and Wexford met three times in the National Hurling League final. All the games were played at Semple Stadium. On 9 May, the result was Cork 2-11, Wexford 2-11; on 16 May, Cork 0-18, Wexford 3-9; and on 22 May, Cork 3-11, Wexford 1-12. It was Cork's first league title since 1980/1981.

Right: Cork captain Brian Corcoran lifts the Croke Cup at Semple Stadium. Photo by Ray McManus, Sportsfile.

1993

Cork Footballers in Command: Munster Senior Football Final

One of the few Munster football finals played at Semple Stadium took place on 18 July, 1993, between Cork and Tipperary. The game was an uphill battle for the home side, after Cork got off to a great start with eight unanswered points, leaving Tipperary trailing by 0-10 to 0-4 at the interval. This pattern continued in the second half, Cork scoring the points and Tipperary squandering many good opportunities. The final score was Cork 1-16, Tipperary 1-8.

Cork: John Kerins, Mark Farr, Mark O'Connor, Brian Corcoran, Ciaran O'Sullivan, Stephen O'Brien, Tony Davis, Shea Fahy, Teddy McCarthy, Don Davis, Joe Kavanagh, Barry Coffey, Colin Corkery, John O'Driscoll, Mick McCarthy (captain). Substitutes played: Liam Honohan, Brian Murphy, Pat Hegarty.

Tipperary: Philly Ryan, John O'Meara, Seán Collum (captain), Seán Brett, John Owens, Tom Macken, Jerry Ryan, Brian Burke, John Costello, Derry Foley, Pat Maguire, Mark Sheehan, Peter Lambert, Anthony Crosse, Davy Hogan. Substitutes played: Tom Anglim, Kevin Coonan, Jimmy Dunne.

Féile '93: Keep on Rocking

The 1993 festival was not as financially rewarding as other years, mainly due to production costs and a drop in numbers attending. Thirty-five acts were on the programme and a weekend ticket cost £45. By the end of 1993, the debt on the stadium was down from £1.28 million to less than £100,000; all in all, the Féile concerts were a wonderful success, achieving their basic aim.

Far right: Semple chairman Michael Lowry (seated) with MCD's Denis Desmond.

Connacht (All Galway), Interprovincial Hurling Champions 1994. Back row (l–r): Dermot Fahy, Joe Rabbitte, Michael Coleman, Richard Burke, Paul Cooney, Liam Burke, Seán Treacy, Pat Malone. Front row (l–r): Micheál Donoghue, Liam Turley, Gerry McInerney, Nigel Shaughnessy, Francis Forde, Noel Power, Brendan Keogh.

1994

Interprovincial Hurling Goes West: Railway Cup Hurling Final

Connacht were ahead by 1-6 to 0-4 at half-time, mainly due to great performances from their midfield pairing of Michael Coleman and Pat Malone. Points from D J Carey, Tom Dempsey and Joe Dooley kept Leinster in contention. Galway's Liam Burke had two points in the final quarter before Meathman Pat Potterton notched a goal at the death, but too late: Leinster surrendered their title. The final score at Semple Stadium on 20 February was Connacht 1-11, Leinster 1-10.

1994

Limerick's First Title Since 1981: Munster Senior Hurling Final

When Clare and Limerick met in the Munster final at Semple Stadium on 10 July, it was their first such meeting since 1981, and hopes were high on both sides of an epic struggle. The attendance of 43,638 saw a confident Limerick give a top-level point-scoring performance against a disappointing Banner team, which failed to do justice on the day. Clare goals by Cyril Lyons and Tommy Guilfoyle came too late to threaten the Shannonsiders. The final score was Limerick 0-25, Clare 2-10.

Above right: Limerick captain Gary Kirby is held shoulder high as he celebrates after the Munster final at Semple Stadium. Photo by Ray McManus, Sportsfile.

Féile '94: The 'Final' One

This year's festival was a reduced version of the original, being a two-day rather than a three-day event. For the 25,000 music lovers that attended, it was very enjoyable. Over five years, the Semple Stadium committee had achieved its goal of clearing a £1.28 million debt. More than 165 bands had played at Féile between 1990 and 1994, and it was regarded as the largest rock festival in Europe. There would be a Féile in 1995, but it was held in Cork's Páirc Uí Chaoimh.

Toomevara, Tipperary Senior Hurling Champions 1994. Back row (l–r): Kevin Kennedy, Tommy Dunne, Jody Grace, Pat Meagher (captain), Terry Dunne, Tommy Carroll, Pat King, Michael Murphy. Front row (l–r): Liam Nolan, George Frend, Michael O'Meara, Declan O'Meara, Tony Delaney, Philip Shanahan, Rory Brislane.

1994

Greyhounds in Full Flight: Tipperary Senior Hurling Final

The early 1990s were brilliant years for Toomevara, who won three county titles in a row in 1992, 1993 and 1994. They kept mostly the same panel of players right through the period, winning in 1992 over Thurles Sarsfields by 0-12 to 1-6 in a replay. The following year, neighbours Éire Óg, Nenagh, fell in the final by 1-14 to 1-13. Toome were well in their stride, maturing into a formidable outfit, and they accounted for Cashel King Cormacs by 3-11 to 1-9 in 1994. Michael O'Meara, Jody Grace and Pat Meagher captained the teams.

> Come! Raise the green and gold again and let us proudly say:
> Three cheers for the gallant 'Greyhounds', Toomevara boys, hurrah!
>
> Br Joseph Perkins, from King, Ó Donnchú, Smyth, *Tipperary's GAA Ballads*

1994

Second for Kilmallock: Munster Senior Club Hurling Final

Kilmallock took the Munster club title for a second time after defeating defending

Kilmallock, Munster Senior Club Hurling Champions 1994. Back row (l–r): Pat Barrett, James Connery, Ger O'Riordan, Paul Dowling, M Cronin, Paudge Tobin, Shane O'Grady, Dave Clarke. Front row (l–r): Maurice Nelligan, Seán Burchill, Mike Houlihan (captain), Tom Hennessy, Paddy Kelly, Donal Barry, Liam Neenan.

champions Toomevara at Semple Stadium on 27 November. The final score was Kilmallock 2-11, Toomevara 1-11.

1995
The Cats Take the League

Bill Hennessy captained Kilkenny to success over Clare in the Church & General National Hurling League final at Semple Stadium on 7 May, 1995. The final score was Kilkenny 2-12, Clare 0-9.

Kilkenny, National Hurling League Champions 1995. Lineout: Michael Walsh, Eddie O'Connor, Pat Dwyer, Liam Simpson, Liam Keoghan, Eddie O'Dwyer, Willie O'Connor, Michael Phelan, Bill Hennessy (captain), Adrian Ronan, John Power, P J Delaney, Eamon Morrissey, D J Carey, Denis Byrne. Substitutes played: C Brennan, Derek Gaffney.

Top left: Match programme for the Munster hurling final 1995.

Top right: Clare captain Anthony Daly, followed by Davy Fitzgerald, leads the Bannermen in the pre-match parade.

Above left: Exultant Clare captain Anthony Daly raises the Munster Cup aloft at Semple Stadium.

Above right: Clare manager Ger Loughnane is fêted at Semple Stadium following the Banner's Munster final success.

Photos courtesy of Clare County Express.

1995
Year of the Banner: Guinness Munster Senior Hurling Final

Clare claimed their first Munster hurling championship since 1932, and only their fourth ever, after beating Limerick at Semple Stadium on 9 July. Davy Fitzgerald scored from a penalty five minutes before the break, crashing the ball high into the town net, before sprinting back to his goal-line. Clare were leading the game by 1-5 to 0-7 at half-time and ended on a scoreline of 1-17 to 0-11. They were captained by Anthony Daly and managed by Ger Loughnane.

The ghosts of sixty-three years were well and truly buried by this long-overdue victory. The release of emotion when Anthony Daly received the cup had to be seen to be believed. Proceedings ended with Daly lifting the cup, the Clare 'Shout' ringing out from the Killinan End, and Tony Considine taking the microphone for his rendition of 'My Lovely Rose of Clare'. Clare's Sean McMahon described the feeling on *Laochra Gael* in 2017:

> For every Clare person, there's a really special day we all longed to see. I had dreamt about playing for Clare and winning a Munster Championship. That day in Thurles was the greatest day for me.

1995
Semple Stadium Debt Cleared

Michael Lowry, the chairman of Semple Stadium committee, informed delegates at the 1995 Tipperary convention that the debt on the stadium had been cleared. Rumours were rife early in the year that Bon Jovi would stage a one-day concert in the stadium in July, but this never materialised. Féile '95 was held at Páirc Uí Chaoimh, Cork.

1995
Remembering Bloody Sunday

On Sunday, 19 November, the seventy-fifth anniversary of Bloody Sunday was commemorated at Semple Stadium with a Dublin/Tipperary senior football game. This was

Top left: The Bloody Sunday memorial plaque at Semple Stadium.

Top right: Photographed at the unveiling of the Bloody Sunday memorial were Mícheál Ó Meára, Seán Mockler, Peter Quinn (former GAA president), Mick Egan (chairman of the commemoration committee), Michael Lowry (Semple Stadium chairman), Seán Fogarty (Tipperary GAA chairman), Fidelma Murphy, Séamus Ó Riain (president, Tipperary GAA), Tomás Ó Baróid (Tipperary GAA secretary), Paddy Power, Séamus Leahy.

Above: Relatives of those who played in Croke Park on Bloody Sunday 1920 at the unveiling of the Semple Stadium memorial.

followed by the unveiling of a plaque, under Ardán Uí Chuinneáin, to the memory of the Tipperary and Dublin teams who played at Croke Park on Bloody Sunday, 1920, and in particular, Tipperary footballer Michael Hogan who was fatally wounded by British forces that day. County GAA president Séamus Ó Riain performed the unveiling.

Tipperary, All-Ireland Under 21 Hurling Champions 1995. Back row (l–r): Liam Barron, Tommy Dunne, Terry Dunne, Brendan Cummins, Aidan Butler, Liam McGrath, Philip Shanahan. Front row (l–r): Paul Shelly, David Burke, Keith Slevin, Darren O'Connor, Brian Horgan, Kevin Tucker, Eddie Enright, Brian Flannery.

1995

Tipperary Win at Home: All-Ireland Under 21 Hurling Final

At Semple Stadium on 10 September, Kilkenny got the dream start with a goal after three minutes; by half-time, they were leading by 1-6 to 0-5. Whatever was said in the Tipperary dressing room by manager Michael Doyle worked wonders, as the team gave a super second-half performance, starting with a stupendous save by Brendan Cummins in the Tipperary goal. They gained heart, and a goal created by a weaving run by Kevin Tucker and finished by Philip O'Dwyer set them on the road to victory. The final score was Tipperary 1-14, Kilkenny 1-10. Attendance on the day was 25,234.

In the replayed All-Ireland Under 21 football final, played prior to the hurling, Kerry defeated Mayo by 3-10 to 1-12.

1995

Historic First for Éire Óg: Tipperary Senior Hurling Final

A marvellous attendance of 14,137 saw Éire Óg, Nenagh, win their first county senior hurling title at Semple Stadium on 15 October. Their opponents Boherlahan/Dualla failed to deliver on their early promise and were well beaten in a one-sided final, 2-25 to

Nenagh Éire Óg, Tipperary Senior Hurling Champions 1995. Back row (l–r): Paul Kennedy, John Heffernan, Con Howard, Noel Coffey, Christy McLoughlin, Eddie Tucker, Frank Moran, John Kennedy. Front row (l–r): Chris Bonnar, Michael Cleary, Darragh Quinn, Conor O'Donovan (captain), Kevin Tucker, Robbie Tomlinson, Robbie Foley.

2-8. After twenty minutes the sides were level, but from that point on the Boherlahan challenge began to falter. At half-time, Nenagh were ahead by 0-12 to 1-5, and in the second half, the crowd witnessed an outstanding Nenagh performance that only became more fluent and perfect as the game progressed.

1996
Number Seven for Galway: All-Ireland Under 21 Hurling Final

Galway had a magnificent win over Wexford in Semple Stadium on 8 September, taking their seventh Under 21 hurling title. The final score was Galway 1-14, Wexford 0-7.

Opposite bottom: Galway, All-Ireland Under 21 Hurling Champions 1996. Back row (l–r): Gregory Kennedy, Gordon Glynn, Eugene Cloonan, Vinny Maher, Cathal Moore, Peter Huban, Liam Hodgins, Fergal Healy. Front row (l–r): Ollie Canning, Donal Moran, Kevin Broderick, Michael Healy, Ollie Fahy, Brian Higgins, Alan Kerins, Darragh Coen.

1996

Kerry Hold the Title: All-Ireland Under 21 Football Final

*Mike Frank Russell, the Kerry corner-forward.
Photo by Stephen McCarthy, Sportsfile.*

On 8 September, at Semple Stadium, Kerry won the Under 21 football final following a 1-17 to 2-10 defeat of Cavan. This was the Kingdom's eighth All-Ireland title overall and their second in a row.

Kerry: Diarmuid Murphy, Kieran O'Driscoll, Brian McCarthy, Morgan O'Shea, Killian Burns, Chris Drummond, Éamonn Fitzmaurice, Darragh Ó Sé, William Kirby, Denis O'Dwyer, Liam Hassett, Dara Ó Cinnéide, James O'Shea, Brian Clarke, Mike Frank Russell. Substitutes played: Jack Ferriter, John Brennan, Ruairí O'Rahilly.

1996

Boherlahan Reach the Promised Land: Tipperary Senior Hurling Final

Just under 10,000 spectators came to Semple Stadium on 27 October to watch Boherlahan/Dualla and Toomevara vie for the Tipperary title. Although Boherlahan

Boherlahan/Dualla, Tipperary Senior Hurling Champions 1996. Back row (l–r): Philip O'Dwyer,
J J McGrath, Aidan Flanagan, T J O'Dwyer, Conor Gleeson, Michael Murphy, Séamus Hickey. Front
row (l–r): Brian O'Dwyer, William Hickey, Liam Maher, Philip Ryan (captain), Ger Flanagan,
Tommy Dwyer, Michael Ferncombe, David Ryan.

had the breeze in their favour in the first half, it was Toomevara who got the breaks and
the scores to give them a five-point lead at the interval, 1-7 to 0-5.

Boherlahan resumed well and took two points in three minutes, but Toomevara came
back with a point from Liam Nolan and a goal by Kevin Kennedy, to put the 'Greyhounds'
seven points ahead. Boherlahan dug deep and responded swiftly with three points by J J
McGrath, Ger Flanagan and Aidan Flanagan. Then a goal by Philip O'Dwyer, and the
game was wide open. The sides were level as the dying minutes approached, until Liam
Maher sent over the bar to give Boherlahan/Dualla the lead for the first time and victory,
by 1-16 to 2-12.

1996

Lohans Lead Wolfe Tones to Glory:
AIB Munster Senior Club Hurling Final

It was something of a miracle that this club final was fit to be played on 24 November,
given the relentless deluge that drenched the country. A small crowd of 5,345 attended

Semple Stadium to see Clare's Wolfe Tones prevail against Waterford's Ballygunner, who looked down and out by half-time, trailing by nine points. The primacy of the Lohan brothers, Brian and Frank, was central to the winners' defence. Wolfe Tones were in total control, limiting their opponents to three points in the first half and cracking in 2-6, the goals coming from Paul O'Rourke and Finbarr Carrig.

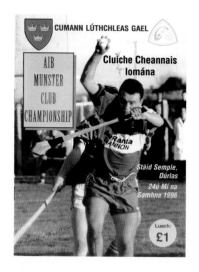

Ballygunner went twelve points behind before they commenced the long haul back. Paul Flynn moved up a few gears and presented a constant threat to Wolfe Tones, ending up with 2-4. He was well assisted by Billy O'Sullivan and Gordon Ryan. When the goals started to fly in, Ballygunner took a grip at midfield, and the match oscilated between a four- and five-point margin for Wolfe Tones until the end, when Flynn's incision down the left created an opening for Ryan, who thrashed home the goal that closed the margin to a point. The final score was Wolfe Tones 4-9, Ballygunner 4-8.

Wolfe Tones na Sionna, Clare: Damian Garrihy, Gerry McIntyre, Brian Lohan (captain), Martin Hartigan, Frank Lohan, Sean Power, Paul Meaney, Denis O'Riordan, Pat O'Rourke, John O'Riordan, Ciaran O'Neill, Paul Lee, Paul O'Rourke, Finbarr Carrig, Paul Keary. Substitutes: Derek Collins, Michael O'Neill, John Markham, Mark Purcell, John McPhillips, Ger Carrig, Fergal O'Shea, Mike McPhillips, Ray Carley, Joe Costello, Andrew Carr, Eddie Mulvihill.

The Voice Now Silent

In November 1996, the news of the death of Mícheál Ó hEithir brought sadness to all GAA followers. He was the voice of Gaelic sport from 1938 to 1985, when his Radio Éireann (later RTÉ) broadcasts kept an eager public glued to the radio on many summer Sundays. During his time, he broadcast on ninety-nine All-Ireland finals.

GAA supporters fill the streets of Thurles before the Munster hurling semi-final.
Photo by Brendan Moran, Sportsfile.

1997

Banter and Brimming Glasses: Munster Senior Hurling Semi-Final

Seán Kilfeather, writing in *The Irish Times* on 21 June, 1997, described the atmosphere in Thurles after the Munster hurling semi-final between Tipperary and Limerick:

The scene was the town square in Thurles after the 1997 Munster hurling semi-final. A jubilant young man in Tipperary colours roared across the street at a group of rather despondent Limerick followers, who were equally well adorned: 'Hey horse,' he roared, 'where are ye from?' As quick as a flash came the reply, 'We don't know. It was dark when we left.'

As an example of repartee and dignity in defeat, it could hardly have been bettered. Later, the two groups could be seen on the same side of the street with brimming glasses, discussing the course of the match.

What is most amazing about Thurles is that, no matter who is playing, they all seem to troop back into the town and mingle in the Square for hours. The good humour and banter between opposing supporters never seems to go beyond the bounds of acceptable behaviour.

1997
D J's Day: Guinness All-Ireland Senior Hurling Quarter-Final

The crowd of 22,826 were treated to hurling fireworks at the All-Ireland quarter-final at Semple Stadium on 27 July. The first half was all Galway, as they tore into Kilkenny and built up a fine lead at the interval of 3-9 to 1-6. Their goals had come from Kevin Broderick, Liam Burke and Joe Cooney, while Kilkenny were dependent on D J Carey, who contributed 1-2. The goal that Carey scored on the day was typical of what made him such a dangerous attacker: Running onto the ball at pace, he left Nigel Shaughnessy in his wake while arrowing towards goal before shortening his grip and firing the sliotar from his left to the roof of the net from close range. Galway were nine points to the good at the break, but it was a renewed Kilkenny team in the second half.

Carey's next goal showcased his ability in the air, as he doubled on a long delivery

from Andy Comerford one-handed to the back of the Galway net for a score that really ignited Kilkenny's second-half comeback. Key also to their resurgence was the introduction of grizzled warrior John Power from the bench. Carey's performance that day was one of his greatest ever, scoring 2-8. In the end, it was a late goal from Ken O'Shea that gave the Cats enough momentum to just about get the job done. But anyone in Semple Stadium that day will surely remember both a classic battle and the supreme individual display by D J Carey, one of the greatest forwards of his generation. The final score was Kilkenny 4-15, Galway 3-16.

Above right: D J Carey, Kilkenny hurling's shining star.

In the county of Kilkenny, we've had many a super star,

From the gallant Ollie Walsh, way back to Lory Meagher,

But now, we have the greatest one, I'm sure you will agree,

The mighty D J Carey will go down in history.

Bob Middleton, Gowran, from Murphy, *The Poetry and Song of Black and Amber Glory*

1997

Goals Count as Rebels Triumph: All-Ireland Under 21 Hurling Final

The Under 21 final was played at Semple Stadium on 21 September, with Cork triumphing over Galway by 3-11 to 0-13. Galway fielded twelve of the team that won the title the previous year. Although playing against the wind in the first half, Cork scored two vital goals to hold a five-point lead at the interval, 2-6 to 0-7. In a hard-fought second half, the Rebels maintained their grip on the game to secure a seven-point victory.

Cork: Donal Óg Cusack, John Browne, Diarmuid O'Sullivan, Wayne Sherlock, Derek Barrett, Dan Murphy (captain), Seán Óg Ó hAilpín, Austin Walsh, Pat Ryan, Brian O'Driscoll (Killavullen), Timmy McCarthy, Mickey O'Connell, John O'Flynn, Darren Ronan, Brian O'Keeffe.

1997

Day Trip to Tipp

On 24 August, a one-day concert was held at Semple Stadium and attended by some 35,000 fans. Top of the bill were the Prodigy, with Manic Street Preachers, Kula Shaker and the Foo Fighters among the support acts. The concert was organised by MCD/Wonderland Promotions and was a great success.

Clonoulty/Rossmore, Tipperary Senior Hurling Champions 1997. Back row (l–r): Kevin Fox (trainer), T J Ryan (manager), Nollaig Heffernan, Barty Flynn, Philip Quirke, Rody Aherne, Michael Hughes, Aidan Butler, Maurice Quirke, Andrew Fryday, Michael Heffernan, Michael Brennan, Michael Ryan, Liam Coen, James Ryan, Joe Hammersley (selector), Michael Coen. Front row (l–r): Dick Martin, John Kennedy, Liam Manton, Alan Kennedy, Declan Ryan, Kevin Ryan, Noel Keane (captain), Michael Heffernan, Michael 'Bonny' Kennedy, Kevin Lanigan-Ryan, Peter Brennan, Seamus Coffey. Mascots: Shane Fryday, Kieran Hammersley.

1997

Keane Leads Clonoulty to Glory: Tipperary Senior Hurling Final

The county hurling final on 2 November at Semple Stadium was Mullinahone's first time to appear, and they were slight favourites. Clonoulty/Rossmore had won their last title in 1989. The contest generated great interest, and a huge crowd of over 17,000 came along, the biggest attendance since the 1950s. Declan Ryan, who played such a pivotal role for Clonoulty in the semi-finals, had a relatively quiet hour. Meanwhile the Mullinahone trio of John Leahy, Brian O'Meara and Paul Kelly, on whom so much depended, did not play to expectation.

It was a murky day and greasy conditions. The sides were level on six occasions in the first half, but by half-time Clonoulty/Rossmore were in front by 0-10 to 0-7. The west men remained in front until Brian O'Meara's goal brought the sides level, and there was all to play for in the final ten minutes. Bonny Kennedy gave Clonoulty/Rossmore a two-point cushion, and with about three minutes to go, Mullinahone got a thirty-yard free. Leahy blasted for goal, but it was saved. He got a second chance and it came off the post, leaving the advantage to Clonoulty/Rossmore and victory by 0-17 to 1-12.

1997

A First for Clarecastle: AIB Munster Senior Club Hurling Final

Semple Stadium was the place to be on 7 December, especially for Clarecastle supporters, who witnessed their club make history by winning the Munster title for the first time. They were up against formidable hurlers in Patrickswell, but the Limerick men got off to a bad start when Ciarán Carey picked up a shoulder injury that curtailed his usual all-action game. Clarecastle led by 1-8 to 0-8 at the break, the goal coming from Alan Neville just two minutes beforehand. With eight minutes remaining, the Well had clawed their way back to equalise. Danny Scanlon – the revelation of the day for the Clare club – stormed through and went to ground. Ken Ralph blasted the ensuing penalty to the net. In a last-minute effort to earn a draw, Gary Kirby attempted a goal from a free, but half of Clarecastle was on the line and Kenny Morrissey turned the ball over for a point, the final score of the game. Kirby had really carried Patrickswell, with a personal tally of eleven points. The final score was Clarecastle 2-11, Patrickswell 0-15.

Clarecastle, Clare: Tommy Hegarty, Ger Canny, Martin Sheedy (captain), Bernard Scanlon, Pat Healy, Stephen Sheedy, Anthony Daly, Kenneth Morrissey, Victor O'Loughlin, Fergus Tuohy, Alan Neville, Danny Scanlon, Robert Fitzgerald, Ken Ralph, Ger O'Loughlin.

1998

Rebels Rock the Déise: Church & General National Hurling League Final

Bathed in glorious sunshine, the League final between Cork and Waterford in Semple

Captain Diarmuid O'Sullivan and Cork supporters celebrate with the Croke Cup following the National Hurling League final at Semple Stadium. Photo by Sportsfile.

Stadium on 16 May was played at a frantic pace. Waterford certainly held their own, until a fantastic strike by Seán O'Farrell just before half-time put Cork a goal in front. Dan Shanahan replied with a point to leave the gap at two points, Waterford 0-7, Cork 1-6. The Déise went ahead in the second half but failed to capitalise on their chances. Alan Browne pounced on a loose hand-pass to kick the ball to the net. Cork led by a goal and never looked back. The final score was Cork 2-14, Waterford 0-13.

Cork: Ger Cunningham, Fergal Ryan, John Browne, Diarmuid O'Sullivan (captain), Mark Landers, Brian Corcoran, Seán Óg Ó hAilpín, Pat Ryan (0-2), Mick Daly, Sean McGrath (0-3), Fergal McCormack (0-1), Kieran Morrison (0-2), Seán O'Farrell (1-3), Alan Browne (1-0), Joe Deane (0-3).

1998

Clare Win Amid Controversy: Guinness Munster Senior Hurling Final

The Munster hurling final and replay between Clare and Waterford were staged at Semple Stadium on 12 and 19 July. It was the sides' first meeting in a Munster final since 1938. Both matches attracted attendances of over 50,000. Clare won the replay, 2-16 to 0-10, having drawn the first match 1-16 to 3-10. In the drawn game, Waterford struggled to keep in touch, but two Anthony Kirwan goals sparked a recovery. Paul Flynn fired a free to the net with the match entering injury time to level the scores. Waterford had an

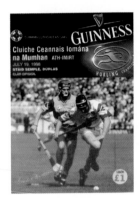

Fergal Hartley of Waterford in action against Jamesie O'Connor of Clare, during the 1998 Munster hurling final at Semple Stadium. Photo by Sportsfile.

opportunity to win it from a long-range free, but Flynn's effort drifted wide.

The replay was a most controversial game. Tension pervaded from the very start and led to the dismissal of Clare full-back Brian Lohan and Waterford corner-forward Micheal White in the fourth minute. Following a hard-fought contest, Clare emerged victors, their goals coming from Niall Gilligan and Conor Clancy.

1998

The Kingdom Marches On: Bank of Ireland Munster Senior Football Final

The Munster football final between Tipperary and Kerry was played at Semple Stadium two weeks after the hurling replay, on 2 August, before an attendance of 27,263. Tipperary were contesting their third provincial final of the 1990s, and hopes were high. At half-time they were just one point behind, 0-7 to 0-6. But Kerry were dominant early in the second half and built up a good lead. A goal by substitute Jim Williams brought Tipperary within three points of Kerry, but this was as close as they got. The final score was Kerry 0-17, Tipperary 1-10.

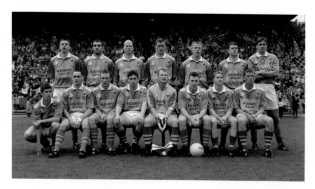 

Above left: Kerry, Munster Senior Football Champions 1998. Back row (l–r): Darragh Ó Sé, Barry O'Shea, Liam Flaherty, Donal Daly, Eamonn Breen, Denis O'Dwyer, Maurice Fitzgerald. Front row (l–r): Éamonn Fitzmaurice, Pa Laide, John Crowley, Stephen Stack, Declan O'Keeffe, Séamus Moynihan, Mike Frank Russell, Dara Ó Cinnéide. Photo by Sportsfile.

Above right: Tipperary, Munster Senior Football Finalists 1998. Back row (l–r): Niall Kelly, Seán Maher, John Costello, Brian Burke (captain), Brendan Cummins, Michael Spillane, Mark Shehan, Conor O'Dwyer. Front row (l–r): Peter Lambert, Bernard Hahessy, Philly Ryan, Declan Browne, Seán Collum, Liam Cronin, Davy Hogan.

Semple Goes Electric

During 1998, in excess of 350,000 patrons attended games in the stadium. One of the many improvements carried out was the installation of an electronic scoreboard and clock. Local man Larry Barrett (pictured) was the scoreboard operator, a role fulfilled by Noel Murphy in the past.

1998
A Thrilling Trilogy: Guinness All-Ireland Senior Hurling Semi-Final

Offaly and Clare met three times in the All-Ireland hurling semi-final. When first they met at Croke Park on 9 August, it ended all square, 1-13 apiece. The replay at the same venue on 22 August ended in confusion, when referee Jimmy Cooney blew the final whistle some minutes early, prompting Offaly fans to stage a sit-down protest; Clare were winning at the time, by 2-10 to 1-16. A refixture at Semple Stadium on 29 August would settle the issue.

Joe Dooley of Offaly during the second semi-final replay at Semple Stadium. Photo by Ray McManus, Sportsfile.

Semple Stadium was in perfect condition before an enthralled attendance of 42,092. Offaly led by 0-9 to 0-6 at the interval and needed to be as good as they were, for this was no collapse by Clare. While both goalkeepers kept clean sheets, the Offaly keeper, Stephen Byrne, had the busier afternoon and stopped an amazing tally of shots. Brilliant also was Offaly's Joe Dooley, who belied his thirty-five years and shot the lights out with five stunning points from play. There was no respite in the second half. The nearest Clare came was when Jamesie O'Connor popped over two points to narrow it down to two with twelve minutes to go. There was still plenty of life left in Clare, and the final period featured the very best of the day's hurling. It had everything, as players strained to the very limits of their endurance.

In the final two minutes, Byrne saved from Fergal Hegarty, Sean McMahon dropped the sixty-five short, Jamesie O'Connor went through but was rewarded only with a sixty-five, Anthony Daly took it, and it fell to the left and wide. The final score was Offaly 0-16, Clare 0-13.

1998

Cork in Control: All-Ireland Under 21 Hurling Final

Cork won their eleventh Under 21 title, beating Galway by 2-15 to 2-10 at Semple Stadium on 20 September. Their scorers were Mickey O'Connell (0-7), Joe Deane (0-7), Brian O'Keeffe (2-0) and John Anderson (0-1). Eugene Cloonan led the Galway scorers with 1-5, while Anthony Kerins scored 1-3 and Pádraic Walshe, 0-2.

Cork, All-Ireland Under 21 Hurling Champions 1998. Back row (l–r): Diarmuid O'Sullivan,
Donal Óg Cusack, Derek Barrett, Dan Murphy (captain), Seán O'Farrell, Wayne Sherlock, Seán Óg
Ó hAilpín. Front row (l–r): Austin Walsh, Michael O'Connell, Neil Ronan, Mark Prendergast, Joe
Deane, Brian O'Keeffe, Luke Mannix, Timmy McCarthy. Photo by Damien Eagers, Sportsfile.

1999

Connacht Turn It Around: Railway Cup Hurling Final

The Railway Cup Interprovincial hurling final was played at Semple Stadium on 21 November, before an attendance of 487. A pedestrian first half ended with Munster ahead by 0-10 to 0-9. In the fortieth minute, Kevin Broderick turned on the style for a great goal. This was followed by Ollie Fahy, with a similar score, and suddenly Connacht were

Connacht, Railway Cup Interprovincial
Hurling Champions 1999. Back row (l–r):
Liam Hodgins, Noel Larkin, Mark Kerins,
Michael Crimmins, Eugene Cloonan, Paul
Hardiman, Rory Grantley, Brian Feeney
(captain), Pádraig Walsh. Front row (l–r):
Kevin Broderick, Ollie Canning, Ollie
Fahy, Joe Rabbitte, Alan Kerins, Cathal
Moore. Photo by Damien Eagers, Sportsfile.

in the driving seat, which they held to the end. Captained by Galway's Brian Feeney, they defeated Munster by 2-13 to 1-15.

Michael Maher, Chairman

During 1999, former all-Ireland hurler Michael Maher replaced Michael Lowry, TD, who retired from the chairmanship of Semple Stadium. Lowry received many plaudits for his success in eliminating the huge debt that existed on Semple Stadium following the centenary All-Ireland.

New chairman Michael Maher had won five senior All-Ireland medals in the late 1950s and early 1960s, lining out at full-back with Tipperary. Following his retirement from the game, Maher emerged as a brilliant committee chairman; he was chair of Tipperary GAA from 1979 to 1981, and of the Munster Council from 1989 to 1991.

Above: Michael Maher (right) with Semple Stadium groundsman Jimmy Purcell.

1999

The Rebels Hold the Edge: Guinness Munster Senior Hurling Final

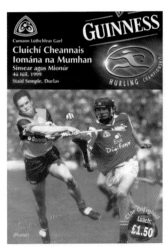

Semple Stadium hosted the Munster hurling final on 4 July, as Cork, captained by Mark Landers, defeated Clare by 1-15 to 0-14 before an attendance of 54,000. Cork had the edge right through this final, but never really established their dominance. The Rebels had a 1-10 to 0-7 lead at half-time. Joe Deane got the only goal of the game in the first half, when a high ball was kept in play on the right by Seánie McGrath for him to flick low past Clare goalkeeper Davy Fitzgerald. With fifteen minutes to play, Clare had come within a point of them; Cork had to call on all their resources to win by four points.

The Rock, Cork's Diarmuid O'Sullivan, jumps for joy as Joe Deane scores a goal. Photo by George Hatchell.

1999
Killinan End renamed Maher Terrace

The Killinan End of Semple Stadium was renamed the Maher Terrace, Lochtán Ó Meachair, on 4 April. A plaque was blessed and unveiled by Monsignor Christopher Lee, commemorating the contribution of the Maher family, Killinan, Thurles, to the GAA locally and nationally. Mícheál Maher, Castlemeadows, and formerly of Parnell Street, Thurles, speaking on behalf of the Maher family, acknowledged the gesture with appreciation.

Above left: Mícheál Maher represented the Maher family at the unveiling.
Above right: Ronan and Padraic Maher, pictured following Tipperary's victory in the 2019
All-Ireland hurling final. Photo by Brigid Delaney.

The Maher connection with Semple Stadium began when Jim Maher was instrumental in the purchase of the grounds in 1910. His brother, Denis, was Tipperary's first senior hurling captain in 1887. Denis's son John captained Tipperary to All-Ireland success in 1945. John's grand-nephews, Padraic and Ronan Maher, are current All-Star hurlers with Tipperary.

1999

Doora Barefield Outgun the Gunners:
AIB Munster Senior Club Hurling Final

Clare's St Joseph's Doora Barefield had a comfortable win over Ballygunner, Waterford, in the Munster club final on 28 November in Semple Stadium. The final score was St Joseph's 4-9, Ballygunner 3-8. The Clare team were defending All-Ireland champions, but they lost the title to Athenry in the final in Croke Park the following March.

St Joseph's Doora Barefield, Clare: Christy O'Connor, Ger Hoey, Donal Cahill, Kenneth Kennedy, David Hoey, Sean McMahon, Darragh O'Driscoll, Ollie Baker, Joe Considine, Colm Mullan, James O'Connor, Noel Brodie, Andrew Whelan, Ciaran O'Neill (captain), Greg Baker. Substitutes played: Fergal O'Sullivan, Dermot Daly.

CHAPTER 9

A NEW MILLENNIUM

2000–2009

2000
Cork Survive Thurles Epic: Guinness Munster Senior Hurling Final

Tipperary and Cork served up a truly absorbing contest in the Munster final at Semple Stadium, on 2 July, before an attendance of 54,586. Tipperary were slow to settle, but their hopes took a dramatic surge when Eugene O'Neill scored their first goal. Cork responded with two points to leave the sides level at the interval, 1-5 to 0-8. Tipperary went ahead in the second period, but Cork gradually got on top and went five in front with three minutes remaining before Tommy Dunne drove in his second goal, followed by a Paul Kelly point. Cork responded as Seánie McGrath fired over an injury-time point. Cork had a star in the form of Joe Deane, who gave a virtuoso performance, scoring ten points. The final score was Cork 0-23, Tipperary 3-12.

2000
First of Limerick's Treble: All-Ireland Under 21 Hurling Final

Limerick took the Under 21 championship after their defeat of Galway in Semple Stadium on 17 September, 2000. It was the beginning of a three-in-a-row for the Shannonsiders; they would beat Wexford in the 2001 final and Galway again in 2002.

Top right: Eugene O'Neill, Tipperary, celebrates after scoring Tipperary's first goal in the Munster final 2000. Photo by Brendan Moran, Sportsfile.

Left: Tipperary senior hurling manager Nicky English.

Below: Tipperary, Munster Senior Hurling Finalists 2000. Back row (l–r): Eddie Enright, Michael Ryan, Brian O'Meara, Philip Maher, Brendan Cummins, Paul Shelly, John Leahy, Eugene O'Neill. Front row (l–r): Mark O' Leary, Paul Ormond, Paddy O'Brien, Tommy Dunne (captain), John Carroll, David Kennedy, Eamon Corcoran.

Limerick, All-Ireland Under 21 Hurling Champions 2000. Photo by Damien Eagers, Sportsfile.

The final score in the 2000 final was Limerick 1-13, Galway 0-13.

Limerick: Timmy Houlihan, Damien Reale, Eugene Mulcahy, Paudie Reale, Paul O'Reilly, Brian Geary, Willie Walsh, John Meskell, Stephen Lucey (0-1), Paul O'Grady (0-1), Seán O'Connor (0-1), David Stapleton (0-1), Donnacha Sheehan (captain, 0-1), Brian Begley, Mark Keane (1-8). Substitute played: Kevin Tobin.

Health and Safety

To the fore in matters dealing with security and stewarding at events at Semple Stadium was Moycarkey/Borris native John Moloughney. John was also a noted piper with the Seán Treacy Pipe Band and regularly played at the venue.

2000
Sixmilebridge Are Munster Champions:
AIB Munster Senior Club Hurling Final

On 26 November, the Munster club title was taken by a Clare team for the sixth year in a row, as Sixmilebridge, under captain Christy Chaplin, won over Waterford's Mount Sion in a close match, ending with a score of 2-17 to 3-8.

Right: Sixmilebridge captain Christy Chaplin celebrates with the cup after the game. Photo by Sportsfile.

Sixmilebridge: Davy Fitzgerald, Kevin McInerney, John O'Connell, Wayne Kennedy, Alan Mulready, Pat Hayes, Declan Murphy, Stiofan Fitzpatrick, Christy Chaplin (captain), Robert Conlon, John Reddan, Martin Conlon, Brian Culbert, Niall Gilligan, John O'Meara. Substitutes: Brian Kennedy, Paul Fitzpatrick, Adrian Chaplin.

2001
Maurice Fitzgerald's Sublime Point:
Bank of Ireland All-Ireland Senior Football Quarter-Final

Semple Stadium was the venue, on 4 August, for the All-Ireland football quarter-final between reigning champions Kerry and Dublin. Kerry dominated for much of the game and were leading by eight points with twelve minutes to play, but then Dublin scored 2-3 without reply and, amazingly, were in front by a point. It was then that Kerry substitute Maurice Fitzgerald worked his magic. His sideline kick from under the Old Stand was out of this world. With injury time ticking away, Fitzgerald swerved over possibly

Above left, top and bottom: The drawn game and replay match programmes.
Above right: Maurice Fitzgerald kicks the equalising point for Kerry. Photo by Ray McManus, Sportsfile.

his most famous score to tie up the game. The final score was Kerry 1-14, Dublin 2-11. In the replay, at the same venue one week later, Kerry won a less memorable game by 2-12 to 2-11. Ruadhan King, a steward at the drawn game, recalled the occasion:

Oddly enough one of my most vivid memories of Semple Stadium is the only big football game I've seen there, Dublin and Kerry in 2001, which ended in a draw. Played on August 4 it was a novel game for the stadium, predominantly used to hurling, and there were stories beforehand that Dublin supporters didn't know where Thurles was, not being used to going further south than Clondalkin!

Kerry conceded two goals near the end to find themselves a point behind, when the ball went out for a Kerry sideline fifty yards out. I was stewarding that day in the Old Stand and was directly behind Maurice Fitzgerald as he faced the goal, thinking 'no way in the world can someone kick a point from there'. He started it off to the left of the post and it just curled beautifully back to right over the black spot, a phenomenal score. I can just recall the ball seeming to gain more and more elevation as it got closer to the goal. It was Fitzgerald's only score, but what a memorable one! What made it more memorable was that Fitzgerald had come on seven minutes before and hadn't actually touched the ball, so the sideline kick was his first one!

And according to Tomás Ó Sé, RTÉ Sports analyst and winner of five All-Ireland senior football medals,

I played there that day myself. Semple Stadium had one of the most electric atmospheres I ever played in.

Coming Home Victorious

Following Tipperary's 2001 All-Ireland final victory over Galway, by 2-18 to 2-15 at Croke Park, a tremendous welcome awaited them at Semple Stadium. Here we see Tipperary captain Tommy Dunne lifting the Liam McCarthy Cup. Photo by Damien Eagers, Sportsfile.

2001

Limerick Retain the Crown:
All-Ireland Under 21 Hurling Final

Limerick held on to their Under 21 hurling title at Semple Stadium on 16 September. They survived a late comeback from Wexford to win by just a single point. The final score was Limerick 0-17, Wexford 2-10.

Timmy Houlihan, Limerick captain, with the Under 21 cup. Photo by Matt Browne, Sportsfile.

2001

First Club Title for Ballygunner: AIB Munster Senior Club Hurling Final

For the first time, Waterford's Ballygunner walked away with the Munster club title after their defeat of Cork's Blackrock in Semple Stadium on 2 December. The final score was Ballygunner 2-14, Blackrock 0-12.

Ballygunner: Ray Whitty, Niall O'Donnell, Alan Kirwan, Rory O'Sullivan, Stephen Frampton, Fergal Hartley, Colin Kehoe, Tom Fives, Paul Power, Paul Foley, Paul Flynn, Andy Moloney, Billy O'Sullivan (captain), Michael O'Mahony, Darragh O'Sullivan. Substitute: Tony Carroll.

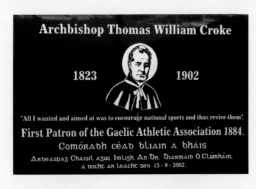

Archbishop Thomas William Croke

1823   1902

"All I wanted and aimed at was to encourage national sports and thus revive them".
First Patron of the Gaelic Athletic Association 1884.
Comóraḋ céaḋ ḃliaiṅ a ḃáis
Arḋeaspaʒ Chaisil aʒus Imliʒh, An Ḋr. Ḋiarmaiḋ Ó Clúmháin,
a nochṫ an Leachṫ ʒeo 15 - 9 - 2002.

Remembering Archbishop Croke

The year 2002 marked the centenary of the death of Archbishop Thomas Croke. The culmination of a series of remembrance events was the unveiling of a commemorative plaque in Ardán Ó Riain on 15 September, prior to the All-Ireland Under 21 hurling final. Appropriately, the plaque, which was the work of local sculptor James Slattery, with an etching by local artist David McElgunn, was unveiled by Archbishop Dermot Clifford, patron of the GAA and successor to Archbishop Croke in the archdiocese of Cashel and Emly. Photo by Tom Ryan Casey.

2002

Whelehan's Masterclass: All-Ireland Senior Club Hurling Final

In this year's club hurling final between Birr of Offaly and Clarinbridge of Galway, a drab first half closed with the Westerners holding a two-point advantage on a scoreline of 1-4 to 1-2. Birr manager Pad Joe Whelehan obviously sparked some much-needed belief into his charges during the break, as they sprung to life by hitting five unanswered points

Below left: Paul Molloy and Donal Franks celebrate with Birr manager Pad Joe Whelahan, left, after victory in the final. Photo by Matt Browne, Sportsfile.
Below right: Birr's Johnny Pilkington in full flight, heading goalwards, in the All-Ireland club final at Semple Stadium. Photo by George Hatchell.

in an eight-minute spell during the second half. The Hanniffy brothers, Gary and Rory, hit ranging scores before Stephen Brown pointed from fifty yards. Simon and Brian Whelehan – sons of manager Pad Joe – slotted over a brace to complete the scoring blitz.

Birr finished off the contest with nine minutes remaining when former Offaly inter-county star Johnny Pilkington kicked home the side's second goal. The final score was Birr 2-10, Clarinbridge 1-5.

2002
Legends of the Lough Shore: All-Ireland Club Football Final

Ballinderry Shamrocks of Derry lit up Semple Stadium on St Patrick's Day with a deserved victory over Cork's Nemo Rangers in the All-Ireland club football final. They thrilled the supporters who had travelled from this small northern parish by weathering a late Nemo storm to hold out in fine style. Nemo trailed by a single point at the break on a scoreline of 1-3 to 0-5. Ballinderry upped their game at the restart and hit four unanswered points to open a commanding lead. Nemo were down but not out and fought back to trail by a point, with the game heading for a thrilling final few minutes.

Ballinderry Shamrocks, AIB All-Ireland Club Football Champions 2002. Back row (l–r): Ronan McGuckin, Niall McCusker, Michael Conlan, Enda Muldoon, Paul Wilson, Barry McOscar, Kevin McGuckin, Seán Donnelly. Front row (l–r): Darren Conway, Jarlath Bell, Conleth Gilligan, Adrian McGuckin (captain), Gerard Cassidy, Declan Bateson, Darren Crozier. Photo by Brendan Moran, Sportsfile.

But Ballinderry struck again, with Ger Cassidy finishing a great move to the net. The same player added a further two points to secure Ballinderry's first All-Ireland club title. The final score was Ballinderry 2-10, Nemo Rangers 0-9.

2002
Kilkenny Clinch Tenth Title:
Allianz National Hurling League Final

In Semple Stadium on 5 May, 2002, Kilkenny, under captain Andy Comerford and manager Brian Cody, took their tenth National Hurling League title. The final score was Kilkenny 2-15, Cork 2-14.

2002
Kelly Secures Replay for Tipp: Munster Senior Football Final

Semple Stadium hosted the Munster football final between Tipperary and Cork, before an attendance of 33,254, on 14 July. Tipperary's All-Star footballer Declan Browne was in brilliant form; five points from play early on, typical trademark shots straight off the turn on the right foot. However Tipperary conceded two goals in that first half, which were hammer blows to the side, leaving Cork ahead by 2-6 to 0-8 at the break.

In a glorious spell in the third quarter, Tipperary fought back and went ahead, 1-11 to 2-7. Cork were not done, however, and in the remaining minutes they took their turn ahead by a point. The equaliser came when substitute Willie Morrissey found Niall Kelly unmarked at the edge of the square, and the Kildangan defender boxed over the point. The match ended in a draw, Tipperary 1-14, Cork 2-11.

In the replay at Páirc Uí Chaoimh, Tipperary never reached their true form and were beaten by 1-23 to 0-7.

Tipperary, Munster Senior Football Finalists 2002. Back row (l–r): Liam England, Bernard Hahessy, Brendan Cummins, Fergal O'Callaghan, Kevin Mulryan, Niall Fitzgerald, Niall Kelly, Damien O'Brien. Front row (l–r): Peter Lambert, Damien Byrne (captain), Paul Cahill, Philly Ryan, Declan Browne, Seán Collum, Seán Maher.

2002
Limerick Claim Third Title: All-Ireland Under 21 Hurling Final

From the throw-in on 15 September, Limerick hummed like a well-oiled machine, and after Mark Keane pointed the way with the opening score in the first minute, there was never any doubt about the outcome; the champions produced what was arguably their best performance of the three years. The final score was Limerick 3-17, Galway 0-8.

Limerick team: Timmy Houlihan; Damien Reale, Eugene Mulcahy, Mickey Cahill, Eoin Foley, Paudie O'Dwyer, Maurice O'Brien, Peter Lawlor (captain), Niall Moran, Conor Fitzgerald, James O'Brien, Kevin Tobin, Andrew O'Shaughnessy, Pat Kirby, Mark Keane. Substitutes played: Pat Tobin, B Carroll, Raymond Hayes.

Above: Mullinahone, Tipperary Senior Hurling Champions 2002. Back row (l–r): Martin Costello, Damien Maher, Aidan Hall, James Comerford, Bill Tobin, Brian O'Meara, Alan Curran, Dan Croke, Conor Arrigan, Dermot Hackett, Vincent Doheny, Tony Dalton, Niall Curran, Danny Morrissey, Edward O'Brien, James Connolly, Jimmy Scott, Michael Scott, Seán Brett. Front row (l–r): Seán O'Meara, Edwin O'Meara, Mark O'Brien, Philip O'Shea, Paul Kelly, Eoin Kelly, Noel Leahy, Pat Croke, Ky Vaughan (captain), John Leahy, Paul Curran, Joey Maher, Stephen O'Brien, Eddie Carey, Niall Doheny. Mascot: Denis Connolly.
Left, top and bottom: Match programmes from the draw and replay.

2002

For the Credit of the Little Village: Tipperary Senior Hurling Final

Mullinahone were ahead by 0-5 to 0-2 at the end of the first quarter, but it was Thurles Sarsfields who were the happier at half-time, retiring to the dressing room with only a two-point deficit, 0-9 to 0-7. Although now facing the wind, Mullinahone went on a scoring spree and opened a six-point margin between the sides by the start of the final quarter. It was at this stage that Sarsfields played their best hurling. They hit four points in a trot to reduce the arrears to 0-12 to 0-10. By injury time the score was 0-14 to 0-12 in favour of Mullinahone, but Sarsfields got two more points; a free from Stephen Mason and a last-gasp point from Pat Lawlor ensured that they lived to fight another day. The final score was 0-14 apiece.

In the replay a week later, it was mostly Sarsfields in the opening half, and they led by

0-9 to 0-2 after twenty-three minutes. Two minutes later Eoin Kelly pounced on a poor Sarsfields clearance and buried the ball in the net. The score was 0-9 to 1-3 at the interval, with Thurles ahead, but they failed to score during the third quarter and Mullinahone took a five-point lead. A Ger O'Grady goal gave Sarsfields hope, but it wasn't enough. Mullinahone had a star performer in Eoin Kelly, who contributed 2-7 of his side's total. The final score was Mullinahone 2-10, Thurles Sarsfields 1-11.

2002

McGrath Seals It for Mount Sion: AIB Munster Senior Club Hurling Final

The first of December was a very wet and windy day at Semple Stadium, as Mount Sion led by 0-9 to 0-4 at half-time against Clare champions Sixmilebridge. Overall the free-taking of Ken McGrath proved significant. The sides were level at 0-10 apiece with three minutes remaining, but two late points by McGrath secured a Déise victory. The final score was Mount Sion 0-12, Sixmilebridge 0-10.

Ken McGrath of Mount Sion. Photo by Matt Browne, Sportsfile.

A Facelift for the Old Stand

The new millennium heralded a demand for higher standards of comfort and safety for players and supporters, and Semple Stadium management, under the chairmanship of Michael Maher, took to their task with gusto. Ardán Uí Chuinneáin/Archbishop Kinnane Stand was extended towards the Town End, accommodating 1,500 extra patrons, and the whole stand was re-roofed. Sixty percent of its capacity now had coverage from the elements, and new seating was installed throughout. Two new tunnels were built to facilitate easier entry and safer egress from the stadium. A new media facility for press, radio and TV was included in an elevated position under the stand. This area also incorporated the control base for the electronic scoreboard and public address. The total project cost in excess of €2.5 million.

2003
Mullane's Hat Trick Not Enough: Guinness Munster Senior Hurling Final

Waterford led Cork by 1-8 to 1-1 after twenty minutes of the Munster final at Semple Stadium on 29 June. By the interval, Cork had reduced their deficit to five points, trailing 1-9 to 1-4. The first eight minutes of the second half saw them draw level. From then to the final whistle was a blur of fury, intensity, sheer drama and a hugely enjoyable experience for the crowd of 52,833.

Cork took the lead in the forty-sixth minute, but Paul Flynn's quick thinking over a free saw him tap the ball to John Mullane, who blasted in his second goal. Cork's Ben O'Connor pointed twice before captain Alan Browne drove in Cork's second goal, and now the Rebels were three points

Waterford's John Mullane in full flight. Photo by Pat Murphy, Sportsfile.

up. But Waterford had the answer in Mullane's third goal, and they were level again. In the fifty-eighth minute, Joe Deane heading cross-field drove the ball to the net. Alan Browne's point put them four clear, and while Waterford twice pared it back to two points, late strikes from Ben O'Connor and John Gardiner guaranteed Cork their first Munster title since 2000. The final score was Cork 3-16, Waterford 3-12.

2003
Eighth Title for the Cats:
All-Ireland Under 21 Hurling Final

Kilkenny, under captain Jackie Tyrrell, took their eighth All-Ireland Under 21 hurling title in Semple Stadium on 21 September, 2003, after beating Galway by 2-13 to 0-12.

Kilkenny, All-Ireland Under 21 Hurling Champions 2003. Back row (l–r): Shane Hennessy, Ken Coogan, Tommy Walsh, John Phelan, Jackie Tyrrell (captain), Canice Hickey, Peter Cleere, Conor Phelan, Colin Dunne, Seán O'Neill. Middle row (l–r): Ger Joyce, Aidan Fogarty, Michael Rice, Richie O'Neill, David Herrity, Mark Phelan, J J Delaney, Brian Dowling, Willie Dwyer. Front row (l–r): Chris O'Neill, Owen McCormack, Michael Grace, Conor O'Loughlin, Niall Moran, Niall Doherty, Martin Phelan, Ned Sweeney.

Newtownshandrum captain John McCarthy lifts the cup with teammate Pat Mulcahy, right, after victory over Patrickswell. Photo by Pat Murphy, Sportsfile.

2003
A First for Newtownshandrum: AIB Munster Senior Club Hurling Final

Cork's Newtownshandrum took their first ever Munster club title over Limerick's Patrickswell, winning by a decisive 2-18 to 2-9 on 30 November in Semple Stadium. They went on to take the All-Ireland crown the following St Patrick's Day.

Hogan Replaces Maher as Stadium Chairman

Photo by Tom Ryan Casey.

At the 2003 Semple Stadium AGM, Michael Maher stood down from his role as chairman. He had served in this position for six busy years and had overseen many necessary improvements and developments at the hallowed ground. Into the position came Con Hogan (pictured), from the Marlfield GAA club in South Tipperary. Con was a former Tipperary GAA chairman with great ability, drive and experience, who had also served on many Croke Park committees.

2004

Déise Best in Classic Final: Guinness Munster Senior Hurling Final

Cork hit top form from the start of this Munster final at Semple Stadium on 27 June, with a goal by Garvan McCarthy, and as the first quarter ended, the Rebels were looking good. However, Dan Shanahan was on top of his game, scoring three of Waterford's opening four points; he would later contribute a vital goal. A stunning solo effort from Eoin Kelly in the fifteenth minute and Déise confidence was on the rise. At the break, they were just three points in arrears, 1-14 to 2-8.

The most significant event after the resumption was John Mullane being red-carded, but to the great credit of the Waterford players, they responded with heroic character. By the fiftieth minute, Waterford were only two points adrift when Paul Flynn's goal from a free, well outfield, put them in front for the first time. This was a sublime piece of hurling skill as Flynn's 'dipper', armed with wristy topspin, deceived Donal Óg, Diarmuid & Co. Joe Deane had Cork level two minutes later. After that Waterford made all the running to the finish. Séamus Prendergast hoisted over the winning point with a minute remaining, and then Ken McGrath plucked a ball out of the clouds to ensure that Cork didn't get a pop at an equaliser. It was their first championship victory over Cork in a final in forty-five years. The final score was Waterford 3-16, Cork 1-21, and attendance on the day was 52,100.

Below left: Tony Browne, Waterford, celebrates victory over Cork in Semple Stadium. Photo by Ray McManus, Sportsfile. Below right: John Mullane, Waterford, in action against Brian Murphy, Cork. Photo by Pat Murphy, Sportsfile.

'I Love Me County'

Following Waterford's great victory – regarded by many hurling aficionados as the best Munster final of all time, with all the ingredients of a classic between two well-matched sides, plenty of goalmouth action and a rapid pace from the opening minute – the Déise supporters burst onto the pitch at Semple Stadium to hail their heroes.

Among the throng was their star forward John Mullane, who had been sent off during the game, now surrounded by loving, loyal Déise supporters as he was interviewed by RTÉ for *The Sunday Game*. A highly emotional Mullane stated, 'I love this county so much … The people of Waterford are my life, and I love me county …'

Former GAA president Paddy Buggy makes a contribution to the collection by travelling troubadour the Pecker Dunne as he plays at the Munster final on 27 June, 2004. Photo by Ray McManus, Sportsfile.

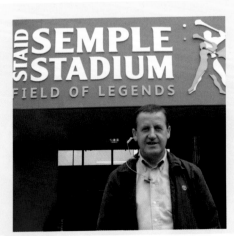

Semple Stadium Management Committee Secretary Mícheál Egan

Mícheál Egan from the Gortnahoe/Glengoole club in Mid Tipperary replaced Tomás Ó Baróid as Semple Stadium Management Committee secretary in 2004. He held this position until 2011. Mícheál currently operates the electronic scoreboard and clock at Semple Stadium.

Eddie Brennan, Kilkenny, celebrates after scoring Kilkenny's third goal.
Photo by Pat Murphy, Sportsfile.

2004

Cats Pounce on Second Chance:
Guinness All-Ireland Senior Hurling Quarter-Final

Kilkenny and Clare played a draw, 1-13 each, in the All-Ireland quarter-final at Croke Park on 25 July. The replay at Semple Stadium a week later never quite lived up to the drama and excitement of the drawn game. At half-time Kilkenny led by 1-4 to 0-3, the goal coming from the on-form Eddie Brennan. There was no upset on the cards, and Kilkenny finished in control, 1-11 to 0-9.

2004

Toome's Unforgettable Win: AIB Munster Senior Club Hurling Final

As half-time approached, with the sides level on 0-8 apiece, Mount Sion won a penalty, which Ken McGrath buried in the Toome net. The half-time score was Mount Sion 1-9, Toomevara 0-8. An early opportunist goal by Willie Ryan gave the 'Greyhounds' the

Toomevara, Tipperary Senior Hurling Champions 2004. Back row (l–r): F Devaney, W Ryan, T Delaney, K Dunne, P Hackett, T Dunne, T Dunne, E Brislane. Front row (l–r): B Dunne (with niece Eva), P Shanahan, M Bevans, J Cottrell (with Michael Delaney), J Boland, D Young, P O'Brien.

lift they needed, and hurling with added determination, they levelled, went in front and stayed there. The final score was Toomevara 1-14, Mount Sion 1-13.

2004

Paul O'Dwyer Rescues the Banner: AIB Munster Senior Club Football Final

The Munster club football final between Waterford's Stradbally and Clare's Kilmurry/Ibrickane, held in Semple Stadium on 5 December, ended in a draw, 0-9 apiece. The scorers for Stradbally were Niall Curran (0-4, 3f), Ger Power (0-2), Michael Walsh, John Hearne and Stephen Cunningham (0-1 each); and for Kilmurry/Ibrickane, Johnny Daly (0-4, 3f), Michael O'Dwyer (0-3), Aongus Corry and Paul O'Dwyer (0-1 each). In the replay, a week later in FitzGerald Park, Clare's Kilmurry edged just ahead of the Waterford team, 0-9 to 0-8.

Kilmurry/Ibrickane, Clare: Dermot O'Brien, Martin Keavey, John O'Connor, Brendan Moloney, Declan Callinan, Martin Cahill, Evan Talty, Peter O'Dwyer, Odhran O'Dwyer (captain), Aongus Corry, Enda Coughlan, Shane Hickey, Michael Hogan, Johnny Daly, Michael O'Dwyer. Substitutes played: Robert O'Dwyer, Gary Donnellan, Martin O'Connor.

D J Carey, Kilkenny, in action against Brian Lohan, Clare, in the Allianz National Hurling League Division 1 final at Semple Stadium. Photo by Brendan Moran, Sportsfile.

2005

When D J Was Barbirolli: Allianz National Hurling League Final

In a power-packed display of hurling, Kilkenny swept Clare to one side in the second half of the National Hurling League final at Semple Stadium on 2 May. The teams were level at half-time: Clare 0-10, Kilkenny 1-7. Peter Barry played a captain's part in central defence, while D J Carey engineered Kilkenny's two second-half goals, finished by Eoin Larkin and Henry Shefflin. The final score was Kilkenny 3-20, Clare 0-15.

Thurles Sarsfields, Tipperary Senior Hurling Champions 2005. Back row (l–r): Eamon Walshe, Shane Ryan, Lee Shanahan, Ciarán O'Connor, Pa Bourke, Eoin Russell, Pat Lawlor, Garry Mernagh, Eddie Enright, Tom King, John Lawlor, Lar Corbett, Declan Ryan, Brendan Carroll, David Kearns, Jamie Murphy, Barry O'Dwyer, Stephen Mason, Aidan Dundon. Front row (l–r): Tony Connolly, Johnny Enright, Jim Mackey, David O'Dwyer, Tommy Collins, Richie Ruth, Wayne Cully, Jim Corbett, Ger O'Grady (captain), Lorna O'Grady (mascot), Paddy McCormack, Stephen Lillis, Brendan O'Sullivan, John Connors, Brian Graydon, Michael Collins, Eoin Costello.

Rhapsody in blue: Sarsfields supporters celebrate their win.

2005

Sarsfields's First in Three Decades: Tipperary Senior Hurling Final

The attendance of 12,710 at Semple Stadium on 16 October saw Thurles Sarsfields live up to their pre-match favourites tag when they defeated Drom/Inch by 1-17 to 0-15. The closeness of the scoring kept spectators on their toes right through. Until about ten minutes into the second half, the outcome lay in the balance, but after that, victory for the Blues became inevitable. At half-time Thurles led by 1-9 to 0-9, the goal coming in the eighth minute, when the Drom/Inch goalkeeper let a sideline cut by Wayne Cully slip between his fingers into the net.

This put Thurles in the driving seat, and even though Drom succeeded in reducing the margin to one point early in the second half, they could never quite obliterate it, and Thurles went on to a well-deserved five-point victory. The win came as a huge relief for Sarsfields, their first in thirty-one years.

2005

O'Connors Steer Newtown to Munster Title:
AIB Munster Senior Club Hurling Final

Cork club Newtown led by 0-8 to 0-7 at the interval, and they increased their advantage to 0-11 to 0-8 by the fortieth minute. However, Waterford's Ballygunner dug in for a real battle, scoring 1-3 without reply, their goal coming from Gearóid O'Connor. Newtown held their nerve over the closing period, ending just in front by 0-16 to Ballygunner's 1-12. It was the Cork club's second Munster title.

Newtownshandrum, Cork: Paul Morrissey, Gerard O'Mahony, Brendan Mulcahy (captain), Dermot Gleeson, Alan T O'Brien, Pat Mulcahy, Philip Noonan, Cathal Naughton, Jerry O'Connor, Donal Mulcahy, John O'Connor, John Paul King, Jerry O'Mahony, James Bowles, Ben O'Connor. Substitute played: Maurice Farrell.

2006
Kilkenny Win Thirteenth Crown: Allianz National Hurling League Final

Brian Cody's Kilkenny were just too good for Limerick at Semple Stadium on 30 April, as they scored at crucial times in an end-to-end decider. Recently back from injury, Henry Shefflin helped himself to a decisive two goals and six points and also set Eoin Larkin up for a twelfth-minute goal.

But the Shannonsiders, in their first league final since 1997, were well primed for a battle and offered much. Kilkenny went in at the interval with a 2-4 to 0-7 advantage. The sides split the first four points of the second half, and as the final quarter approached, there were just two points between them, 2-7 to 0-11. But Kilkenny put in a telling spurt, scoring 1-2 in the space of four minutes to all but end Limerick's fight. The final score was Kilkenny 3-11, Limerick 0-14.

2006
Rebels Win Titanic Battle: Guinness Munster Senior Hurling Final

A crowd of 53,500 packed into Semple Stadium on 25 June, as age-old rivals Tipperary and Cork battled for Munster supremacy. Hurling's enchasing pull was illustrated with a sizzling summer smiling on the noisy, colourful scene. Lar Corbett got Tipperary's opening goal of the game when he shot low to beat Cork goalkeeper Donal Óg Cusack in

Above left: Michael 'Babs' Keating began his second stint as Tipperary hurling manager in 2006.
Photo by George Hatchell.
Above right: Pat Mulcahy lifts the Munster trophy. Photo by Ray McManus, Sportsfile.

the fourth minute. Cork goals from Ben O'Connor and Brian Corcoran had Tipperary five points behind, but points mainly from Eoin Kelly had the sides level at the interval, 1-9 to 2-6. The second half was tit for tat but the Cork forwards were getting a better and more plentiful supply of the ball, where Joe Deane was amounting his total of eight points. Tipperary only managed to score five points in the second half to Cork's eight. The final score was Cork 2-14, Tipperary 1-14.

Semple Stadium Caretaker Philip Butler

Jimmy Purcell, who had been a fixture at Semple Stadium since late 1984, retired at the end of 2006. A native of Loughmore but living in Thurles for many years, Jimmy contributed significantly to the maintenance of what is generally regarded as the best playing surface for hurling in the country. He took great pride in his work and ensured

Above left: Seán Fogarty (left), chairman of the Munster Council, makes a presentation to Semple Stadium groundsman Jimmy Purcell at the 2006 Munster final, just before Purcell's retirement. Photo by Brendan Moran, Sportsfile. Above right: Jimmy Purcell and Philly Butler.

that the venue was always in peak condition. Philip Butler of Thurles replaced Jimmy as groundsman. Philly had proven his ability as caretaker of Dr Morris Park since 1997.

2006

Hogan's Goal Mattered Most:
Erin All-Ireland Under 21 Hurling Final

A brilliant, opportunist goal by Paddy Hogan in the twenty-first minute steered Kilkenny to victory over Tipperary in a thrilling Under 21 final replay at Semple Stadium. The final score was Kilkenny 1-11, Tipperary 0-11.

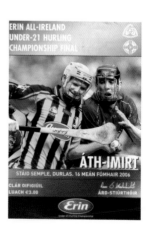

Kilkenny: Liam Tierney, Seán Cummins, John Tennyson, Kieran Joyce, Pat Hartley, John Dalton, Damien Fogarty, James 'Cha' Fitzpatrick, Michael Fennelly (captain), Paddy Hogan, Austin Murphy, T J Reid, Richie Power, Richie Hogan, David McCormack.

Waterford, Allianz National Hurling League Champions 2007. Back row (l–r): Dan Shanahan, Tony Browne, Declan Prendergast, Clinton Hennessy, Ken McGrath, Stephen Molumphy, Séamus Prendergast, John Mullane. Front row (l–r): Eoin Kelly, Eoin Murphy, James Murray, Jack Kennedy, Aidan Kearney, Michael Walsh (captain), Shane Walsh. Photo by Ray McManus, Sportsfile.

2007
Déise Rising: Allianz National Hurling League Final

This was as good a hurling classic as one could wish for so early in the season. Waterford put in a titanic battle and had the better of Kilkenny in the first half; they were ahead by 0-11 to 0-9 at the interval. The Déise defence was in sparkling form, with Ken McGrath the commanding figure.

The margin was the same after twenty minutes of the second period, 0-13 to 0-11, but then Kilkenny started to motor and levelled at 0-16 apiece. Richie Power put the Cats a point ahead, but John Mullane levelled, 0-18 each. The Déise dug deep; Eoin Kelly, who scored a total of eight points, put them ahead, and Séamus Prendergast, sweeping across to his left, fired over the final point in a wonderful Waterford triumph. Sheer joy was palpable as Michael 'Brick' Walsh raised the cup, a national title at last – their first league title since 1963. The final score was Waterford 0-20, Kilkenny 0-18.

Mícheál Ó Muircheartaigh at work in his commentary position at Semple Stadium. Photo by Brendan Moran, Sportsfile.

The Voice of the GAA

Mícheál Ó Muircheartaigh was a well-known and familiar, friendly face around Semple Stadium for many decades. The renowned radio commentator was born in Dún Síon, just outside Dingle, in 1930. Until he announced his retirement from broadcasting in 2010, he was the voice of Gaelic games in a marvellous career that spanned six decades. In more recent years, Ger Canning, Brian Carthy and Marty Morrissey have continued the broadcasting tradition.

Mick Plays His Part

Lisdowney native Mick Carroll has given immeasurable service to Semple Stadium over many years in his voluntary role as advisor on pitch maintenance. The much-admired playing sod is maintained to a top standard by the groundsmen under Mick's direction, where his expertise in pitch management has contributed to making it the Field of Legends. A former Teagasc employee, Mick is the twin brother of the late Ted Carroll, former All-Ireland medal winner and Kilkenny GAA secretary. Mick is currently president of Dúrlas Óg GAA in Thurles.

2007

Hat Trick for Déise Dan: Guinness Munster Senior Hurling Final

Semple Stadium welcomed 48,371 supporters to the Munster final on 8 July. When Brian Begley flicked in a goal off a long-range Brian Geary free in the seventh minute, Limerick were beginning to look good. They protected a narrow lead through much of the first half before Waterford edged ahead with a Séamus Prendergast point just before half-time, 0-9 to 1-5. The second half belonged to Dan Shanahan, who scored 3-3 from play. Overall Waterford's greater big-time experience stood to them, and they injected power and precision into their game to out-score Limerick by 2-3 to 0-2 over the last eight minutes. The final score was Waterford 3-17, Limerick 1-14.

Dan Shanahan, Waterford, shows concentration, timing and skill at Semple Stadium. Photo by Brendan Moran, Sportsfile.

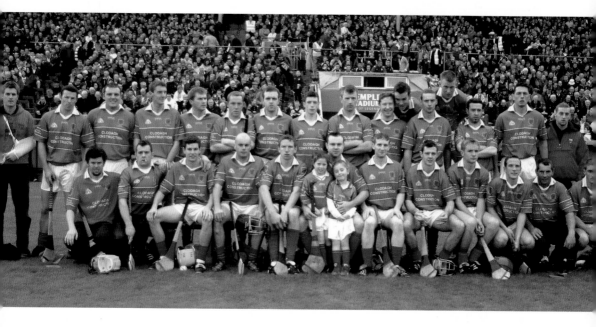

Loughmore/Castleiney, Tipperary Senior Hurling Champions 2007. Back row (l–r): Tommy Ormond, John Paul Foy, James Egan, Tom King, Paul Ormond, Ger Morris, Colm Campion, John Campion, David Kennedy, Derek Bourke, Eoin Ryan, Paul Brennan, Martin Ryan, Alvy Stapleton, Micheál Webster, Diarmuid Brennan. Front row (l–r): Jody Sweeney, David McGrath, Evan Sweeney, Gary Sweeney, Eddie Connolly, Johnny Gleeson (captain), Amy and Patricia Gleeson (mascots), Ronan Stapleton, Ciaran McGrath, Noel McGrath, James Connolly, Séamie Bohan, Tommy Long.

2007

Sweeney Points Loughmore to Victory: Tipperary Senior Hurling Final

On the day it was a one-sided final in which Loughmore/Castleiney hit the ground running and never gave up, while Drom/Inch strove to get going for the hour. Drom had their only bright moment in the first few minutes when Séamus Callanan gave them the opening score. After that it was to be Loughmore all the way, inspired by a brilliant display by half-forward Evan Sweeney, who scored nine points, earning him the Man of the Match award. Loughmore led by 0-13 to 0-5 at half-time, and the pattern continued right through the remaining half. With six minutes remaining, they led by 0-22 to 0-8 – that was a better reflection of their superiority than the final score of 0-22 to 0-13.

2007
Pulsating Victory for the Rebels:
Cadbury's All-Ireland Under 21 Football Final

An injury-time free from Daniel Goulding saw Cork take the All-Ireland Under 21 Football title for the first time since 1994, following a pulsating win over Laois. The final score was Cork 2-10, Laois 0-15.

2007
Refurbishment of Ardán Uí Chuinneáin

In 2007, the modernisation of Semple Stadium was high on the agenda of management committee chairman Con Hogan. With support funding from the GAA and a sports capital grant, he spearheaded further development work, initially on the Dr Kinane Stand, involving expenditure of €5.5 million.

The project was managed by a design team led by Wilson Architecture, Cork, with Duggan Brothers, Templemore, as the main contractors. Four new dressing rooms, a referee room, a drug-testing room, upgraded toilet facilities, medical treatment rooms, new facilities for ticketing and programme sales, and modern turnstiles were installed. This modernisation, coupled with some necessary structural improvements to the stand, made the stadium more attractive for both player and spectator.

*John Mullane basks in
De La Salle euphoria.*

2008
Glory for De La Salle:
AIB Munster Senior Club Hurling Final

Having won the Waterford crown for the first time ever just three weeks before, De La Salle turned around the Munster club final, held in Semple Stadium on 30 November, in the final minutes. Limerick champions Adare had a five-point interval lead, but it was dashed by John Mullane, who scored 1-2 in the second half, and his teammates, leaving the final score at De La Salle 1-9, Adare 0-10.

De La Salle: Steven Brenner, Alan Kelly, Ian Flynn, Michael Doherty, Darren Russell, Kevin Moran, David Greene, Brian Phelan, Conan Watt, Paidi Nevin, Brian Farrell, Lee Hayes, Dean Twomey, John Mullane (captain), James Quirke. Substitutes played: Stephen Daniels, Thomas Kearney, Seamus Richardson, Alan O'Neill, Dermot Dooley.

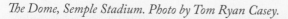

2008

Stadium Modernisation Continues Apace

As refurbishment and modernisation work continued, the focus of attention moved to Ardán Ó Riain. New seating was installed in the stand, as well as medical rooms, a stewards room, new press facilities and an event control base. The need for bar facilities, merchandise shops, and hot and cold food outlets was recognised and provided for. Seomra an Uachtaráin and VIP facilities were fitted out appropriately. Signage was upgraded, and a new entrance was made from the Nenagh Road, running alongside the grounds of Thurles Crokes AC; this would ease access and egress from the stadium. Extra parking and picnic areas were also provided.

Another exciting addition came in the form of the Dome, a multipurpose sports

The Dome, Semple Stadium. Photo by Tom Ryan Casey.

building that was a joint venture between Semple Stadium management and North Tipperary VEC. This 21.3m x 54.4m building included changing rooms, toilets, shower facilities, storage areas and a mezzanine level for fitness equipment. The sports hall accommodated a full-sized basketball court suitable for national standard competitions, and was also lined for badminton, volleyball etc.

This multi-functional hall is used by the local school, Coláiste Mhuire Co-Ed, during the week for sports, exams, drama and assembly, and in the evenings and on weekends for training by the Tipperary hurling and football teams. On match days, the Dome accommodates many GAA and sponsor guests for refreshments, corporate lunches and functions. It is also used as a music venue – singer Tommy Fleming performed the first concert there on 13 November 2009.

Wilson Architecture, Cork, and Horganlynch Consulting Engineers worked in conjunction with Duggan Brothers of Templemore, as did quantity surveyors James Sheehan Associates and mechanical engineers Overy+Associates, Clonmel, in the delivery of these projects.

Epic Encounters, Etched in Memory

Nickey Brennan, GAA president, 2006–2009. Photo by Ray McManus, Sportsfile.

Those of us who have grown up in a hurling environment will have special memories of Semple Stadium. Down through the decades the famed Thurles sod has hummed to the sound of hurlers and hurling people. The biggest names in the sport will attest to the wonderful arena that is Semple Stadium. The venue has a special aura for hurlers. Down through the years some of our Association's most compelling hurling games took place here. These epic encounters remain etched in the minds of many people to this day.

I have many happy memories of playing in Semple Stadium with both St Kieran's College and with Kilkenny. It almost felt like playing at home. The atmosphere was always electric and being located in hurling heartland, it also attracted more than just people from the participating counties. The jewel in the crown with Semple Stadium has always been the pristine condition of the pitch. The green sward was welcoming to every camán, and no hurler could point to the pitch as a reason for a bad result or performance. Groundsmen manicured the pitch better than their own gardens.

Nickey Brennan, Allianz Hurling League match programme,
14 February 2009

2008
Toomevara's Decade of Glory: Tipperary Senior Hurling Championship

These were glory days for Toomevara hurling, as they won six county championships between 1999 and 2008. This year's success showed that their hunger for glory hadn't waned; they had three points to spare over old rivals Thurles Sarsfields in the final at Semple Stadium on 19 October, winning by 2-14 to 0-17.

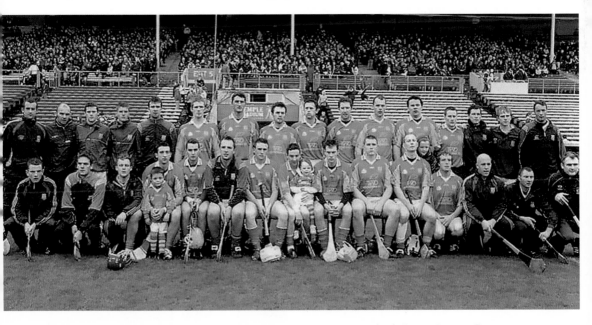

Toomevara, Tipperary Senior Hurling Champions 2008. Back row (l–r): Barry Dunne, Denis Kelly, Kieran Brislane, Conor O'Meara, David Kennedy, Francis Devaney, Padraig Hackett, Paul McGrath, Ken Dunne, John O'Brien, Terry Dunne, Eoin Brislane, Thomas McCarthy, Ronan Ryan, David Nolan, Andrew Ryan. Front row (l–r): Paddy Grace, Kieran McGrath, Darren Cuddihy, Benny Dunne, Willie Ryan, James McGrath, Patrick Tuohy, Michael Bevans (captain), Joseph McLoughney, David Young, Paddy O'Brien, John Delaney, Justin Cottrell, John Boland, Tony Delaney. Mascots: Mikey Delaney, Ava Bevans, Eva Dunne.

Field of Legends

A new Semple Stadium logo and the iconic slogan 'Field of Legends' were adopted in 2009.

2009
Lights On!

On 14 February, 2009, GAA president Nickey Brennan officially reopened Semple Stadium, and the switching on of its new floodlights took place. Musco Lighting were contractors for the installation, which saw four masts erected at the four corners of the pitch. The occasion was the first in a programme of celebrations in Tipperary to mark the founding of the GAA at Hayes's Hotel in 1884, 125 years previously. A plaque was unveiled to mark the historic occasion. The iconic stadium – this 'Field of Legends' – in the GAA's birthplace had copper-fastened its status as the Association's number-two

Above left: A fine aerial view of the completed development. Photo by Star Systems, Thurles.
Above right: Switching on the floodlights at Semple Stadium were (l–r) Jimmy O'Gorman, chairman, Munster Council; Barry O'Brien, chairman, Tipperary GAA; Uachtarán CLG Nickey Brennan; Con Hogan, chairman, Semple Stadium; and Padraic Duffy, GAA Árd Stiurthóir. Photo by Bridget Delaney.

Above: Snowflakes fell as GAA president Nickey Brennan unveiled a plaque at Ardán Ó Riain to mark the completion of major refurbishment and floodlighting at Semple Stadium. Left to right: Mícheál Egan, secretary, Semple Stadium; Nickey Brennan, Uachtarán CLG; Con Hogan, chairman, Semple Stadium; and Barry O'Brien, chairman, Tipperary GAA.

venue after Croke Park, now having a capacity of 53,500.

The addition of floodlights also marked the completion of the major refurbishment that began in 2006. The work on the Kinane Stand side of the stadium involved expenditure of €5.5 million, with the overall cost of the stadium upgrade estimated at €18 million. The entire programme was financed by grant aid from GAA Central Council, who provided €10 million, and by Munster GAA, government funding, term ticket sales, ongoing earnings and borrowings. The project had been completed on time and within budget under the stewardship of stadium chairman Con Hogan.

2009
David Morgan, First Stadium Director

Limerick native David Morgan, from Cappamore, was appointed Semple Stadium director this year, with responsibility for running the stadium and the Dome on a commercial

basis. David was the commercial and operations manager of the Irish Greyhound Board prior to taking up his appointment at Semple Stadium.

Semple Stadium director David Morgan (right) chats with chairman Con Hogan. Photo by Tom Ryan Casey.

Kilkenny captain Henry Shefflin receives the National Hurling League Cup from Christy Cooney, who succeeded Nickey Brennan as GAA president in 2009.

2009

Richie Hogan Leads Cats' Recovery: Allianz National Hurling League Final

Both Kilkenny and Tipperary clearly deemed the league title a prize worth fighting for, hence the ferocity of the exchanges from start to finish at Semple Stadium on 3 May. James Woodlock kicked Tipperary's first goal in the third minute, and John O'Brien buried a great pass from Shane McGrath for their second, five minutes later. Brendan Cummins blocked a rasper from Henry Shefflin just before half-time, which had Tipperary 2-7 to 0-8 ahead. They increased the advantage to eight points when Callanan scored their third goal, following a Lar Corbett pass. Tipperary supporters in the 17,087-strong crowd were beginning to feel confident. But not for long, as Richie Hogan's goal hailed Kilkenny's recovery. The Cats weren't finished, and Aidan Fogarty smashed Kilkenny's second goal in the fiftieth minute. Tipperary just managed to stay in front until the sixty-eighth minute, when a Fogarty point levelled it up for the first time. Points were exchanged, with Noel McGrath getting the equaliser: Tipperary 3-14, Kilkenny 2-17.

Kilkenny had the psychological edge as the game went into extra time, and they made

Tipperary's Lar Corbett receives close attention from Kilkenny's Jackie Tyrrell and Paul Murphy.

it count when it mattered most. Noel McGrath's goal had Tipp ahead by 4-16 to 2-20 early in the second period, before points by Reid and Hogan brought the sides level. From there to the end, it was all Kilkenny, who scored point after point. The final score was Kilkenny 2-26, Tipperary 4-17 (after extra time).

2009

Corbett Goals Prove Decisive: Munster Senior Hurling Final

Playing in their fifth Munster final of the decade, at Semple Stadium on 12 July, Waterford went full throttle from the start. However, it was Tipperary who would take their second Munster title in a row for the first time since 1988. Over 40,000 spectators were treated to a rip-roaring first half, with Waterford's Eoin Kelly and John Mullane scoring 1-2 apiece, and Seamus Callanan, Eoin Kelly and Lar Corbett netting for Tipperary.

Tipperary all but won the match during an eleven-minute spell before half-time, during which they hit 3-3, and led by 3-10 to 2-04 at half-time. Corbett fired home their fourth goal six minutes after the break, and the margin was now eleven points. The Mullane-inspired Déise hit the game's final six points, but the damage had been done. Liam Sheedy's men deservedly held on to march into the All-Ireland semi-final as provincial champions.

Twenty-year-old Seamus Callanan maintained his goal-a-game ratio, while eighteen-year-old Noel McGrath continued to sparkle. A bloodied and bruised Mullane did his best to carry the fight, ending the game with 1-5 from play. But the likes of Padraic Maher stepped up to the mark, producing a fine defensive display including a very brave block as Maurice Shanahan went for goal around the hour mark. The final score was Tipperary 4-14, Waterford 2-16.

2009

GAA 125

A number of events took place this year to mark the 125th anniversary of the founding of the GAA in Hayes's Hotel, Thurles, on 1 November, 1884. Before the Munster final in Semple Stadium on 12 July, all of those captains who led their teams to Munster hurling victory between 1984 and 2008 lined up for the photo below, which was taken by George Hatchell.

Back row (l–r): Declan Carr (Tipperary, 1991), Ger Fitzgerald (Cork, 1992), Michael O'Meara (Tipperary, 1993), Gary Kirby (Limerick, 1994), Anthony Daly (Clare, 1995, 1997 and 1998), Mark Landers (Cork, 1999), Fergal Ryan (Cork, 2000), Fergal Hartley (Waterford, 2002), Alan Browne (Cork, 2003), Ken McGrath (Waterford, 2004), Pat Mulcahy (Cork, 2006). Front row (l–r): Ciarán Carey (Limerick, 1996), Ger Cunningham

(Cork, 1985), Richard Stakelum (Tipperary, 1987), John Fenton (Cork, 1984), Jimmy O'Gorman (chairman, Munster GAA), Pat O'Neill (Tipperary, 1988), Kieran McGuckian (Cork, 1990), Bobby Ryan (Tipperary, 1989), Tommy Dunne (Tipperary, 2001), Tomás Walsh, representing Michael 'Brick' Walsh (Waterford, 2007), James (Jim) Kelly, representing Eoin Kelly (Tipperary, 2008). Missing from photo: Tom Cashman (Cork, 1986) and Sean Óg Ó hAilpín (Cork, 2005).

The most notable of the GAA 125 events was a torch relay run from the birthplace of Michael Cusack at Carron, County Clare, to Hayes's Hotel, Thurles. On the day of the Munster final, the torch was carried by relay from the hotel to Semple Stadium and brought onto the pitch by former Tipperary hurler Jimmy Doyle, while the Artane Band supplied appropriate musical fanfares.

Munster Council chairman Jimmy O'Gorman (left) receives the torch from Jimmy Doyle. Photo by George Hatchell.

2009
Newtown's Ben Strikes Twice: AIB Munster Club Hurling Final

About 3,000 dedicated fans made the journey to Semple Stadium on 29 November for the Munster club hurling final. They defied the sleet and biting wind to witness a contest of quality from Newtownshandrum and Ballygunner. The Déise boys played with the strong wind but for most of the game looked a pale shadow of themselves.

Newtown were firing on all cylinders to lead at the break by six points, 1-7 to 0-4. Halfway through the second half, the gap had stretched to ten points, 2-9 to 0-5. Even in the dark depths of winter, change can come, and it did as the Gunners fired in 2-4 in the next eleven minutes without a reply from the stunned Cork champions, leaving the game tied, 2-9 apiece, and heading into injury time.

Newtownshandrum needed leadership as the tide turned against them, and up stepped the evergreen and ever-reliable Ben O'Connor to shoot two points to see them home. The final score was Newtownshandrum 2-11, Ballygunner 2-9.

Newtownshandrum's Ben O'Connor celebrates victory at the final whistle. Photo by Brendan Moran, Sportsfile.

CHAPTER 10

THE LEGEND LIVES ON

2010–2020

2010
Kavanagh Takes Galway All the Way:
Allianz National Hurling League Final

Semple Stadium was bathed in sunshine on 2 May, through seventy magnificent minutes of hurling. Galway and Cork went at it toe to toe from the start, thrilling the 14,200-strong crowd. Galway led 2-12 to 1-11 at the interval, after playing into the slight breeze in this battle that saw almost a score a minute. Their goals came from Damien Hayes and a young Joe Canning. Cork's goal was special, a pass from Ben O'Connor to his Newtown clubmate Cathal Naughton for a run which ended with him booting the ball to the net from distance.

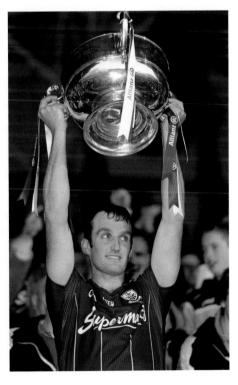

Galway captain Shane Kavanagh lifts the league cup. Photo by Ray McManus, Sportsfile.

The second half was also played with great intensity, but Galway held the whip hand all the way through to the finish. They outgunned Cork and never allowed them closer than four. The Rebels had their chances, and Colm Callanan made a couple of fine saves including a Horgan penalty. The final score was Galway 2-22, Cork 1-17.

2010

Tony Browne's Heroics in Attack and Defence:
Munster Senior Hurling Final

Waterford and Cork finished level on 11 July at Semple Stadium, with the final score reading 2-15 apiece, before an attendance of 35,347. Cork looked to be set for their first provincial victory since 2006, but Waterford had a saviour in Tony Browne, who reacted quickest to fire home the rebound to the Cork net, after Eoin Kelly's twenty-metre free had been saved. Prior to that, goals from Aisake Ó hAilpín and Ben O'Connor had turned the game for Cork, who had trailed by four points early in the second half.

The replay at the same venue, under lights, on 17 July, attracted an attendance of 22,763. It was another epic contest in wet and misty conditions. At half-time Waterford were leading by four points, 0-8 to 0-4. In the forty-fifth minute, a Ben O'Connor free

Tony Browne of Waterford in action against Aisake Ó hAilpín of Cork during the Munster final replay at Semple Stadium. Photo by Brendan Moran, Sportsfile.

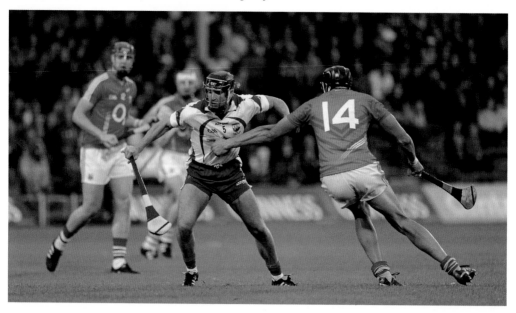

from out on the right touchline streaked past Clinton Hennessy, putting Cork in the lead for the first time, 1-8 to 0-9. It looked like the Rebels were on their way to a win, but four points in a row showed the true character in this Waterford team. At the sixtieth minute, the sides were level, 1-10 to 0-13, and level again as they headed into extra time, 1-11 to 0-14.

Tony Browne's long-range free had the Déise ahead at half-time in extra time. Three minutes into the second half, a Waterford attack saw Eoin McGrath breaking through and giving an inch-perfect pass to Dan Shanahan, who tucked in neatly in the Rebels' net at the Killinan End, just out of the reach of the diving Donal Óg, who managed to make contact, but not enough. Typically, Cork came back, hurling frantically now. The game had slipped into injury time when Cathal Naughton unleashed a rocket to the Town End goal, only for Tony Browne's defensive heroics to intervene with a remarkable block, the sliotar ricocheting off his helmet to safety. A night to remember for Waterford hurlers. The final score was Waterford 1-16, Cork 1-13 (after extra time).

Order of Malta

Since the 1940s, the Thurles Order of Malta have been a regular feature at all games and events at Semple Stadium. Their role is a vital one, as they are first in line with emergency first aid and ambulance cover for both players and spectators, a service that is very much appreciated by all.

Left: Crowds at the Welcome Home celebration at Semple Stadium. Right: Tipperary manager Liam Sheedy sings, accompanied by his mother, Biddy. Both photos by Bridget Delaney.

2010
Welcoming Home the Champs

Tipperary won the All-Ireland by beating Kilkenny 4-17 to 1-18, having qualified for the final via the backdoor system. The Tipperary team, captained by Eoin Kelly, were given a hero's welcome as 45,000 turned out in Semple Stadium to celebrate. The victors travelled by train to Thurles, then an open-top bus brought them through the streets of the town to their official reception at Semple Stadium.

2010
Tipperary Win Lopsided Final: Bord Gáis Energy All-Ireland Under 21 Hurling Final

Six days after Tipperary won the senior All-Ireland final, on 11 September spirits were high as the Under 21s welcomed Galway to Semple Stadium. The home team were absolutely unstoppable; an early blast of goals from Brian O'Meara and John O'Dwyer gave them a lead which was never relin-

Padraic Maher lifts the Cross of Cashel trophy following the Under 21 All-Ireland final. Photo by Ray McManus, Sportsfile.

quished, while Seán Carey's goal made it 3-4 to 0-2 inside fifteen minutes. Featuring five players who started in the senior All-Ireland, Tipperary were in excellent form and led 3-7 to 0-9 at the break. Galway needed a good second-half start, but instead it was Tipperary making and taking all of the chances, and for the rest of the game they continued to reel off scores. In the end, they won by 5-22 to Galway's 0-12.

It was Tipperary's first Under 21 All-Ireland in fifteen years, and the first time since 1989 that they completed the senior and Under 21 double: a perfect end to a perfect week.

2011
One Hundred Years of Girl Guides

On 7 May, 2011, over 6,200 members of the Irish Girl Guides gathered at Semple Stadium to celebrate the centenary of their organisation. The day was officially opened by Minister for Children and Youth Affairs Frances Fitzgerald TD.

Galway, All-Ireland Under 21 Hurling Champions 2011. Back row (l–r): Conor McDonagh, Gearoid McInerney, Robert Mitchell, Eoin Fahy, Niall Quinn, Colm Flynn, Rory Foy, Niall Donoghue, Niall Burke, Jamie Ryan, Conor Cooney, Jason Grealish, Donal Cooney, Paul Gordon, Donal Fox, Ronan Burke, Stephen Page, Martin Dolphin, Richie Cummins. Front row (l–r): Alan Armstrong, David Burke, Bernard Burke, Tadhg Haran, Declan Connolly, Barry Daly (captain), Johnny Coen, Fergal Flannery, James Regan, Ger O'Halloran, John Brehony, Davy Glennon. Photo by Ray McManus, Sportsfile.

2011

Galway Take the Crown:
Bord Gáis Energy All-Ireland Under 21 Hurling Final

Galway's abundance of natural hurling talent was in evidence at Semple Stadium on 10 September, when their victory over Dublin was never in doubt. The final score was Galway 3-14, Dublin 1-10.

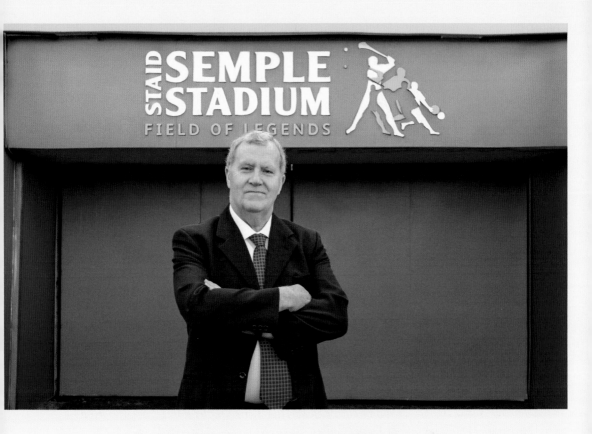

Tom Maher, Semple Stadium Secretary

Tom Maher, from the Moyne/Templetuohy club in Mid Tipperary, replaced Mícheál Egan as secretary of Semple Stadium management committee this year. On match days, from his position in the players' tunnel, Tom ensures that the day's events are carried out efficiently. Photo by Tom Ryan Casey.

2011
A First for Drom/Inch: Tipperary Senior Hurling Final

The county final between Clonoulty-Rossmore and Drom/Inch started slowly but came alive in the tenth minute, when a good Clonoulty movement combined for the game's first goal, by Seán Maher. It wasn't long, however, before Pat Lupton hit back with a Drom goal. During the remainder of the half, Drom edged more into contention and were only a point in arrears at half-time, 1-9 to 1-8.

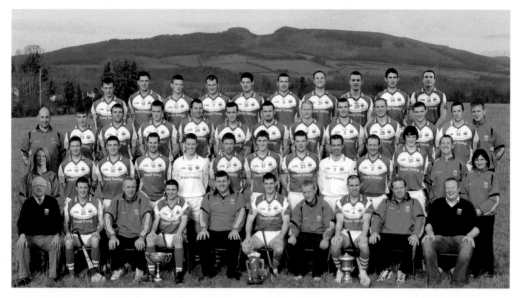

Drom/Inch, Tipperary Senior Hurling Champions 2011. Front row (l–r): Austin Broderick, Kevin Butler, Martin Butler, Johnny Ryan, Tadhg Kennedy, Séamus Callanan (captain), Seán Prendergast, Michael Costello, Andy Bourke, Pat Egan. Second row (l–r): Corina Daly, Séamus Butler, Philip Looby, Matthew Ryan, Shane Hassett, Paul Collins, Liam Ryan, Michael Everard, Damien Young, Martin Butler, Jamie Moloney, Trevor Hassett, Helen Ryan. Third row (l–r): Lorcan Looby, Pádraig Stapleton, James Woodlock, David Butler, Eric Woodlock, Joe Lupton, Eddie Costello, Éamonn Buckley, Mícheál Butler, John Kennedy, David Collins, Declan Ryan, Paul Kennedy. Back row (l–r): Mike Purcell, Paddy Kennedy, Pat Lupton, James Ryan, Donncha Kennedy, Paul Stapleton, Jerome Ryan, Shane Delaney, Enda Walshe, MacDara Butler.

Clonoulty resumed the stronger after the interval, and John O'Neill rifled home a goal in the thirty-second minute to stretch their lead to five points. Drom moved Seamus Callanan into full-forward, and the tide began to turn in their favour. By the forty-fifth minute, Drom had drawn level, 1-15 to 2-12, and the momentum eased them in front; there they remained, winning by 1-19 to 2-14.

2011
Na Piarsaigh Take a Second Chance: AIB Munster Club Hurling Final

Na Piarsaigh, Limerick, and Crusheen, Clare, finished level at Semple Stadium on the last Sunday in November. A mere 2,893 supporters braved the elements and were disappointed as this expected Munster showpiece failed to fire. Early points were exchanged before Shane Dowling goaled for Na Piarsaigh with a bullet-like penalty in the seven-

Na Piarsaigh, Munster Club Hurling Champions 2011. Back row (l–r): Paul McNamara, Pa Guinane, Aidan Hennessy, Declan O'Connor, Kieran Bermingham (captain), Kieran Breen, Padraic Kennedy, David Lynch, David Breen, Kieran Kennedy, Shane O'Neill, Cathal King, David Sheppard, Damien Quigley. Front row (l–r): Brian Shannon, James O'Brien, Kevin Ryan, Pat Gleeson, Alan Dempsey, Brian Hartnett, Kevin Downes, Shane Dowling, John Madden, Brian Buckley, Bradley Russell.

teenth minute. The remainder of the opening half was all Crusheen, with five successive points leaving them in front at the break, 0-9 to 1-3.

The second period was point for point, and by the fiftieth minute the sides were level, 0-12 to 1-9. Crusheen goalkeeper Donal Touhy was a busy man in this period and made three fine saves. Excitement grew as the minutes ticked down, with neither side able to grasp the initiative. The final score was a draw: Na Piarsaigh 1-11, Crusheen 0-14.

For the replay the following Sunday, Semple Stadium was bitterly cold, but the biting winds and heavy showers didn't deter the players from serving up a contest to stir the blood and warm the heart. The attendance of 2,486, down from the previous week, enjoyed a keenly contested first half that finished 0-5 to 0-4, Crusheen ahead. The Claremen were three clear, 0-9 to 0-6, with only fourteen minutes left. The final quarter, however, was all Na Piarsaigh – they notched up 1-6, with no reply from Crusheen. Star substitute Adrian Breen got the goal with two minutes remaining, after a fine attack by Dowling and Downes. Na Piarsaigh's young guns had done the business. It was their first Munster club title. The final score was Na Piarsaigh 1-13, Crusheen 0-9.

2012
Kilkenny Put Rebels to the Sword:
Allianz National Hurling League Final

Cork were rocked on their heels at Semple Stadium on 6 May by a ruthless Kilkenny team that sent them home wondering about their hurling prospects for the season. The Cats took control in the opening minutes and never relinquished it, with all six forwards scoring from play. Eoin Larkin registered the first goal, and five minutes later

Left: Kilkenny captain Eoin Larkin celebrates victory.

his pass to Colin Fennelly was finished to the Cork net. Patrick Horgan picked off a scattering of points from frees, but the Kilkenny lead was increasing all the while. Just before half-time T J Reid pounced on Coleman's poor clearance in the Cork goal to fire home Kilkenny's third goal. At half-time they were ahead by 3-11 to 0-6.

The second half was more of the same; Kilkenny never allowed Cork to make significant inroads into their lead. The final score was Kilkenny 3-21, Cork 0-16.

2012
Michael Portillo Visits Semple

Left to right: Dr Patrick Bracken, Joanne Ryan, Michael Portillo and Noel McGrath.

In June 2012, the former British Conservative minister Michael Portillo visited Semple Stadium to record an item for the BBC television series *Great British Railway Journeys*. While there, he spoke with historian Dr Patrick Bracken, Thurles, about the impact the emergence of the railways in Victorian Tipperary had on the growth of sport. Tipperary hurling and camogie stars Noel McGrath and Joanne Ryan were also on hand to demonstrate the art and skills of hurling.

As he ran out the player's tunnel onto the pitch, Portillo remarked, 'I'm probably the first British minister to run out the tunnel at Semple Stadium.'

2012
Hear the Almighty Roars

No Irish summer is complete without getting up close and personal with the hurling championships. There is nothing like it anywhere in the world.

The atmosphere ferments into something quite electric once you get inside Semple Stadium. It's the action on the pitch, the commentary and craic from the stewards and the people that make the day. You don't hear songs at GAA games – what you hear are almighty roars. In the stands, the lack of fan segregation makes for great banter between counties. And the games are open to everyone. There's no age limit – you'll see everyone from babies to old men and women. I recall the All-Ireland quarter final match last year, Galway and Waterford, which everyone assumed that Galway would win. An up-and-coming Waterford were outplayed for most of the game but managed to turn it around. The end result can often surprise everyone.

Joanne Cantwell, *The Irish Times*, May 2010

Clare, All-Ireland Under 21 Hurling Champions 2012. Back row (l–r): David McInerney, Conor Ryan, Aaron Cunningham, Shane Golden, Tony Kelly, Conor McGrath (captain), Seadna Morey. Front row (l–r): Padraic Collins, Pat O'Connor, Ronan Taffe, Cathal O'Connell, Cathal McInerney, Colm Galvin, Paul Flanagan, Killian Ryan.

2012
Tenacious Clare Beat Kilkenny: All-Ireland Under 21 Hurling Final

Clare enjoyed an excellent start on 15 September, with Cathal O'Connell scoring the game's first goal as he beat Dylan Walsh with an excellent finish. Colm Galvin and Patrick O'Connor were also among the point-scorers, and Clare led by 1-5 to 0-2 after only eight minutes, but points from Walter Walsh, Geoff Brennan and Kevin Kelly kept Kilkenny in the game. Coming up to the interval, John Power scored a penalty following a David McInerney challenge on Power. The Cats added another goal soon after as Ger Aylward latched on to Power's long ball, and Kilkenny finished the half in style, ahead by 2-7 to 1-7.

Clare were in determined form in the second period, and at the three-quarter stage they had doubled their points tally – including a Conor McGrath goal from close range – with a sole point the Kilkenny response. Shane Golden, Cathal McInerney and Tony Kelly made sure Clare ultimately ran out comfortable winners, lifting the trophy for only the second time in their history, 2-17 to 2-11.

2012

Fifteenth Title for Commercials: Tipperary Senior Football Final

The county football final, between Clonmel Commercials and Thomas MacDonaghs, was played at Semple Stadium on 4 November. The first half was a dull affair, with Commercials getting the first two points by Ian Barnes and Colman Kennedy and Mac-Donaghs not scoring until the twenty-second minute, via Joe Carroll. Padraic O'Meara

added a second before the break to leave the sides level at 0-2 each.

Commercials resumed a different outfit and added three points through Aldo Matassa and Ian Barnes (2) in a seven-minute spell. MacDonaghs responded with a Séamus Hennessy point, but then came Colman Kennedy's fine goal, followed by another Barnes point, which left Commercials ahead by 1-6 to 0-3 entering the last quarter. The Clonmel team stayed in front, and substitute Alan Lonergan managed their last point to give them a 1-9 to 0-5 victory and their fifteenth county title.

Fergal Condon, captain of Clonmel Commercials, raises the O'Dwyer Cup aloft.

Leading the Parade

The Seán Treacy Pipe Band, from the parish of Moycarkey/Borris, just outside Thurles, have a long association with Semple Stadium. Founded in 1934, the band has been leading teams in pre-match parades and entertaining the crowds at Thurles Sportsfield, later Semple Stadium, since the 1940s. They are now a well-established part of the pageantry, where the skirl of the pipes and their precision drumming add immensely to the sense of occasion and magical atmosphere of Thurles on big match days.

2013
Three Out of Five for Clare: All-Ireland Under 21 Hurling Final

This game was effectively over by half-time, with Clare ahead by 2-16 to 0-4, as Antrim failed to mount a serious challenge. Seadna Morey, Cathal Malone and Davy O'Halloran contributed early points, and Clare stormed into a 0-13 to 0-2 lead after only twenty minutes. Shortly after, Davy O'Halloran got the game's first goal. As half-time approached,

Clare captain Paul Flanagan receives the Cross of Cashel trophy from GAA president Liam O'Neill.

Shane O'Donnell's goal from a difficult angle confirmed Clare's dominance. To their credit, Antrim didn't give up and they improved slightly in the second half, with points from Stephan McAfee, Ciaran Clarke and Chris McGuinness, but the result was never in doubt. The final score was Clare 2-28, Antrim 0-12.

2014

A Breathtaking Battle: Allianz National Hurling League Final

League specialists Kilkenny recorded the county's first three-in-a-row after a breathtaking final at Semple Stadium on 4 May. Extra time was needed to separate them from their timeless rivals, Tipperary, under the gaze of 21,601 spectators. In the end T J Reid set up Richie Hogan to shoot the winning point.

Tipperary started the match better, and by the half-hour they had outscored their opponents by 1-11 to 0-4. The goal was a well-taken flick to the net by John O'Dwyer, who got on the end of Noel McGrath's line ball. At the very end of the first half, Kilkenny were granted a penalty, dispatched by T J Reid to leave the half-time score 1-11 to 1-9, with Tipperary ahead.

In the fiftieth minute, the home side led by three when Kilkenny got a penalty, which Reid drove home to level, 2-11 to 1-14. The match swung from one side to the other in final quarter, with the levelling point coming from Tipperary's Kieran Bergin, who grabbed a pass from Patrick 'Bonnar' Maher, making it Kilkenny 2-17, Tipperary 1-20. In extra

T J Reid, Kilkenny, celebrates after scoring his side's second goal from a penalty. Photo by Diarmuid Greene, Sportsfile.

time, Kilkenny led by one at the break, 2-21 to 1-23. In the closing ten, Noel McGrath and Seamus Callanan, with a free and a sixty-five, pushed Tipperary back in front. However, Pádraig Walsh had the match level in the final minute when Reid and Hogan sealed it with a point. The final score was Kilkenny 2-25, Tipperary 1-27 (after extra time).

2014
Kelly Inspires Clare to Three in a Row:
Bord Gáis All-Ireland Under 21 Hurling Final

On 13 September, 2011, at Semple Stadium, Clare were in control all the way through the Under 21 final, but hard-working and brave Wexford made them earn their title. The sides traded scores early on, then in the thirteenth minute Wexford suddenly broke through on goal and Kevin Foley's shot looked bound for the net – only to crash off the crossbar and out the field. Action now swung to the other end, where Shane O'Donnell left the Wexford defence in ribbons before hand-passing across to Reidy, who finished to the net, bringing the score to 1-2 to 0-2. Now Tony Kelly, Ballyea, went to work and fired over four brilliant points from play in an eight-minute spell to leave Clare deservedly five clear at the interval.

Wexford started the second half well with points from McDonald and Guiney, but Clare responded with scores from Colm Galvin and Bobby Duggan to go four clear again before they broke through for their second goal from Aaron Cunningham. Clare now led by eight points and were cruising to victory, but Wexford fought back and had the ball in the net moments later courtesy of substitute David Dunne. Three Duggan points in quick succession and one from Kelly stemmed the Wexford fight back

Clare captain Tony Kelly raises the Cross of Cashel trophy aloft following the final.

and sent Clare eight clear again, but then a second Dunne goal – a fine finish with eight minutes to go – gave Wexford half a chance. When Conor McDonald slammed a shot past Hogan and into the roof of the net two minutes later, a comeback suddenly looked possible. But Clare didn't panic and closed out the win ruthlessly with points from Colm Galvin and Tony Kelly. The final score was Clare 2-20, Wexford 3-11. Attendance on the day was 15,081.

Galway camogie players Ailish O'Reilly, Sarah Dervan and Tara Kenny celebrate their win. Photo by Ray McManus, Sportsfile.

2015
Galway Best in Camogie Final

Galway came out strong from the beginning of the Irish Daily Star National Camogie League Division 1 final at Semple Stadium on 3 May, 2015, destroying the Cork defence in the first half. The Rebels made more headway after the interval, bringing the gap to just three points at the final whistle, but the winners were never in doubt. The final score was Galway 2-15, Cork 2-12.

Galway team: S Earner, T Kenny, S Dervan, H Cooney, S Coen, S Healy, L Ryan, N Kilkenny, E Kilkelly, A Donohue, N McGrath, AM Starr, O McGrath, M Dunne, A O'Reilly. Substitutes played: F Keeley and J Gill.

2015

Déise Marksman Mahony Delivers: Allianz National Hurling League Final

Waterford defeated Cork in the league final on 3 May at Semple Stadium. In front of 17,559 spectators, their ace marksman Pauric Mahony was on song, registering 0-11. Team captain Kevin Moran was awarded Man of the Match following an inspirational display capped by three fine points. But Waterford had other stars all over the pitch, with Noel Connors and Austin Gleeson excellent at the back. Gleeson scored two stunning first-half points, one a sideline cut and the other from play, and Waterford led by 0-11 to 0-7 at half-time. Goalkeeper Stephen O'Keeffe performed heroics to beat away Séamus Harnedy's fierce drive in the twentieth minute. The Déise had nine different scorers, and latecomer Tom Devine got the game's only goal with six minutes of play remaining. Best of the Rebels were Conor Lehane, who scored five points from play, and Séamus Harnedy in flashes. The final score was Waterford 1-24, Cork 0-17.

Pauric Mahony, with eyes focused on the ball, takes a free for Waterford in the Hurling League final. Photo by Ray McManus, Sportsfile.

Remembering Jimmy Doyle

Following the untimely death in 2015 of Tipperary hurling legend Jimmy Doyle, his funeral cortège passed Semple Stadium flanked by a guard of honour led by GAA Uachtarán Aogán Ó Feargháil and Michael Maher, chairman of Thurles Sarsfields. A huge outpouring of sympathy saw thousands attend to pay their tribute to a man regarded as one of the best hurlers of all time. Photo by Bridget Delaney.

'He was the flawless version of the Celtic art.'

Top left: President of Ireland Michael D Higgins, accompanied by Robert Frost, Munster Council chairman, waves to the crowd before the 2015 Munster final at Semple Stadium. Photo by Ray McManus, Sportsfile.

Top right: Tipperary captain Brendan Maher lifts the Munster Cup following his side's victory. Photo by Stephen McCarthy, Sportsfile.

Above: Tipperary supporters invade the pitch at Semple Stadium following the Munster hurling final. Photo by George Hatchell.

2015
Tipperary Gather the Points: Munster Senior Hurling Final

Just over 43,000 packed Semple Stadium on 12 July, but they weren't treated to the expected classic Munster final between Tipperary and Waterford. The home team enjoyed a fine spell at the start of the game that yielded a four-point lead. Na Déise worked their way back in the second quarter, thanks largely to Maurice Shanahan's excellence up front, and were just a point down at the break, 0-10 to 0-9.

The game turned into an arm wrestle in the second half, but Tipperary kept their noses just about in front, helped along by Waterford's poor shooting. Tipperary started with Padraic Maher as a deep-lying sweeper, and he cleaned up in the full-back line and fed a constant supply of long diagonal balls to his inside-forward line, bypassing the influential Tadhg de Búrca. In the closing stages, it was first Lar Corbett, then Patrick Maher and finally Shane Bourke who nailed the scores that at last shook off Waterford's challenge. The final score was Tipperary 0-21, Waterford 0-16.

Above left: Groundsman Dave Hanley. Above right: Hanley (right), Seán Kiely and Pa Bourke take a break from field maintenance to admire the hurling. Photo by Eamonn McGee.

Semple Stadium Caretaker Dave Hanley

Dave Hanley from Adamstown, Templemore, has been head groundsman since 2013, when he took over from Philly Butler. Dave is immensely proud of Semple Stadium, and along with local man Pa Bourke, a former Tipperary hurler, always seeks perfection in the preparation of the pitch. As Dave says himself, 'I wouldn't want to be anywhere else.'

2015
Limerick Shatter Wexford Dream:
Bord Gáis Energy All-Ireland Under 21 Hurling Final

This annual hurling showpiece at Semple Stadium on 12 September attracted 18,544 spectators. From the throw-in, it was obvious that Limerick were really up for the battle, while Wexford looked rather leg-weary. The displays of Richie English, Pat Ryan, Barry Nash, Ronan Lynch and Tom Morrissey were a sight to behold and kept the scoreboard busy. Wexford suffered heartbreak three minutes before the interval when Kevin

Limerick, All-Ireland Under 21 Champions 2015. Back row (l–r): Barry Nash, Ronan Lynch, David Dempsey, Colin Ryan, Pat Ryan, Darragh O'Donovan, Gearóid Hegarty, Diarmaid Byrnes, Barry O'Connell, Tom Morrissey, Séamus Flanagan, Seán Flanagan, Eoghan McNamara. Front row (l–r): Jack Kelleher, Mark O'Callaghan, Jody Hannon, Peter Casey, Mike Casey, David McCarthy, Cian Lynch, Richie English, Seán Finn, Andrew La Touche Cosgrave, Liam O'Sullivan. Photo by Diarmuid Greene, Sportsfile.

Foley's hard-earned goal was disallowed because an earlier free had been flagged. Conor McDonald pointed twice, and Wexford trailed 0-11 to 0-4 at the break.

On the resumption, Limerick cantered into a 0-14 to 0-5 lead. A ray of hope for Wexford came in the fiftieth minute with a sublime goal from Conor McDonald, but its effect was wiped out by a spate of frees. The final score was Limerick 0-26, Wexford 1-7.

Chief Steward Robert Ryan

A native of Knock, Roscrea, Robert Ryan has been involved in security and stewarding at the stadium since the early 1990s. Always with the health and safety of players and spectators top of his agenda, he ensures that everybody gets to enjoy the games and is treated in a friendly and welcoming manner. Photo by Ray McManus, Sportsfile.

2015
King Wins the Crown: AIB Munster Senior Club Hurling Final

It was bitterly cold for the 2,320 spectators who braved Semple Stadium on 22 November. Waterford's Ballygunner, playing with the breeze, had the better of the first-half exchanges and were full value for their interval lead of 1-7 to 1-4. They were operating without the Mahony brothers – Philip suspended and Pauric injured – but Limerick's Na Piarsaigh were also without county star Kevin Downes. David Dempsey netted the opening goal of the game for Na Piarsaigh in the twentieth minute, but Ballygunner hit back with one of their own eight minutes later, Tim O'Sullivan on target.

Na Piarsaigh, under captain Cathal King, were a team transformed for the second half, which they began with five unanswered points. After hitting the front, they never looked back. Ballygunner rallied to within two points when Brian O'Sullivan netted a late goal, but Na Piarsaigh finished with a flourish as Limerick ace Shane Dowling rattled home a brilliant goal in the final minute, ending 2-18 to Ballygunner's 2-11. It was Na Piarsaigh's third Munster crown in five seasons.

Shop assistants Sarah and Lorraine Hayes, along with manager Marion Graham, wait for customers before a game at the GAA merchandise shop under the Old Stand. Photo by Brendan Moran, Sportsfile.

Match Programmes (Clár Oifigiúil)

Thurles Sarsfields have been in charge of the production and distribution of match programmes at Semple Stadium for many decades now. Over the years, great experience has been gained in this field, and top-quality, award-winning programmes have been produced. Always working to a deadline, the programme editor is assisted by an important team of journalists, statisticians, photographers, historians, printers, etc. Since the 1970s, the official programmes have been compiled and edited by Donal O'Gorman, Liam Ó Donnchú (this author), John McCormack, and presently by Ger Corbett. For many years now, Tom Beirne, Kilkenny, has taken charge of the design and layout. Ed Donnelly, former Tipperary GAA PRO and now Communications Manager at Munster GAA, looks after the programmes for Munster Council games, while DBA Publications produce programmes for all GAA Central Council competitions. Distribution at Semple Stadium is organised through Thurles Sarsfields GAA Club.

Left: Programme editor John McCormack receives the McNamee Media Award from GAA president Seán McCague in 2000.
Below left: Selling match programmes under the Dr Kinane Stand at Semple Stadium (l–r): Peter Donnelly, James Meehan, Ger Donnelly, Laura Donnelly, Jo Anne Meehan, Tom Meehan Snr, Tom Meehan Jnr, Andy Ryan.
Below right: Programme editor Ger Corbett receives the McNamee Media Award from GAA president Criostóir Ó Cuana (left), accompanied by Padraic Duffy, GAA director general, in 2011.

2016

A Great Year for Kilkenny Camogie

Kilkenny confirmed their dominance by taking their twelfth Irish Daily Star National Camogie League Division 1 title on 1 May, 2016, in Semple Stadium. It was yet another blow for rivals Galway, who also had defeats in the Division 2 and minor A championship deciders over the weekend. The final score was Kilkenny 2-7, Galway 0-7. Photo by Piaras Ó Mídheach, Sportsfile.

Kilkenny team and scorers: A M Lennon, J Frisby, D Tobin, C Dormer, S Quirke, E Keane, S Kent, K A Doyle, A Farrell (1-1), A Dalton (0-1), J A Malone (1-1), D Gaule (0-3), S A Quinlan (0-1), M Walsh, S Farrell. Substitutes: C Phelan, M Quilty.

2016

Kelly Points Clare to Glory: Allianz National Hurling League Final

At Semple Stadium on 1 May, 2016, Maurice Shanahan rescued Waterford with a dramatic equalising point from a free to leave the final score Waterford 0-22, Clare 0-22 (after extra time). The sides had been level at the end of normal time, and again at half-time in extra time. Both teams were relieved to survive for another day.

The replay was at the same venue on the following Sunday. Waterford, in front for

Tony Kelly, in brilliant form, played a major role in Clare's success. Photo by David Fitzgerald, Sportsfile.

much of the game after Patrick Curran and Jake Dillon struck first-half goals, looked on course for victory, although Clare answered with a wonderful goal by Tony Kelly after he was picked out by Aaron Cunningham. When Waterford substitute Brian O'Halloran clipped over a point with five minutes left, it pushed them in front, 2-19 to 1-19, but the Bannermen timed their run to the finish line to perfection. Colin Ryan and Darach Honan cut the deficit to two points in injury time, then Clare brought it level before Kelly shot over the match-winning score in the fourth minute of added time. They had landed their first hurling league title since 1978, with a final score of 1-23 to Waterford's 2-19.

2016
Hawk-Eye Comes to Semple Stadium

Hawk-Eye official Dickie Murphy, Wexford, watches as the technology is put to use in Semple Stadium. Photo by Stephen McCarthy, Sportsfile.

The score-detection technology Hawk-Eye was first used in Croke Park in 2013. In 2016, Semple Stadium became the only other venue in Ireland to use the technology. Its first outing was the Munster senior championship quarter-final meeting of Tipperary and Cork on 22 May. Eight cameras form an integral part of the new technology.

2016

Incredible Drama Sees 'Cats' Through:
All-Ireland Senior Hurling Semi-Final

This replay was another epic battle at Semple Stadium on 13 August, with 30,358 in attendance. On the previous Sunday, Kilkenny forced a draw with Waterford after an exhilarating contest at Croke Park that ended Kilkenny 1-21, Waterford 0-24. The replay began with a bang, Austin Gleeson scything through for a goal, but Kilkenny didn't hesitate, hitting back with a brace of goals by the dangerous Colin Fennelly. The game's fourth goal came at the end of the first quarter, Jake Dillon coming onto a Shane Bennett pass, and now the score read 2-4 to 2-2. Kilkenny dominated the second quarter and had them three ahead at the break, 2-10 to 2-7.

On fifty minutes, it was a two-point lead thanks to Maurice Shanahan's point, but Kilkenny had stretched it to four three minutes later. With four minutes left, Pauric Mahony's free made it a one-point game, and Jamie Barron tied it up. In the closing seconds, Richie Hogan latched onto an Eoin Murphy clearance to score the insurance point. The final score was Kilkenny 2-19, Waterford 2-17.

Richie Hogan, Kilkenny, celebrates scoring a point during the All-Ireland semi-final replay at Semple Stadium. Photo by Piaras Ó Mídheach, Sportsfile.

'A Choking Grasp on an Irishman's Heart'

I have many different passions but there's a special one that rages in my middle-aged heart. Many people may think I am mad, but it is the idealism of the majestic, elusive All-Ireland Hurling Championship that makes my heart beat faster day after day.

Close your eyes ... Think of summer. What do you see? I see midges swooping and dancing through a languid sunset. I see heat-drenched Limerick jerseys shuffling through the streets of Thurles, where bellows of banter waft along with the whiff of cider that floats from the open doors of packed pubs in Liberty Square. Inside D D Corbett's, a bitter alcoholic draws tears from the crowd with a soft, sweet rendition of 'Slievenamon'. On a street corner a humming chip van mumbles its invitation to giddy children as the June sun beats down. The Pecker Dunne sits perched on a flat stone wall, plucking and strumming, twanging banjo chords as he winks at those who pass. A smile broadens his foggy beard as coins glint and twinkle from the bottom of his banjo case. Hoarse hawkers flog melted chocolate and paper hats on the brow of a humpbacked bridge, as we move closer to the Field of Legends. The drone of kettle-drums and bagpipes rise from the Seán Treacy Pipe Band, as they parade sweat-soaked warriors around the green hallowed sod. A whistle rings on high, ash smacks on ash and the sliothar arrows between the uprights. A crash of thunder and colour erupts from the terraces ... I see the championship!!!

The championship is something special. What else has such a choking grasp on an Irishman's heart? What else has the power to cram Knockaderry Church on a Saturday night and leave it sleeping on Sunday championship mornings? What else draws the likes of Mike Quilty and Mike Wall and sits them among roaring, red-faced lunatics in the shadow of the crowded Old Stand? What else exists that plucks the cranky farmer from the milking parlour and flings him into a concrete cauldron sixty miles across the province? There are those who swear the apocalypse would not have the same effect ...

Some of my earliest memories are of the championship. I remember travelling with my father in Tom Howard's black Morris Minor for the Munster semi-final in 1962 to see Ringy and the Rebels take on the might of Tom Cheasty, Ned Power and Frankie Walsh's Waterford. Another day in Cork saw me crammed like a sardine behind the city goal as I watched Cregan and Grimes emerge to mesmerise the Premier County. Another vivid memory is of Glenroe's own 'Banger' O'Brien with blood streaming from his temple, raising a fist to the crowd, 'Waterford are bate and Limerick are in the All-Ireland!' ... But oh to be a hurler ... To sprint from the tunnel in Limerick like a greyhound from the traps. To hear the eruption from forty thousand sunburnt fans, to see the swish of flags among a sea of faces. It's only something I can dream about, but nonetheless it's the greatest passion that rages in my heart.

The championship is more precious than life for many. I've seen grey-haired men gazing into half empty glasses reeling off the names of the great ones, like prayers. I'm afraid I too follow suit. Ask me who's the Minister for Finance and your question will be greeted with indifference. I simply couldn't care less. 'Bless me father, for I'm a fanatic!' But oh to be a hurler ...

If the truth be known I couldn't hurl spuds to ducks. The boss of my hurley has seen the arse of a Friesian cow more often than it has the crisp leather stitching of an O'Neill's sliothar! Okay, I've had my own All-Irelands up against the gable end and in and around the mother's flowerbeds, but that's as far as it went for me. My dad was the same, but come June and the chirp of the sparrow, you can be guaranteed we'd be stuck in that long snake of traffic, as it slithered its way to Cork, Limerick, Thurles and other far-flung fields. The terrace is where the real nectar of hurling comes to a head – when every Joe Soap in the country stands together on the same patch of cement with their eyes fixed on the same lush, green carpet ...

Because for me, and thousands like me, the 'one absolutely beautiful thing' ...

IS THE HURLING CHAMPIONSHIP!

Vincent Hanly, Knockaderry, Limerick

2016
Tipperary Welcomes McCarthy Cup Home

Following Tipperary's All-Ireland success, beating Kilkenny by 2-29 to 2-20 at Croke Park on Sunday, 4 September, thousands poured into the streets of Thurles to welcome the champions home the next day. Captained by Brendan Maher, they had put a stop to Kilkenny's gallop and won Tipperary's first senior All-Ireland in six years. A joyous, noisy atmosphere permeated the air as Tipperary hats, flags, headbands, trumpets and posters were out in force. Car number plates reading '16-T-LIAM' sold like hot cakes as the adoring hordes headed for Semple Stadium. The cheers were getting louder and building

Above left: Tipperary captain Brendan Maher holds the Liam McCarthy Cup aloft at the Welcome Home celebrations at Semple Stadium. Above right: They came in their thousands to celebrate the All-Ireland victory. Both photos by Bridget Delaney.

to a crescendo until the players, with Liam McCarthy in safe hands, made their public appearance on stage. There were cheers for manager Michael Ryan, but the loudest were reserved for Man of the Match Seamus Callanan.

Waterford, All-Ireland Under 21 Hurling Champions 2016. Back row (l–r): Mark O'Brien, Gavin Power, Billy O'Keeffe, Niall Fives, Ross Browne, Micheál Harney, Austin Gleeson, Tom Devine, Jordan Henley, Conor Prunty, Adam Farrell, Stephen Bennett, Michael Kearney, Dermot Ryan. Front row (l–r): Jack Fagan, Patrick Curran, Barry Whelan, Colm Roche, Conor Gleeson, Darragh Lyons, William Hahessy, Shane Bennett, Peter Hogan, D J Foran. Photo by Ray McManus, Sportsfile.

2016

Dazzling Déise Surge Past Tribesmen: All-Ireland Under 21 Hurling Final

Na Déise flicked the power switch and surged to their first success at this level since 1992. It was a swashbuckling display against Galway, decorated with amazing score-taking and out-of-this-world approach play. By the end of the first quarter, Waterford were well in command, leading by eleven points, 3-5 to 0-3, with the goals coming from D J Foran, Patrick Curran and Stephen Bennett. Waterford held a commanding 3-10 to 0-6 interval advantage.

Galway made a stirring start to the second half with five quick-fire points from Seán Linnane (2), Conor Whelan, Brian Molloy and Eanna Burke to reduce the deficit to eight. But Waterford's fourth goal arrived in the fiftieth minute, Shane Bennett's ground-stroke a delicate first-time effort to the bottom right corner of the net. Three minutes from the end, Stephen Bennett notched his second goal when he whipped a sensational shot to the net from an impossible angle. The final score was Waterford 5-15, Galway 0-14.

2016

Ballyea Make History: AIB Munster Senior Club Hurling Final

Tony Kelly was at his brilliant best at Semple Stadium on 20 November, as Ballyea were crowned Munster senior club hurling champions. On a bitterly cold afternoon, before

Ballyea, Munster Senior Club Hurling Champions 2016. Back row (l–r): Niall Lynch, Eamonn Breen, Conor Harkin, Brian Carrig, Cillian Brennan, Mark Crowe, Aonghus Keane, Gary Brennan, Barry Coote, Ryan Griffin, David Sheehan, Niall Deasy, Brian Murphy, Brandon O'Connell, Cian Meaney, John Ryan, Peter Casey. Front row (l–r): Conor Lynch, Liam Crowe, James Murphy, Eoghan Donnellan, Tadhg Lynch, Aaron Griffin, Tony Kelly, Martin O'Leary, Oisin Hennessy, Sean Meaney, Jack Browne, Pearse Lillis, Micky Nagle, Joe Neylon, Brian Casey. Photo by County Express.

an attendance of 4,593, Ballyea established a nine-point lead, 1-10 to 0-4, at half-time. Their goal was by Pearse Lillis, as he latched onto Gearoid O'Connell's pass before cracking it home in the thirteenth minute.

But Cork's Glen Rovers were not gone home, and corner-forward Conor Dorris rocked the Clare champions with two goals early in the second half. With ten minutes left, Rovers were just three behind, when Cork senior star Patrick Horgan landed a sixty-five, but Ballyea finished excellently, with leading scorer Niall Deasy accurate on placed balls and from play throughout. In the final eleven minutes of playing time, plus the extra three minutes, Ballyea outscored Rovers by 0-7 to 0-2. In their very first provincial final appearance, Ballyea showed fine composure on a landmark day for the club. The final score was Ballyea 1-21, Glen Rovers 2-10.

Attendance Numbers 2016/2017

In 2016, 292,000 patrons attended games at Semple Stadium, while 260,128 passed through the turnstiles the following year.

2017
Nash's Puck-Outs Set Up Rebel Victory: Munster Senior Hurling Final

A sunny Semple Stadium hosted the Cork/Clare final on 9 July, 2017, in front of 45,558 spectators. Both sides traded points until Cork's Alan Cadogan broke free of his marker in the eleventh minute and finished a great goal, off his left, low past Andrew Fahy. Anthony Nash's accuracy with his puck-outs proved vital as time after time he picked out a Cork player, and the attack was on. In the eighteenth minute, Shane O'Donnell was fouled and the ensuing penalty

Cork goalkeeper Anthony Nash in action during the Munster final at Semple Stadium. Photo by Piaras Ó Mídheach, Sportsfile.

went over the bar from Tony Kelly. Cork led by 1-10 to 0-8 at the interval, with Cadogan and Patrick Horgan scoring most of the points.

The highlight of Clare's recovery in the second half was when John Conlon broke through in the fifty-fifth minute and passed a great ball to Conor McGrath, who crashed it low beyond Nash's reach to leave Clare trailing by just 1-16 to 1-13. Cork's defence showed great character and withstood much Clare pressure from there to the end. The Rebels claimed a first Munster title in three years, their fifty-third in total. The final score was Cork 1-25, Clare 1-20.

2017

Semple Stadium Wins Inaugural Pitch Award

This year, the Thurles venue was the inaugural winner of the nationwide Pitch of the Year award. Assessment of the grounds was completed by Stuart Wilson, Croke Park pitch manager, and Dr Stephen Barker of the Sports Research Institute.

The decision process involved scoring and feedback from referees during the Allianz Leagues in spring. It took into consideration a Pitch Quality Assessment based on performance standards, construction, management programme, environmental conditions and usage levels.

At the Pitch of the Year award presentation were Croke Park head groundsman Stuart Wilson, Semple Stadium groundsman Dave Hanley, Tipperary GAA chairman Michael Burke, Uachtarán CLG Aogán Ó Fearghail, and committee chairman Kieran McGann of the National Pitch Maintenance Work Group. Photo by Ray McManus, Sportsfile.

At the announcement, GAA president Aogán Ó Fearghail said:

I would like to congratulate the team at Semple Stadium on winning this award. We have all witnessed many great games in Thurles over the years, and while the talents of hurlers and footballers catches the eye of many, the conditions for them to play is always top class, so I salute the work undertaken by all.

David Morgan, stadium manager, Mick Carroll, pitch advisor, Dave Hanley, head groundsman, and Pa Bourke, assistant groundsman, along with their families visited Croke Park to mark the event and to receive the award on 13 August.

Ardán Ó Riain was also re-roofed during this year, by local contractors Fitzgibbons.

2017
Bright Future Ahead for Limerick:
Bord Gáis Energy All-Ireland Under 21 Hurling Final

Limerick supporters travelled in strength to Semple Stadium on 9 September, and they made up the majority of the 15,485 crowd. They had plenty to cheer about from the off, as Aaron Gillane, Cian Lynch and Barry Nash demonstrated some flashes of real class up front. Limerick started with wind advantage, and by the time the interval rolled around, they led by 0-11 to 0-4, which was an accurate reflection of their supremacy.

Kyle Hayes controlled the defence from centre-back, while at centre-field Robbie Hanley was in the thick of everything. With ten minutes remaining, the Shannon-siders were 0-14 to 0-6. Kilkenny struck five points in eight minutes with Alan Murphy sharp from frees, but Limerick weren't going to be denied. The final score was Limerick 0-17, Kilkenny 0-11.

Limerick captain Tom Morrissey lifts the James Nowlan Cup after the All-Ireland Under 21 final. Photo by Piaras Ó Mídheach, Sportsfile.

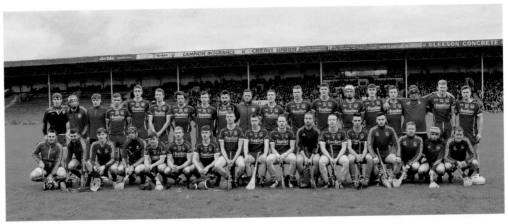

Thurles Sarsfields, Tipperary Senior Hurling Champions 2017. Back row (l–r): Willie Tierney, Lar Corbett, Michael Purcell, Kevin O'Gorman, Jack Derby, Rory Dwan, David Corbett, Seanie Butler, David Maher, David Kennedy, Michael Cahill, Padraic Maher (captain), Billy McCarthy, Ronan Maher, Cathal Moloney, Tommy Doyle, Declan Ryan, Denis Maher, Pa Dunne. Front (l–r): Barry O'Dwyer, Aidan Ryan, Rory Purcell, Mossy McCormack, Cian Treacy, Paul Maher, Conor Stakelum, Stephen Maher, Stephen Cahill, Stephen Lillis, Paddy McCormack, John Maher, Aidan McCormack, Mikey O'Brien, Richie Ruth, Conor Lanigan, Pa Bourke.

2017

Four in a Row for the Blues: Tipperary Senior Hurling Final

Borris/Ileigh set up their team with Brendan Maher acting as sweeper in defence. Both teams seemed nervous and cagey early on, but Thurles Sarsfields eventually started to pick off scores and led by seven points after twenty minutes, 0-9 to 0-2. Sarsfields' defenders were at the top of their game, and Borris/Ileigh found it hard to penetrate. However, they did manage a few points from out the field towards the end of the first half. The margin then was four points, with Thurles ahead, 0-11 to 0-7.

Sarsfields began the remaining half determined to do the business, and Denis Maher, Aidan McCormack and Stephen Cahill ratcheted up points without reply. When Conor Stakelum netted with ten minutes remaining, the match was over as a contest. In the end, Sarsfields won by sixteen points, Aidan McCormack the top scorer with nine. When the final whistle sounded, Sarsfields had achieved their target of four titles in a row for the first time in over fifty years. Padraic Maher, who led from the front, received the Dan Breen Cup and the Man of the Match award. The final score was Thurles Sarsfields 1-24, Borris/Ileigh 0-11.

2017
Late Breen Goals Give Na Piarsaigh the Title:
AIB Munster Senior Club Hurling Final

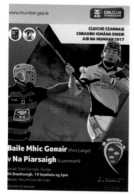

Ballygunner showed their potential in the opening half at Semple Stadium on 19 November. In the tenth minute, Conor Power ran onto Shane O'Sullivan's long pass to give his side a 1-2 to 0-2 lead. Pauric Mahony stretched it to four points, but Na Piarsaigh finished the half strongly with Ronan Lynch, Peter Casey and Adrian Breen pointing, to leave them one behind at the interval, 1-4 to 0-6.

At the restart, Mahony, Peter Hogan and Billy O'Keeffe all pointed in quick succession, and the Waterford lads were looking good. Na Piarsaigh weren't playing well, but things were about to change. Kevin Downes sent a great pass to David Breen, who rattled the roof of the net. This was followed by a point from Adrian Breen, and suddenly Na Piarsaigh were ahead, 1-8 to 1-7, with fourteen minutes remaining. Points were exchanged, and two minutes from time Peter Hogan fired a great goal for Ballygunner to put a point between the sides. However, Adrian Breen and David Breen hit back with two goals to see the Limerick team run out convincing winners. The final score was Na Piarsaigh 3-15, Ballygunner 2-10.

Come Rain or Shine

The vagaries of the Irish weather can be difficult on playing pitches, as was seen at Semple Stadium in late February and early March 2018. A thick carpet of snow on the

playing surface ensured that the fixture plan was thrown into disarray.

Long periods of drought can also have a detrimental effect on the pitch. Grass growth is impaired and discolouration can result. Luckily, Semple Stadium possesses its own well, and an appropriate watering programme is followed on such occasions.

2018
Horgan and Harnedy Engineer Cork Triumph:
Munster Senior Hurling Final

Semple Stadium hosted the Munster final on 1 July, before an attendance of 45,364. Clare settled quickly, with John Conlon causing chaos among the Cork backs and scoring three points by the twelfth minute. David Reidy broke through in the seventeenth minute to lash home a great Clare goal, following a surging Tony Kelly run. As the clock approached the interval, a long-range free by Donal Tuohy was met with a flick of Peter Duggan's hurley and another green flag being raised. Cork looked in trouble, but their hopes were rescued somewhat when Luke Meade finished neatly to the net after being set up by Séamus Harnedy. Four points in it at the break, 2-11 to 1-10, with Clare in front.

Cork struck the first three points of the second half, then Clare's Peter Duggan pointed, but Cork hit four more without reply to edge in front, 1-17 to 2-12, with twenty minutes left. The result was in the balance, and the tension was palpable as Cork's wing-forward, Séamus Harnedy, finished to the net after a fine move. Cork now had their tails up, notching points, and an Ian Galvin goal came too late for Clare. Patrick Horgan, Cork, was top scorer with 0-11. The final score was Cork 2-24, Clare 3-19.

Right: A masterclass, as Patrick Horgan of Cork takes a free during the Munster final. Photo by Ray McManus, Sportsfile.

2018
Galway Keep the Crown: Leinster Senior Hurling Final

Galway and Kilkenny finished all square at Croke Park on 1 July, 0-18 apiece. The venue was unavailable for the replay, so history was made when Semple Stadium hosted its first Leinster final the following Sunday, before a crowd of 25,102. President Michael D Higgins was in attendance, as was the Artane Band. The pace was frantic from the start, and Jonathan Glynn was unstoppable, scoring Galway's first goal after fourteen minutes. He shot a point two minutes later and laid on three other scores for his teammates in a stunning first-half performance. By the twentieth minute, Galway were 1-9 to 0-1 ahead, with Kilkenny looking helpless at times, but Ger Aylward's goal a minute from the break gave them some hope. The Glenmore man did well to score, considering he lost his hurley, but he seemed to take too many steps before he kicked the ball to the net from close range.

Galway led 1-16 to 1-07 at half-time, but Kilkenny soon recovered, and spearheaded with goals by Colin Fennelly and Richie Hogan, they came within one point of the westerners, 1-20 to 3-13, with fifteen minutes remaining. But that was as good as it got for them, as Galway went on a point-scoring spree. The final score was Galway 1-28, Kilkenny 3-15.

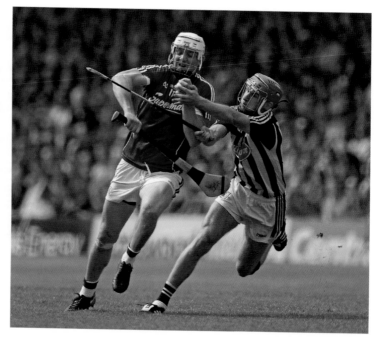

Joe Canning of Galway in action against Cillian Buckley of Kilkenny during the Leinster final replay at Semple Stadium. Photo by Ray McManus, Sportsfile.

2018
Brilliant Limerick Survive the Fight:
All-Ireland Senior Hurling Quarter-Final

Kilkenny were in Semple Stadium on the following Sunday, 15 July, for what turned out to be a classic clash with Limerick. Before an attendance of 18,596, the Shannonsiders showed real steel to get the better of the Cats. It was a high point-scoring first half, with Kilkenny dominating early on, but Limerick fought back to hold a 0-15 to 0-12 interval lead.

Limerick were 0-17 to 0-13 in front when Eoin Murphy pulled off his third point-blank save, this time from Gillane in the forty-sixth minute. Three quick Kilkenny points left them trailing by one ten minutes later, 0-19 to 0-18. A point by substitute Peter Casey and a stunning sideline from Darragh O'Donovan edged Limerick three clear. John Donnelly set up Richie Hogan, who swivelled and lashed his shot past Nickie Quaid to put the Cats into the driving seat. But Limerick retained their composure and scored three points in a row for a 0-25 to 1-21 lead, before Richie Leahy levelled it again in the sixty-eighth minute. The game was now hectic, but Tom Morrissey kept a cool head to give Limerick the lead in the seventy-first minute, and Aaron Gillane finished it off. The final score was Limerick 0-27, Kilkenny 1-22.

T J Reid of Kilkenny grabs possession despite the close attention of Seán Finn, Dan Morrissey and Diarmaid Byrnes of Limerick. Photo by Ray McManus, Sportsfile.

2018
The Trip to Tipp Returns

Féile, now known as Féile Classical, returned to Semple Stadium on 21 and 22 September, 2018. The lineup was a throwback to the 1990s glory days, with The Stunning, Hothouse Flowers, An Emotional Fish, Something Happens, The 4 of Us, and The Frank and Walters all taking to the stage and performing with the Irish Chamber Orchestra in what turned out to be a veritable nostalgia tsunami. The event brought some 20,000 patrons to Thurles and injected around €7-10 million into the local economy.

2018
Acheson Inspires the Rovers: Tipperary Senior Football Final

Moyle Rovers had eight points to spare over Ardfinnan in the county final at Semple Stadium on 14 October. Man of the Match Peter Acheson – who made three return trips from Dubai to line out with his club – was the powerhouse and inspiration for Rovers' success. Ardfinnan had a good first half and led by 0-6 to 0-5 at the break. However, Moyle Rovers totally dominated the second, outscoring Ardfinnan by 1-10 to 1-1. The final score was Moyle Rovers 1-15, Ardfinnan 1-7.

Moyle Rovers: Ciaran Kenrick, Paddy Morrissey, Alan Campbell (captain), Morgan Irwin, David McGrath (0-1), Ross Mulcahy (0-1), Luke Boland, Richard Power (0-1), Peter Acheson, Dara Ryan, Stephen Quirke (0-1), Seán Carey (0-1), Liam Boland (0-5), Shane Foley (1-2), Danny Owens (0-1). Substitutes played: Aidan McGrath, Tadhg Fitzgerald, Diarmuid Foley (0-2), Riain Quigley, Darragh Dwyer, Jack Harney.

2018

A Win at Last for the Gunners: AIB Munster Senior Club Hurling Final

Ballygunner were crowned Munster club champions in Semple Stadium on Sunday, 18 November, the Waterford side collecting their first title since 2001. Ballygunner were one up against Limerick's Na Piarsaigh as the first half ended, 1-7 to 1-6, and Pauric Mahony's free-taking kept the Déise lads ahead right through the second period. The final score was Ballygunner 2-14, Na Piarsaigh 2-8.

2019

Séamus Callanan and Team Receive Magnificent Reception

Tipperary secured an emphatic 3-25 to 0-20 win over Kilkenny in the All-Ireland hurling final at Croke Park on 18 August. An estimated 30,000 fans showed up at Semple Stadium to give the players and management a hero's welcome home.

Séamus Callanan, Tipperary captain (left), and his manager Liam Sheedy with the Liam MacCarthy Cup at the homecoming celebration at Semple Stadium. Photo by Sam Barnes, Sportsfile.

2019
Féile and Fringe

Féile Classical was held again at Semple Stadium on 20 and 21 September. It was Sinéad O'Connor's first major festival in a few years, and there was an outpouring of admiration and support for her. A festival fringe programme included a music trail, photo exhibition, pop-up gigs, a silent disco, a walking tour of Thurles, and 'surprise guests' performing 'in the most unexpected places'.

2019
Devaney Stars in Borris Victory: Tipperary Senior Hurling Final

Two north Tipperary clubs, Borris/Ileigh and Kiladangan, met in the county final at Semple Stadium on 3 November. Over 7,000 spectators saw Borris/Ileigh sow the seeds of their victory in the first half as they built up a five-point lead chiefly due to the fine display by one of the youngest players on the field, J D Devaney. His goal in the twenty-eighth minute put daylight between the sides at half-time, on a scoreline of 1-9 to 0-7.

Kiladangan got a much-needed lift when Dan O'Meara netted soon after the restart, but it just didn't happen for them and they were still four adrift, 1-9 to 1-13, after forty-five minutes. During the closing minutes, the points were shared, and Borris/Ileigh were county champions, 1-15 to 1-12.

James 'J D' Devaney, Borris-Ileigh, in action against Declan McGrath of Kiladangan in the county final. Photo by Ray McManus, Sportsfile.

The Semple Stadium Team, 2019

Con Hogan, chairman; Tom Maher, secretary; this author, Liam Ó Donnchú, PRO; Éamonn Buckley, treasurer; Matt Hassett, society solicitor; Niall Hackett, safety officer; John Devane, county chairman; Tim Floyd, county secretary; Michael Power, county treasurer; Michael Bourke, Central Council. Committee members: Seán Nugent, John O'Donovan, John Ryan, Liam Hennessy, John Costigan, Michael Lanigan, Pat Hickey, P J Maher, Jim Max, Mícheál Egan.

2020

League Title Stays Shannonside: Allianz National Hurling League Final

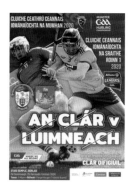

Played at Semple Stadium on 25 October, with no spectators present due to COVID-19 restrictions, this meeting of Clare and Limerick was two competitions in one: the winners would be crowned National Hurling League champions and also secure a Munster semi-final spot. This game is remembered for Tony Kelly's masterclass in point-scoring. The Ballyea marksman notched seventeen and kept the Banner in contention especially in the opening half, which ended with the sides locked at 0-15 to 0-15.

Limerick's superior threat and balance did eventually storm to the surface in the second period. On the restart, they set a blistering pace to pick off the first six points in just five minutes through Graeme Mulcahy, Gearóid Hegarty, Kyle Hayes, Aaron Gillane, Cian Lynch and Tom Morrissey, leaving the sides at 0-21 to 0-15. Clare did rally once more to lessen the gap to just the minimum, but they weren't able to sustain that challenge. The final score was Limerick 0-36, Clare 1-23.

2020

Empty Stands and Terraces: Munster Senior Hurling Semi-Final

This was the unusual scene during the Munster semi-final at Semple Stadium on 31

October, 2020. Due to COVID-19 restrictions, the game took place behind closed doors, with no spectators present. Waterford qualified for the final, defeating Cork by 1-28 to 1-24. Photo by George Hatchell.

2020

Limerick Pass Déise Test: Munster Senior Hurling Final

This mid-November Munster final was played in an eerily quiet atmosphere, without spectators. Waterford put up a fight, but it was once again Limerick's ability to spring top-class substitutes that proved decisive. The Shannonsiders' sheer size gave them an edge when the ball was there to be won on the ground, but Waterford kept scrapping for all they were worth, and at times they punched above their weight in those ferocious contests for possession. When the half-time whistle blew, Limerick led 0-14 to 0-11.

Waterford ripped into Limerick from the start of the second half and were level by the fortieth minute, thanks to two frees by Stephen Bennett and a nice score on the run by Jack Prendergast. The Déise lads' self-belief was visibly building, and when the superb Bennett put them ahead for the first time with a brilliant point from play on fifty-one minutes, their subs in the stand rose to their feet in acclamation. But substitute Séamus Flanagan scored with his very first touch to once again highlight the strength of the Limerick panel. Limerick had put Munster titles back to back for the first time since 1981. The final score was Limerick 0-25, Waterford 0-21.

Match Day Event Controller Con Hogan

Con, as event controller, works from the control room in Ardán Ó Riain. With him is the chief Garda on site, along with Michael Lanigan on communications. With access to CCTV and a top-class communication network, they play a vital role in the safe management of events at the stadium. Con also takes charge of the pre-event meeting, approximately one week before the match, where the statutory bodies and all involved in the production meet and plan all facets of the day.

Right: Con Hogan with this author in the shadow of Ardán Uí Chuinneáin. Photo by Bridget Delaney.

2020
Kiladangan's Dramatic First: FBD Tipperary Senior Hurling Final

Loughmore/Castleiney ripped through the Kiladangan defence in the first half, showing great combination and scoring three goals through Evan Sweeney, Tomás McGrath and John McGrath. But Kiladangan also finished the half well, scoring four points. It

Kiladangan captain Paul Flynn joins his teammates to celebrate with the Dan Breen Cup. Photo by Ray McManus, Sportsfile.

was 3-5 to 0-12 in Loughmore's favour at half-time.

In the third quarter, Kiladangan began to play in a commanding fashion as they out-scored their opponents 0-5 to 0-3. The action ebbed and flowed from there, Loughmore pushing ahead 3-12 to 0-19 with four minutes left on the clock in normal time. Then Kiladangan produced a scoring surge that saw them overhaul their opponents, and captain Paul Flynn knocked over a point that looked the winner. But Noel McGrath levelled, making the final score of normal time Loughmore/Castleiney 3-14, Kiladangan 0-23.

With both sides tiring, mental errors were noticeable in extra time, but Loughmore edged the first period 0-3 to 0-2 and in a frantic second period managed to go two in front. Kiladangan's Bryan McLoughney proved the match winner, coming back on to score two points from play before the match-winning goal. The final score was Kiladangan 1-28, Loughmore/Castleiney 3-20 (after extra time).

Kiladangan: Barry Hogan, Darragh Flannery, James Quigley, Fergie Hayes, Decky McGrath, David Sweeney, Alan Flynn, Willie Connors, Tadhg Gallagher, Sean Hayes, Joe Gallagher, Billy Seymour, Dan O'Meara, Paul Flynn (captain), Bryan McLoughney. Substitutes played: Andy Loughnane, Martin Minihan, Darren Moran.

2020

Commercials Keep the Title: FBD Tipperary Senior Football Final

Clonmel Commercials retained the county football title as Loughmore/Castleiney came up just short in another epic decider at Semple Stadium. Commercials' point-scoring from all angles had them in control from the off, and they were ahead by 0-13 to 0-7 at half-time.

Loughmore were always going to respond, and a thirty-second-minute goal from Conor McGrath brought them right back into the game.

They continued to dominate the ball in the second half, with substitute Liam Treacy, Conor Ryan, John McGrath and Evan Sweeney bringing the sides level at forty-four minutes. A Sean O'Connor free edged Commercials ahead at the

Clonmel Commercials captain Jamie Peters and his teammates with the O'Dwyer Cup. Photo by Ray McManus, Sportsfile.

second water-break, but all the momentum was with Loughmore, and points from John McGrath and Evan Sweeney nudged them in front at fifty-one minutes.

Then came the score of the game – worthy of winning any final – as Man of the Match Michael Quinlivan ran onto a ball sixty-five yards out, and burning past two Loughmore defenders, fired to the roof of the net from fourteen yards. Again, Loughmore came back with Conor Ryan (free) and Evan Sweeney bringing the sides level at fifty-nine minutes, before Jack Kennedy slotted over what would prove to be the winner. The final score was Clonmel Commercials 1-16, Loughmore/Castleiney 1-15.

Clonmel Commercials: Michael O'Reilly, Jamie Ahearne, Liam Ryan, Jamie Peters (captain), Kevin Fahey, Seamus Kennedy, Pauric Louram, Conal Kennedy, Jack Kennedy, Colman Kennedy, Michael Quinlivan, Ross Peters, Jason Lonergan, Sean O'Connor, Ryan Lambe. Substitute played: Cathal McGeever.

2020
A Pillar of the Local Economy

Photo by Bridget Delaney.

Semple Stadium makes a significant contribution to the economic life of Thurles. The stadium and its commercial partner, D-Vine Catering, spend €1.5 million per year directly in the local community on wages, goods and services. Semple draws all of its maintenance, catering and cleaning staff from the local community; they can number more than one hundred on big match days. Goods and supplies are purchased locally whenever possible, and local contractors are employed for structural, engineering and development projects.

In addition, as the GAA's largest stadium aside from Croke Park and hosting many of the Association's major games, the stadium attracts business to Thurles; an average of 280,000 patrons attend sporting events here every year, bringing an annual spend in excess of €20 million to the town. Semple Stadium operates a green environment policy, recycling waste and practising energy conservation where possible.

2020
Green Light for Old Stand Redevelopment

In April 2020, conditional planning permission was granted for the redevelopment of Ardán Uí Chuinneáin, the Old Stand at Semple Stadium. The plans will see a second level created over the concourse at the back of the stand. The proposed works include modifications to the ground floor: identified turnstiles will be removed and a new exit gate installed, and three new service cores will provide access to upper floor levels. The works also include the development of an additional floor under the existing stand to provide for a gym, physio room, changing room, media facilities, function space and bar, kitchen, reception, meeting room, plant store and associated circulation areas. The reconfiguration of some seating will provide dedicated VIP and disabled access areas.

There will be minimal change to the existing capacity of the stand, which stands at 14,500. The project will be financed by GAA grants, sports capital funding and revenues generated by stadium events.

Con Hogan, chairman of Semple Stadium Management Committee, said the plan is 'shovel ready and as soon as we can, we will be moving on it'. However, the COVID-19 pandemic has caused this project to be temporarily put on hold.

2020
The Yellow Sliotar Appears

This year, the GAA decided to replace the traditional white sliotar with a yellow one for championship hurling, a decision made for the benefit of both players and spectators. The yellow sliotar was identical in composition, size and weight to the white one, but it was much easier to see.

The new ball was used for the first time in a national final at the Allianz National Hurling League final at Semple Stadium on 25 October.

2020
The Very Centre of the Hurling Universe

'It is popular because it is supremely magnificent.'

So it goes with Semple Stadium. The old Thurles Sportsfield comes infused with so much history and cliché and all that whispery-echo stuff that it can tend to obscure the genius of the venue itself. But there's no need to be coy about it – Thurles is the best place to go to see a hurling match …

Everybody knows that Semple Stadium has the best pitch. They know it in their bones. It sometimes gets likened to a bowling green or a snooker table but while they'll take the compliment in the spirit it's meant, that's not what they're going for. Hurlers don't need the pitch to be smooth, they need it to be like the first cut of rough on a good golf course. They know they'll get that in Thurles.

They know it in the way Ronan Maher or Joe Canning will point a sideline ball from

seventy yards. They know it in the fact that there's never a false bounce or a surprising ricochet to a ball hopping your way. They know most of all that if you can't hurl in Thurles, you won't hurl anywhere.

Build all the stands ye like, lads. The pitch will still be the thing.

Malachy Clerkin, *The Irish Times*, 8 August, 2020

Top: A fine aerial view of a thronged Semple Stadium at the 2017 Munster hurling final.
Above: Planning the future, April 2021: David Morgan, manager; Con Hogan, chairman; Tim Floyd, Tipperary GAA secretary; Joe Kennedy, Tipperary GAA chairman; this author, Liam Ó Donnchú, PRO; Tom Maher, secretary. Photo by Tom Ryan Casey.

'Semple Stadium'

Gaeldom revels at this revelation –

Edifice to a great figure, on and off the field.

What memories Semple Stadium evokes?

Its sod, its atmosphere on Munster Final day.

The actors that have trod its stage seem infinite.

Some great performers come to mind.

Dinny Barry-Murphy scoring from his own line.

Stakelum on the ground or in the air.

Finn the half-back supreme.

Phil Cahill scoring in full flight.

Ring without question the most successful player.

Mackey, the colossus, thundering goalwards.

Jimmy Doyle the greatest hurler –

He was the flawless version of the Celtic art.

From the four corners they come to Semple Stadium.

The kith and kin of all the Gael

To see the ancient Celt exhibit

His treasure of a hundred – a thousand years.

Gerard Ryan, Inch, in King, Ó Donnchú, Smyth, Tipperary's GAA Ballads

INDEX OF NAMES